DATE DUE

DEMCO 38-296

The Female Marine and Related Works

THE
FEMALE MARINE
and Related Works

NARRATIVES OF CROSS-DRESSING
AND URBAN VICE IN
AMERICA'S EARLY REPUBLIC

Edited with an introduction by
Daniel A. Cohen

University of Massachusetts Press   *Amherst*

Copyright © 1997 by
The University of Massachusetts Press
All rights reserved
Printed in the United States of America
LC 97-20655
ISBN 1-55849-123-6 (cloth); 124-4 (pbk.)
Designed by Milenda Nan Ok Lee
Printed and bound by Thomson-Shore, Inc.
Library of Congress Cataloging-in-Publication Data

The female marine and related works : narratives of cross-dressing and
urban vice in America's early republic / edited with an introduction
by Daniel A. Cohen.
p.   cm.
Includes bibliographical references and index.
ISBN 1-55849-123-6 (alk. paper). — ISBN 1-55849-124-4 (pbk. :
alk. paper)
1. American prose literature—Massachusetts—Boston.   2. Wright,
N. Hill (Nathaniel Hill), 1787–1824—Authorship.   3. United States—
History—War of 1812—Women—Fiction.   4. City and town life—
Massachusetts—Boston—Fiction.   5. Women merchant mariners—United
States—Fiction.   6. Prostitutes—Massachusetts—Boston—Fiction.
7. Women sailors—United States—Fiction.   8. American prose
literature—1783–1850.   9. Transvestism—New England—Fiction.
10. Coverly, Nathaniel, 1775?–1824.   11. Popular literature—New
England.   12. Didactic fiction, American.   13. Narration (Rhetoric)
14. Literary form.   I. Cohen, Daniel A.   II. Female marine.
PS549.B6F46   1997
818'.20808–dc21
97-20655
CIP

British Library Cataloguing in Publication data are available.

This book is published with the support and cooperation of the
University of Massachusetts, Boston.

To the Memory of My Grandparents

Emanuel Cohen (1896–1996)

and

Anna Frank Cohen (1899–1996)

CONTENTS

ILLUSTRATIONS

PREFACE

Over the past several years, cross-dressing has emerged as one of the hottest topics in the academic hothouse of "cultural studies," a thriving interdisciplinary field that combines elements of literary criticism, cultural history, feminist theory, and progressive social commentary. However, as several practitioners of cultural studies have helped to remind us, cross-dressing has actually been a hot topic in British and Anglo-American popular culture over the past several *hundred* years. This volume makes a few of the earliest and most popular American cross-dressing narratives easily available again to scholars, students, and general readers.

In the immediate aftermath of the War of 1812, a somewhat disreputable Boston printer and bookseller named Nathaniel Coverly Jr. issued *The Adventures of Louisa Baker*, a fanciful but timely narrative that struck a responsive chord among New England readers. Sales of the pamphlet were so encouraging that Coverly issued a sequel, quickly followed it with another, and then combined the first two installments, sometimes with excerpts from the third, into a succession of composite editions entitled *The Female Marine*. Coverly's ephemeral best-sellers recounted the unlikely adventures of a young woman from rural Massachusetts who was seduced by a false-hearted lover, fled to Boston to conceal from her parents the resulting pregnancy, and was entrapped in a Boston brothel. After working there as a prostitute for a few years, Coverly's heroine escaped by disguising herself as a man, served with valor on board the American frigate *Constitution* during the War of 1812, and eventually married a wealthy young gentleman from New York City. Although no fewer than nineteen printings or editions of the various installments and composite narratives were issued by Coverly and others between 1815 and 1818, no more would appear until the publication of the first modern edition of *The Female Marine* by Da Capo Press in 1966.

Unfortunately, the Da Capo volume reprints one of the composite editions that does not include the Third Part of the series, containing the story's happy denouement. By contrast, the text in this volume is based on the longest of the nineteenth-century composite editions, which includes an abridged version of the Third Part; I have also interpolated many omitted passages of text from the earlier separate installments, resulting in a new composite edition that includes virtually all of the text from the original three parts. In addition, this volume appends the texts of two related "spinoffs" that Coverly produced in a further effort to cash in on *The Female Marine*'s remarkable success. The first, Rachel Sperry's *A Brief Reply to the Late Writings of Louisa Baker,* purports to be the response of the madam of a Boston brothel to the female marine's allegations of coercion; the second, *The Surprising Adventures of Almira Paul,* is the narrative of another cross-dressing female sailor and prostitute reportedly lodged in the Boston jail in 1816. The final nineteenth-century text in this volume is an abridged reprint of *A Brief Account of the Origin and Progress of the Boston Female Society for Missionary Purposes* (1818), which contains several reports by two evangelical ministers who conducted an early domestic mission in the same West Boston vice district described in *The Female Marine.*

From a strictly scholarly point of view, this volume should serve a variety of laudable purposes. For students of early American literature and popular culture, *The Female Marine* is a fascinating blend of several highly significant eighteenth- and nineteenth-century Anglo-American genres; it is, among other things, a Female Warrior narrative, a sentimental novel, and one of the earliest American urban exposés. For those interested in women's history, Coverly's pamphlets help illuminate gender relations and popular attitudes toward sexuality shortly before the emergence of antebellum America's dominant gender ideology of True Womanhood. For sociologists of deviance and historians of prostitution, the female-marine narratives, together with the pious reports of the Boston Female Society for Missionary Purposes, provide unusually graphic accounts of early-nineteenth-century brothels and their inmates. For historians of urban geography and of the African American experience, the texts in this volume provide some of the earliest available descriptions of "Negro Hill," a notorious Boston vice district and the city's largest black residential neighborhood. And for scholars of New England political history, the female-marine narratives shed valuable light on the region's uneasy upsurge of patriotism at the close of the War of 1812. All of those serious topics are explored in this edition's scholarly introduction.

But fortunately *The Female Marine* can never be contained by laudable purposes, scholarly or otherwise. Although the last installment of the narrative is entitled *The Awful Beacon* and explicitly presented to young readers as a cautionary tract, it is, despite its moralistic hyperbole, nothing of the kind. To the contrary, Coverly's cross-dressing pamphlets are all animated by a playful vitality and good humor that defy early-nineteenth-century moralists and late-twentieth-century pedants alike. Were its original publisher somehow to get his hands on a copy of this new scholarly edition, Nathaniel Coverly might initially scratch his head in puzzlement—but he would soon be slapping his thighs and enjoying a good laugh. This volume will allow a new generation of readers to join in the fun.

ACKNOWLEDGMENTS

The first draft of the essay that has evolved into the introduction to this volume was written in 1986 during the American Antiquarian Society's Summer Seminar in the History of the Book in American Culture, led by the late Stephen Botein. A subsequent revision was delivered in July 1992, both at the American Antiquarian Society as a Summer Lunchtime Colloquium and at the Fourteenth Annual Meeting of the Society for Historians of the Early American Republic in Gettysburg, Pennsylvania. A longer version of the essay was then published in the *Proceedings of the American Antiquarian Society*, vol. 103, part 2 (October 1993). I would like to thank the American Antiquarian Society for supporting my research on *The Female Marine* with a Stephen Botein Fellowship during the summer of 1992, for providing many of the illustrations for this book, for providing access to several of the nineteenth-century pamphlets whose texts are reprinted in this volume, and for permission to use material that previously appeared in its *Proceedings*. Thanks are also due to Paul Wright, Pam Wilkinson, and Catlin Murphy of the University of Massachusetts Press, and to the copyeditor, David Hopkins, for shepherding a somewhat complex manuscript through the editorial and production processes. Finally I am grateful to Richard D. Brown, Elizabeth Bussiere, Sueann Caulfield, Morris L. Cohen, Patricia Cline Cohen, Robert A. Gross, John Hench, Susan E. Klepp, Rosalind Remer, Lois Rudnick, Caroline Sloat, Elizabeth Young, Mary S. Zboray, and Ronald J. Zboray for their assistance and encouragement.

INTRODUCTION

Our textbooks assure us that the War of 1812 was an extremely unpopular conflict throughout much of New England, especially in Federalist port towns like Boston. Despite the fact that the hostilities stemmed largely from British attacks on American commercial shipping, merchants of the region had for years seen more economic harm in the retaliatory embargoes imposed by congressional Republicans than in the British blockades, seizures, and impressments. As diplomatic tensions mounted, many New Englanders greeted Congress's preparations for combat with alarm. In late April 1812, less than two months before the official declaration of war, no fewer than 455 Boston merchants frantically petitioned Congress for a postponement of hostilities. Their warnings seemed to be vindicated by the generally disastrous course of the conflict that ensued, as American defeat followed defeat, climaxed by the burning of the nation's capital.[1]

Yet Boston's entrepreneurs seem to have been less upset by their country's humiliation than by their own economic woes. By the autumn of 1813, there were 250 ships sitting idly in Boston harbor and people were leaving the city in search of employment. "We are in a deplorable situation," a Massachusetts Federalist lamented in October 1814, "our commerce dead; our revenue gone; our ships rotting at the wharves. . . . Our treasury drained—we are bankrupts." The following December and January, with the situation looking grim, representatives of the New England states met at Hartford in an ill-timed expression of regional dismay over government policies. But when news of a peace treaty and of Andrew Jackson's great victory at New Orleans reached them in February 1815, even disgruntled New Englanders responded with relief and jubilation.[2]

Still, Bostonians could not rest entirely easy while their beloved *Constitution* remained in danger—not the document, about which many of them felt somewhat ambivalent, but the ship, which remained subject to British attack despite the peace. Affectionately dubbed Old Ironsides, the frigate *Constitution*, built and based in Boston, had achieved one of the first American naval victories of the war in August 1812 and thereafter became a potent symbol of national military prowess, much celebrated in popular ballads. Even New Englanders who ardently opposed the war, and suffered its deprivations, expressed patriotic pride in the *Constitution*'s triumphs. "No nation ever possessed a vessel which had more . . . deserved popularity," the editor of Boston's leading Federalist newspaper declared in mid-April 1815, "and the solicitude for her safety is general, affectionate and profound."[3]

While the war was officially over by then, hostilities persisted at sea, and Boston newspaper readers anxiously followed a series of updates on the status of the *Constitution*. On April 19, for example, the *Columbian Centinel* cited a report that the American vessel had been captured; a week later it happily reported that Old Ironsides had successfully evaded a British squadron. When the *Constitution* finally arrived safely in Boston harbor at the end of May, the inhabitants of the town responded with exuberance. As the ship cast anchor and its officers disembarked, flags waved, artillery roared, and a band played patriotic tunes. Crowds of citizens of both sexes filled the streets, wharves, vessels, and house windows, adding to the general commotion with their hearty cheers and shouts. It may have been a bad war but it certainly was an exhilarating peace—after all, the *Constitution* had come through with colors flying.[4]

I

One canny Boston entrepreneur named Nathaniel Coverly Jr. saw the happy conclusion of the war and the triumphant return of the *Constitution* as occasions not only for patriotism but also for profit. The son of an itinerant printer, publisher, and bookseller, Coverly followed in the footsteps of his father, earning a precarious livelihood in Boston by printing cheap pamphlets and broadsides for common readers, often on criminal or military themes.[5] The younger Coverly is probably best remembered today as the publisher of almost all of the 300 or so broadside ballads purchased by the great American printer Isaiah Thomas in 1814 and donated by him to the American Antiquarian Society as a permanent record of popular—or, as he put it, "vulgar"—taste. Many of those ballads related to American victories in the then ongoing war with England, and several dealt specifically with the famous naval victories of Old Ironsides.[6] Even in Federalist Boston there seems to have been a ready market for such works. After all, close to one-third of the inhabitants voted for Republican candidates throughout the war and, as noted above, even those who did not support the Republican war effort took pride in the martial exploits of American, particularly local, ships and sailors.

According to one source, Boston sailors were themselves among Coverly's chief patrons.[7] Yet whatever his readership, Coverly was no novice at cashing in on patriotism. Some of his publications suggest that he knew how to appeal not only to patriotic passions but to prurient ones as well.[8] In the aftermath of the *Constitution*'s triumphant return to Boston, Coverly came up with a formula that would appeal to both.

In mid-August 1815, Coverly inserted notices in two of Boston's Republican newspapers advertising a pamphlet entitled *An Affecting Narrative of Louisa Baker*. The title page of the first edition indicated that it had been printed in New York by one Luther Wales. However, that imprint was almost certainly a fiction contrived by Coverly, perhaps as a "cover" in the event that Boston authorities were offended by the racy work. The narrative was typical of Coverly's output—and his name appeared proudly on three subsequent editions. A few months later, in November 1815, Coverly advertised a sequel to the Baker narrative entitled *The Adventures of Lucy Brewer*, followed in May 1816 by a third installment of the series, entitled *The Awful Beacon to the Rising Generation*. Several composite editions of the narratives appeared throughout 1816 and thereafter under the title *The Female Marine*. In all, copies survive of at least nineteen printings or editions of *The Female Marine* and its shorter components, all produced between 1815 and 1818. For a period of a few years, they must have been among the most widely circulated pamphlets in Boston.[9]

Although many of them list no printer or publisher on their title pages, most of the female-marine pamphlets were almost certainly issued by Nathaniel Coverly Jr. While it is possible that he wrote the narratives himself, it seems more likely that they were compiled by a hack author in his employ. According to an unidentified nineteenth-century newspaper clipping in the collections of the American Antiquarian Society, Coverly "kept a poet, or ready writer, who manufactured for him all prose and verse articles which were called for by the occasions of the time." The clipping described that author—appropriately named Mr. Wright—as "a comical genius, who could do the grave or the gay, as necessity demanded, and with equal facility." Such a good-humored and versatile "genius" would have been just the sort to have concocted the playful and eclectic story of the female marine.[10]

The author referred to in the newspaper clipping was probably Nathaniel Hill Wright, an obscure printer, publisher, editor, and poet who produced several volumes of verse under his own name during the early decades of the nineteenth century.[11] Wright had been born in Concord, Massachusetts, in 1787, the youngest of twelve children of Amos Wright, a local tavernkeeper. The elder Wright died in the smallpox epidemic of 1792 and it is possible that his youngest boy was

Patriotic front paper cover of an 1816 edition of *The Female Marine,* with a vignette of the great seal of the United States. Courtesy, American Antiquarian Society.

apprenticed to one of the Coverlys at some point thereafter. In fact, it seems probable that the Wrights would have become acquainted with Nathaniel Coverly Sr. in 1794, when he briefly operated a printing office in Concord.[12] Whatever his training, Nathaniel Wright first appeared on the literary scene in 1805, at about the age of eighteen, when he penned a patriotic broadside *Ode* for a Republican celebration of the Fourth of July.[13] He married in 1809 at Newburyport and his wife gave birth to a boy just six months later.[14] Several years after that, apparently while living in Vermont, he produced two small volumes of poetry that featured patriotic verses on American naval exploits in the War of 1812, including a couple of pieces relating to the frigate *Constitution*.[15] Back in Massachusetts in 1819, he composed a pamphlet entitled *Boston: or A Touch at the Times,* a poetic tour of the city that was alternately "descriptive, serious, and satirical." Toward the end of the pamphlet, in some verses that are surely autobiographical, Wright describes a dejected poet who feels obliged to abandon his higher literary aspirations in order to churn out "doleful ditties, murders, and the like" that appeal to the "wondering multitude."[16]

At the time of the first appearance of *The Female Marine,* Nathaniel Hill Wright was in his late twenties, a family man with a wife and at least one small child, evidently struggling to make ends meet.[17] While none of this *proves* that Wright was the author of the female-marine narratives, his political affiliation, sexual history, literary predilections, self-characterization, and personal circumstances—along with the newspaper reference identifying "Mr. Wright" as Coverly's hack—all tend to make him a very plausible candidate. If, indeed, Wright (or any other male author) was the creator of the ostensibly autobiographical accounts, it would be a fitting irony for the playful story of a woman disguising herself as a man to have been written by a man presenting himself to his readers as a woman.[18]

According to the American Antiquarian Society's helpful clipping, the main customers for Coverly's broadsides were "sailors," "the Ann street population of that day" (i.e., prostitutes and their compatriots), and "juveniles."[19] Coverly probably intended a similar readership for the female-marine narratives, though in this case he seems to have particularly targeted the "juveniles." A note on the title page of the Third Part pronounces it "worthy the perusal of young persons of both sexes, and of all classes."[20] With the First and Second Parts priced at a very modest twelve and a half cents each—roughly equivalent to the cost of a mass-market paperback to an unskilled laborer in the late twentieth century—the pamphlets would have been accessible to all but the most impoverished of readers.[21] It may be significant that at least three of the four early owners' signatures on surviving copies are those of women, probably young women. One of them neatly noted inside the front cover—underlining for emphasis—that *The Female Marine* was "a very interesting Book Indeed." Other readers seem to have agreed; about half of the known editions survive only in a single copy—typically worn and tattered— suggesting that many of the modest volumes were literally read to pieces by their eager purchasers.[22]

And no wonder, as a quick plot summary will make clear. The First Part describes the adventures of Louisa Baker, a teenage girl from rural Massachusetts who is seduced by an insincere lover. The fallen and pregnant young woman soon moves to Boston, where she finds shelter in a brothel and gives birth to a baby. After the infant dies, Louisa is coerced into prostitution, a vocation that she follows for three years. At that point, in 1812 or 1813, she disguises herself as a man, escapes from her brothel, and enlists as a United States marine. She serves bravely on board the *Constitution* for two or three years and, in 1815, reassumes her female identity, returning as "a true penitent" to her parents.[23]

In the Second Part, the young veteran, now identified as Lucy Brewer (alias Louisa Baker), becomes restless living at home with her parents and decides to travel. She again disguises herself as a man and boards a stagecoach heading southward. During the trip one of her fellow passengers, a wealthy young woman from New York named Miss West, is abused by an impertinent midshipman. Lucy intervenes and rescues the girl by accepting the sailor's challenge to a duel. Thoroughly intimidating the young man with a clever bluff, Brewer avoids any actual bloodshed. Lucy then travels to New York, where she spends some time with Miss West and her brother. Returning to Boston still dressed as a man, she visits her old brothel and some former shipmates before returning to her parents.[24]

In the Third Part, Mr. West, the brother of the girl whom Lucy had rescued on the stagecoach, discovers that the good samaritan was, in fact, a woman and travels up to Massachusetts to court her. The two visit Plymouth Rock, where Mr. West launches into a patriotic disquisition on the Pilgrims. Later West proposes to Lucy; she accepts; her father agrees to the match (one imagines with a good deal of relief); and the former Boston prostitute is happily married to the wealthy New Yorker. In addition to the main plot line, the Second and Third Parts also include several supplementary warnings and moral sketches, further illustrating the destructive consequences of sexual vice.[25]

The first installment of the female marine and its two sequels were so popular with New England readers that Coverly produced at least two additional spinoffs. In late June 1816, Coverly advertised a pamphlet entitled *A Brief Reply to the Late Writings of Louisa Baker* by Mrs. Rachel Sperry. The ostensible author, identified as the madam of the brothel in which Baker claims to have been entrapped, reveals that Baker's real name is Eliza Bowen and indignantly denies that Bowen had been an unwilling participant in prostitution. Sperry also defends her own involvement in the sex trade as a necessary recourse, following the sudden death of her husband, to save her family from "misery and want."[26]

In early September 1816, Coverly advertised yet another pamphlet, entitled *The Surprising Adventures of Almira Paul.* This new heroine has an even more varied and unlikely career than "the female marine," serving in male disguise on board English, American, and Algerine naval vessels before becoming engaged to an English war widow in Portsmouth, England. Although Paul is determined to "convince the world that the capacities of *women*" are "equal" to those of "the *men,*" she eventually chooses to abandon her disguise and work in the vice districts of Baltimore, New York, and Boston as a prostitute. It was not until October 1816 that Coverly finally beat a belated retreat from the daring themes of female sexuality, autonomy, and adventure, advertising *A Brief Account of the Happy Death of Mary Ann Clark,* the narrative of a much more conventional heroine. Perhaps as an antidote to its immediate predecessors, the story of Miss Clark was designed to provide "an example of meekness and submission," along with "the clearest evidence of early Piety."[27]

II

Although all editions of *The Female Marine* and its component parts are presented as factual accounts—and have been taken as such by uncritical readers ever since—they are almost certainly works of fiction. Such, at least, was the considered judgment of Alexander Medlicott Jr., the first academic historian to study the narratives. Medlicott systematically checked the vital records of all twenty-six towns in early national Plymouth County, the putative site of the female marine's birth, and found no evidence whatsoever of the existence of any Louisa Baker, Lucy Brewer, Lucy West, or Eliza Bowen, as the female marine is variously designated in Coverly's several pamphlets. He also checked the muster rolls of the frigate *Constitution* and found no marine aboard the ship with the first or last name of George, the moniker under which the female marine supposedly served. More recently, I have undertaken similar investigations of the elusive marine with no more success than Medlicott.[28]

Even if one accepts its general designation as fiction—and it would have been difficult for contemporary readers to be sure—*The Female Marine* is far from being a simple work to categorize. "Like most novels of the early nineteenth century in America it is a composite," Medlicott explains, "a blend of many types of popular contemporary styles, themes, and techniques: romance, memoir, pseudo-history, adventure, picaresque tale, autobiography, and sermon." The ambiguity in genre is paralleled by the multiple uncertainties and misperceptions experienced by characters within the plot itself. Male or female, vice or virtue, bravery or cowardice, happiness or sorrow, youth or old age, dream or reality—all of those conventional, and conventionally self-evident, polarities are confused or blurred at one point or another by various characters within the narrative itself.[29]

That sort of problematizing of perception both for actors within the plot and for "external" readers is characteristic of a type of complex narrative identified by literary scholar Thomas Kent as "epistemological texts." In such texts, Kent explains, "epistemological uncertainty may be seen to function on two levels: on the narrative level within the text where characters and events are interwoven, and on the extra-textual level, or audience level, where judgments must be made by the reader about the meaning of the text." In the case of *The Female Marine*, even that most basic distinction between text and audience is subverted when characters in the Third Part of the narrative are influenced by their own reading of the First Part; thus the fragmented text itself becomes an active agent within the plot— serving, ironically, to correct a key misperception by one of its central characters. Kent contrasts complex "epistemological texts" to the relatively simple and highly formulaic dime novels of the late nineteenth century, which he describes as "automatized texts." Part of the epistemological havoc generated by *The Female Marine* is caused by its selective appropriation of motifs from a number of popular formulaic genres—or "automatized texts"—familiar to early-nineteenth-century readers.[30]

Prominent among the generic influences on Coverly's pamphlets was a long tradition of Female Warrior ballads and narratives in early modern popular literature. In *Warrior Women and Popular Balladry*, literary scholar Dianne Dugaw locates no fewer than 120 different Anglo-American Female Warrior ballads printed mostly in Great Britain between the seventeenth and nineteenth centuries, along with many prose narratives on the same theme. Indeed, she claims that "the Female Warrior and masquerading heroines like her were an imaginative preoccupation of the early modern era, appearing not only in popular street ballads but in a host of other genres as well: epic, romance, biography, comedy, tragedy, opera, and ballad opera." According to Dugaw, the early modern tradition of Female Warriors emerged at the dawn of the seventeenth century, reached the height of its vogue during the 1700s, and declined in popularity during the early nineteenth century.[31] At least a few of the Female Warrior ballads identified by Dugaw seem to have been printed and sold by the Coverlys (father and son) of early national Boston.[32] In addition, American *prose* narratives of cross-dressing female soldiers were published in connection with the Revolution, the War of 1812, the Mexican War, and the Civil War. The first of those accounts—the narrative of a Revolutionary war veteran named Deborah Sampson Gannett—is repeatedly cited by the heroine of *The Female Marine*, both as the inspiration for her own exploits and as a documented precedent to bolster the credibility of her tale.[33]

It should be noted that the popular image of the Female Warrior stemmed not only from a literary tradition but from a social tradition as well. In an age when harried military and naval officers often struggled to fill their regiments and crews—and were none too scrupulous about the quality of their recruits—hundreds, if not thousands, of cross-dressing women (along with underaged boys) served in European and North American armies and navies between the sixteenth and nineteenth centuries. For example, Rudolph M. Dekker and Lotte C. van de Pol have documented the cases of more than eighty cross-dressing Dutch women who served as soldiers or sailors during the seventeenth and eighteenth centuries; they indicate that those confirmed cases probably represent "only the tip of the iceberg." Contemporary observers and modern scholars have similarly calculated that at least dozens, if not hundreds or even thousands, of disguised women served in the Union and Confederate armies during the American Civil War.[34]

Indeed, several of the best known American Female Warrior narratives were at least loosely based on the lives of women who actually did serve in the armed forces. Such, for example, were the cases of the Revolutionary heroine Deborah Sampson Gannett—who eventually received a pension from the federal government—and the two most celebrated cross-dressing soldiers of the Civil War, Sarah Emma Edmonds and Loreta Janeta Velazquez. Those two latter cases vividly illustrate the complex interrelationship of the social and literary traditions of the Female Warrior. Modern scholars have now established that the bestselling narratives of Edmonds and Velazquez were based, at least in part, on their actual military experiences. But much as the fictive Lucy Brewer cited Deborah Sampson Gannett's "memoirs" as a personal model, so did the flesh-and-blood fighting women of the Civil War cite earlier narratives of Female Warriors as sources of inspiration for their own martial exploits. Loreta Janeta Velazquez recalled that her juvenile imagination had been fired by stories of "the glorious deeds of Joan of Arc," while Sarah Emma Edmonds reportedly attributed her martial aspirations to her girlhood reading of a popular piece of cheap American fiction of the 1840s—Maturin Murray Ballou's *Fanny Campbell, the Female Pirate Captain*—given to her by a kindly peddler in rural Canada. Although such published reminiscences may not be *entirely* reliable, there can be little doubt that the social and literary traditions of the Female Warrior were intricately intertwined in the lives and imaginations of both narrators and readers.[35]

Female Tar.

J. Pitts, Printer. & Wholesale Toy Warehouse
6. Great st, Andrew street 7 Dials.

COME all you blooming damsels & listen to my song
And all you pretty maidens that know what to love
It is of pretty Sally I unto you shall name,   (belong,
That for the sake of her true love Jemmy did plow the
                                    raging main,   [did ply.
Young Jemmy was a Waterman at Wapping he did
Pretty Sally loved him dearly and lived hard by,
And oft abroad in boat or skiff where silver streams did
                                    flow,

This loving pair to take the air together they would go
Like a pair of turtle doves this young couple did agree
And vow'd to each other true and constant for to be,
But at length young Sally's father the same came to
                                    know,

I'll part you both he then did say Jemmy to sea shall go
Dear honoured father the young damsel then did say,
Pray doon't be cruel as to force my love away,
For my Jemmy's my delight we have vow'd ne'er to
                                    part,   (heart,
Whilst life remain no other swain shall ever gain my
Then seventeen miles from London Sally was sent away
Unto a rich old uncle guarded both night and day.
While her father cruel hearted had Jemmy sent to sea
In hopes that he might ne er return his son in law to
Thus those two lovers were forced to part,   (be,
Which grieved pretty Sally quite sorely the heart,
But fortune did befriend this pretty maiden fair,
And soon she did follow her true love that she did love
                                    so dear,

Twas early in the morning just as day light did appear,
Fretty Sally from her uncle's house got both safe and
                                    clear,
Drest in man's apparel to London came straightway,
And soon she found that Jemmy's ship in Sheerness lay
With jacket blue and heart true trowsers so neat and
                                    white,
Pretty Sally ty'd back her hair and follow d her love
                                    outright.   )in.
And when she came unto the ship that Jemmy he was
Straigrtway she enter'd on board and sail'd along with
                                    him   (the sea,
Scarcely days more than eight or nine had they sail don
When a French ship they spy'd sailing with a stiff breeze
All hands were called then to pursue the enemy,
No sooner we came up witt them but a shot we let fly
Four hours and some minutes these two ships did engage
At length their colours down did fall and yield to Bri-
                                    tons brave,

But altho' the battle was so fierce and hot,
Pretty sally well escap d the fire and shot.
Our ship she did return with her prise to England's
                                    shore,   (ador'd,
Young sally she made herself known to Jemmy she
While Jemmy gaz'd upon her he unto her did say,
Now I'll make you my lawful bride without any more
                                    delay,   (hand,
Then these two loyal lovers two church went hand in
And a number of the ship s company which made a je-
                                    vial band
The first lieutenant also who gave the bride away,
While bells in steeples they did ring and music swee
                                    did play.

THE SHIP CARPENTER.

YOU loyal lovers far and near,
  A true relation you shall hear,
Of a young couple who prov'd to be
A pattern of true loyalty.
A merchant did in Bristol dwell,
As many people know full well ;
He had a girl of beauty bright,
In whom he plac'd his whole delight.
He had no child but only she,
Her Father lov'd her tenderly,
Many to court her thither came,
Gallants of worthy birth and fame.
Yet notwithstanding all their love,
A young ship carpenter did prove
To be the master of her heart,
She often said we'll never part.
As long as life and breath remain
Your company I'll not refrain,
No cursed gold, nor silver bright,
Shall make me wrong my heart's delight:
Now when her Father came to know
That she did love this young man so,
He caus'd him to be press'd to sea,
To keep her from his company.
Now when the damsel this did hear,
Without the thoughts of dread or fear,
She drest herself in Seaman's hue,
And after him she did pursue.
Into the Captain she did go,
  said right worthy Sir 'tis so,
  u do want men I understand,
  m   to fight with heart and hand.
The Captain straitway did reply,
Young man you're welcome heartily :
A guinea in her hand he gave,
She passed for a seaman brave.
Soon after this the ship did sail,
And with a fair and pleasant gale,
But this ship carpenter (her dear,)
Did not think his love so near.
She then appeared for to be
A person of no mean degree.
With pretty fingers long and strait,
She soon became the surgeon's mate.
It happen'd so that this same ship,
In storming of the town Dieppe,
She lay at anchor, something nigh,
Where cannon bullets they did fly:
The first man who was wounded there,
Was this young bold ship carpenter,
When drums did beat and trumpets sound
He in his breast receiv'd a wound.
Then to   surgeon's care was he
Brought   n with speed immediately,
Where the pretty surgeon's mate
Did courteously upon him wait.
She drest the woeful wounded part,
Although the sight did pierce her heart,
Sh   then did use her utmost skill,
To cure him with a right good will.

She cur'd him in a little space,
He often gaz'd upon her face,
The merchant's daughter of Bristol, who
Had to her truelove proved true,
When many storms were overblown,
Unto her love herself made known,
The season of the year being past,
The ship was homeward bound at last.
When in the harbor she did get,
The seamen all on shore were set,
Not yet of all the whole ship's crew
Bot a soul among them knew
That they a woman had so near,
Until she told it to her dear.
Not long time ago said she,
You told me that such eyes as mine
Did formerly your heart confine ;
Then without any more ado,
Unto his arms strait way she flew
And said my love this is thy own,
This have I done for you alone,
His heart was fill'd with joy likewise,
When as the tears stood in his eyes,
Thou hast shown a valiant heart
And likewise play'd a truelove's part.
And then without the least delay,
He deckt her like a lady gay,
And then married they were with speed,
As formerly they had agreed,
Then to her Father's house he went,
And found him in much discontent ;
He ask'd him for his daughter dear,
Which pierc'd her father's heart for her.
He with a mournful voice reply'd
I wish she'd in her cradle dy'd,
But now I ne'er shall see her more,
My jewel whom I did adore,
Had I a kingdom now in store,
Nay had I that and ten times more,
I'd part with all her face to see,
Daughter would I have dy'd for thee.
The young man hearing what he said,
Reply'd your daughter is not dead,
For you within a few hours space,
Shall surely see your daughters face.
He rode as fast as he could hie,
And brought her home immediately
And set her in her father's hall,
Where on her knees she strait did fall ;
Thrice welcome home thou art, said he,
Once more my jewel unto me.
To him the truth she did relate,
How she had been the surgeons mate,
He then did smile and was right glad,
And gave them all that e'er he had.
She now is made a loving wife,
And liveth free from care and strife,
Young lovers all a pattern take,
When you a solemn contract make.

Early-nineteenth-century American edition of a British Female Warrior ballad, probably printed somewhere in New England.

Front paper cover of an 1846 edition of Maturin Murray Ballou's *Fanny Campbell, the Female Pirate Captain,* reportedly the inspiration for Sarah Emma Edmonds's martial exploits during the American Civil War.

THE FEMALE VOLUNTEER;

OR THE

LIFE, WONDERFUL ADVENTURES AND MIRACULOUS ESCAPES OF

MISS ELIZA ALLEN,

A YOUNG LADY OF EASTPORT, MAINE.

Being a truthful and well-authenticated narrative of her parentage, birth and early life—her love for one whom her parents disapproved —his departure for Mexico—her determination to follow him at all hazards—her flight in man's attire—enlistment—terriffic battles of Mexico—her wounds—voyage to California—the shipwreck and loss of her companions—her miraculous escape—return to her ·native land—meeting of the lovers—reconciliation of her parents— marriage and happy termination of all her trials and sorrows.

SOLD BY AGENTS ONLY.

Front paper cover of *The Female Volunteer* (1851), an American Female Warrior narrative of the Mexican War.

Whether adopting social-historical or literary approaches, many modern scholars, particularly feminist scholars, have been fascinated by the gender politics embedded in Female Warrior ballads and narratives. Cross-dressing women certainly destabilize the culturally constructed distinction between male and female. However, one might argue that Female Warrior ballads do so in ways that privilege masculine virtue; after all, Female Warriors are celebrated—and they almost invariably *are* celebrated in the popular literature—for their adoption of conventionally male behaviors.[36] In addition, Female Warriors in the early modern literature are generally motivated by a traditional feminine goal: their desire to be reunited with husbands or lovers gone off to war. Thus Dugaw explains that "almost all" of the ballads and "most" of the prose narratives "make [heterosexual] love the heroine's ultimate motive."[37] By contrast, Lucy Brewer goes to war not to "stand by her man" but rather to escape her entrapment within an exploitative system of commercialized sex. Her conventional marriage at the end of the narrative is not presented as the motive for her exploits but rather as a reward for her aggressive pursuit of autonomy and personal fulfillment. In that regard, at least, *The Female Marine* is distinctly more radical than most earlier Female Warrior narratives.

One could further argue that *The Female Marine* is radical even by the demanding standards of recent "cultural studies" theory. In her much-acclaimed *Gender Trouble: Feminism and the Subversion of Identity*, feminist philosopher Judith Butler asserts the fundamentally unstable and "performative" quality of gender identity. All people, she insists, whatever their biological characteristics, sexual preferences, style of dress, and public demeanor, constantly "play" gender "roles" of one sort or another, if only the ones prescribed by dominant social norms. Gender identities, then, are not biological essences but cultural constructions and individual performances. While Butler's insights may rightly pass for "cutting edge" in the late-twentieth-century academy, they would have been dull commonplaces to the authors, protagonists, and readers of early modern Female Warrior narratives.[38]

Along those lines, the heroine of *The Female Marine* appears to have taken particular pleasure in destabilizing or subverting conventional gender-based conceptions of "virtue"—particularly "female" chastity and "male" valor. Not only does Lucy Brewer (as protagonist) transcend her many violations of sexual propriety and repeatedly demonstrate physical courage in combat, she also ridicules and humiliates a man who seems to claim martial valor as a sexual prerogative. In a humorous description of her confrontation with the midshipman who insults and harasses a young woman on board a stagecoach, Brewer (as narrator) repeatedly identifies her antagonist with his phallus: "the little weapon that hung by his side." She not only refers to him as the "*dirkman*" and "the valiant young knight of the *dirk*," but describes how the midshipman "appeared to wilt considerably, and walked less erect" when confronted by Brewer's own "cocked pistol." The female marine's ability to emasculate the "*dirkman*" with the aid of an unloaded pistol neatly demonstrates the "performative" quality of gender; shortly before staging her abortive duel with the midshipman, Brewer assures a collaborator that she intends to "act" not "a tragedy" but "a farce." The incident also illustrates the simpler insight, central to the entire Female Warrior tradition, that courage, like cowardice, knows no sex.[39]

Nathaniel Coverly's pamphlets not only reflect a venerable early modern tradition of Female Warrior narratives; they also stand near the beginning of what was to become a prolific nineteenth-century tradition of urban exposés. According to Lyle Wright, a pioneer bibliographer of American fiction, only two out of sixty-nine novels of "city life" published in the United States between 1800 and 1850 appeared before 1820. According to Adrienne Siegel's more comprehensive count, only eighteen "urban novels" appeared in America during the period between 1774 and 1830, in contrast to the hundreds that poured from American presses during the 1840s and 1850s. Having thoroughly canvassed that vast output, Siegel suggests that mass-market fiction of the mid-nineteenth century conveyed an ambivalent vision of urban America. Many of the novels exposed the material hardships, social inequities, and moral dangers of city life. But at the same time, they tended to reinforce the claims of urban boosters that American cities were great repositories of cultural abundance and social opportunity.[40]

The Female Marine conveys a similarly split image of early national Boston. On the one hand, Lucy Brewer presents an extremely graphic portrait of Boston's seamy vice district on West Boston Hill (this refers to the north slope of Beacon Hill, as it is called today, often designated "Negro Hill" or "Nigger Hill" by white Bostonians of the early republic). Her unromanticized descriptions of dance halls, brothels, seductive call girls, coarse streetwalkers, child prostitutes, and interracial sexual encounters surely shocked early-nineteenth-century readers. At one point, the narrator suggests that Boston may have a "greater proportion" of whores than any "town of equal size in the Union." Judging from her lurid narrative, that is easy to believe. As an urban exposé with vivid descriptions that allow readers to indulge vicariously in that which they presumably deplore, *The Female Marine* is an early precursor to what David Reynolds has described as a vast antebellum literature of "immoral didacticism" or "subversive reform."[41]

But on the other hand—and in Coverly's multivalent narrative there almost always is an other hand—several descriptions of Boston contained in *The Female*

Map of Boston, Massachusetts (ca. 1810–25). The arrow points toward West Boston Hill, also known as "Negro Hill," the largest African American neighborhood and one of the two main vice districts in the city during the early nineteenth century.

Marine make it read more like an advertisement than an exposé. In the First Part of the narrative, an informed observer claims of Boston that "there is not a city or town in any part of the United States, that can boast of a greater proportion of honest, kind and hospitable inhabitants." Much later, in the Third Part, Mr. West describes the "Capital of New England" in similarly laudatory terms; Lucy's future husband

> represented the town, for pleasantness, &c. far surpassing his expectations, while upon its inhabitants, for their natural good humour and polite attention to strangers, he bestowed the highest encomiums. . . . [T]he many excellent bridges which connect the neighbouring villages with the town, for convenience and beauty of structure, he represented as far surpassing any that he had ever before seen—the State-House, for beauty, &c. he thought equal and far more pleasantly situated than the City Hall of New-York, nor did he conceive the Bowery of that city half so pleasant as the justly admired Mall of Boston.[42]

Not only do Coverly's pamphlets anticipate both the muckraking and the boosterism of antebellum city novels, one of them even reconciles those two seemingly incompatible stances toward urban life. In her *Brief Reply* to Louisa Baker, Rachel Sperry claims that vice districts like "Negro Hill" actually purify the civic environment by segregating disreputable elements:

> [T]hat the existence of such places are essential to the security of the innocent and defenceless, in large commercial towns and cities, I have no doubt. What would be the situation of Boston, and what the danger attending the evening excursions of its female inhabitants, were not a peculiar class of their fellow-creatures priviledged with a place of resort like the Hill?—should those of easy life, peculiar to sea ports, be denied a residence here, they would privately seek one in more respectable parts of the town—then would every female, however innocent and respectable, be liable to be insulted in their houses, and venture abroad in the evening at the risk of their lives. . . . [S]ailors, soldiers, &c. who now uniformly resort to the hill, would then parole [*sic*] the public streets in search of company, and to whose insults and abuse every female, young and old, would be liable. Large towns and cities have found it always necessary to erect suitable places of deposit for all nuisances, filth, &c. whereby the health of its inhabitants are endangered—so for public good, in every large town and city, ought there to be a place allotted those who prefer a life of debauchery, and who are esteemed as a public nuisance—so far we consider the Hill, and its inhabitants . . . of public benefit to the town.[43]

By ignoring the coercion and exploitation that often pervade zones of urban vice, the author introduces a rationale for tolerating such districts that would be widely embraced by policymakers of the nineteenth and twentieth centuries, who often tried to contain or regulate prostitution rather than extirpate it.[44] However, it is probably significant that Coverly (or his hack) distances himself from that complacent position by attributing it to an author of dubious character. The more credible account of Louisa Baker—to which Sperry's narrative is opposed— features sharp and intolerant diatribes against the procurers, madams, and harlots of "Negro Hill." As a group, Coverly's pamphlets thus present a multivalent vision of urban life—and of urban vice—that defies any simple formula.

Another conventional genre that *The Female Marine* impersonates but ultimately transcends is the sentimental seduction tale—the dominant form of early American fiction. Samuel Richardson's *Clarissa*, first published in England in 1748, provided an archetype for such early American novels as William Hill Brown's *The Power of Sympathy* (1789), Susanna Rowson's *Charlotte Temple* (1791), and Hannah Foster's *The Coquette* (1797). In all of those works, women are seduced by insincere lovers and then die, or commit suicide, out of shame and remorse.[45] Although seduction tales conveyed seemingly conservative messages of filial obedience and sexual restraint to their predominantly female readers, such modern feminist scholars as Cathy N. Davidson have argued that early sentimental novels were actually a subversive genre that warned young women against male depravity, called for female solidarity, and assailed the sexual double standard.[46]

In some respects *The Female Marine*, particularly in its early pages, fits comfortably into the canon of early American sentimental fiction. As Alexander Medlicott observes, the author employs "almost every device known to the writers of romance in the eighteenth century: parental warnings; headlong-heedless love; seduction by a dastardly villain; flight through storms; temporary sanctuary with a kindly protectress; ensnarement by a wretched deceiver; a pitiful death of an unwanted child; sermons and lectures on moral fibre; and years of depravity and disillusionment as a fallen woman." Most important, Lucy's seduction is remarkably similar to those depicted in the earlier novels. "I was all innocence, and knew no sin, until that fatal period when the vile and insinuating author of my ruin deluded and deceived me," Lucy recalls. "I never once reflected that the man who could stoop to seduction, would not hesitate to forsake the wretched object of his passion." In short, the opening episodes of Coverly's narrative faithfully replicate the definitive motifs of the sentimental seduction tale.[47]

The Female Marine also resembles other works of early American fiction in claiming a serious didactic purpose. Thus the narrator inserts a cautionary statement, typical of early sentimental novels, at the end of the first installment: "If what I have exposed to public view is sufficient to induce youths of my sex never to listen to the voice of love, unless sanctioned by paternal approbation, and to resist the impulse of inclination, when it runs counter to the precepts of religion and virtue, then, indeed, have I not written in vain." That moralistic warning was, in fact, taken nearly verbatim from Susanna Rowson's *Charlotte Temple,* the most popular American novel of the early republic. Just like Lucy Brewer, Rowson warns her young female readers to "listen not to the voice of love unless sanctioned by paternal approbation" and to "resist the impulse of inclination when it runs counter to the precepts of religion and virtue." At least one other extended passage from the *The Female Marine* is taken verbatim from *Charlotte Temple;* an attack on the sexual double standard in *The Awful Beacon* echoes Rowson's rhetoric of outrage; and there is other evidence of direct literary borrowing.[48]

The main obstacle to incorporating *The Female Marine* into the traditional canon of sentimental fiction is that Coverly's playful narrative flagrantly defies the main tenet of the formulaic seduction tale—that a sexual fall must be followed by anguished suffering and penitent death. Although Lucy does go through some hard times immediately following her seduction, she eventually turns her reversal to advantage, surviving three years of heroic military service and finally winning the hand of the wealthy Mr. West. Far from exhibiting the passive anguish of violated womanhood, Lucy demonstrates active courage, resourcefulness, and even good humor in the face of adversity.

The utter subversiveness of Lucy's story is accentuated by its juxtaposition to one of the supplementary tales appended to the Third Part of the narrative. That brief sketch tells the sad story of Maria D——, a sweet and pure, but naive, young woman who innocently marries a "weak, vicious and debauched man." Her unworthy husband soon becomes a patron of Boston's vilest brothels, leading to poor Maria's passive decline and early death.[49] The sharp contrast between the fates of Lucy Brewer and Maria D—— suggests that a bad marriage could be a greater disaster than an outright seduction. In the treacherous world of gender relations depicted by *The Female Marine,* a young woman's autonomy was ultimately more important than her virginity. Although it seems unlikely that Nathaniel Coverly Jr. (or Nathaniel Wright) had women's liberation in mind when he set his literary pot to boiling, that message of female autonomy may help explain the narrative's appeal to the young ladies of early national Boston—and to enlightened academics today.

Yet another literary ancestor to *The Female Marine* is the picaresque, a fictional form that originated in early modern Spain. Picaresque novels are episodic narratives that depict the travels and comic adventures of young plebeian "rogues" trying to get ahead in a hierarchical society. Although female *pícaras* occasionally appear in early modern Spanish novels, Cathy Davidson has argued that the early American picaresque genre—in which "politics is the central issue"— "virtually excludes women precisely because women *were* excluded from the politics of the new Republic." Despite that caveat, Davidson goes on to describe several early American examples of the "female picaresque," including the "memoirs" of the cross-dressing Revolutionary warrior, Deborah Sampson Gannett. But Davidson emphasizes the problematic character of such works, suggesting that the *pícara* of the early republic necessarily plays a "specious and surreptitious" role that ultimately challenges "neither the status quo nor the [sexual] double standard." Davidson is especially dismissive of "the fad for female adventures" that "became particularly popular throughout the first half of the nineteenth century." Citing *The Female Marine* in a short list of examples, Davidson implicitly condemns such narratives as "fantasies" lacking "a hard core of realism."[50]

While it is certainly true that the anonymous author of *The Female Marine* neglects to demand the political enfranchisement of women, Davidson is much too quick to discount the ideological challenges that such female *pícaras* posed to the sexual "status quo" of the early republic. As Natalie Zemon Davis pointed out long ago, popular representations of "women on top," however comical or unrealistic, can sometimes "prompt new ways of thinking about the [gender] system," serve as "a resource for feminist reflection on women's capacities," and even "hint at the possibility of a wider role of citizenship for women." Along those lines, I would argue that *The Female Marine*—with its exuberant depictions of female patriotism, resourcefulness, valor, and autonomy—conveys messages at least as radical and subversive as those attributed by Cathy Davidson to such conventional sentimental tales as *Charlotte Temple.*[51]

The playful gender radicalism of *The Female Marine* is perhaps best understood when situated near the beginning of a popular American literary tradition of antiheroines or "confidence women." Literary scholar Kathleen De Grave has recently described a series of narratives of female criminals, adventuresses, soldiers, and spies, among others, that gained popularity during the nineteenth century. Although she discusses a few stray examples published prior to 1850, she suggests that the literary image of the "confidence woman" did not become a "powerful force" until the decades between the Civil War and World War I. According to De Grave, such unconventional women "first and foremost had confidence in themselves, a sense of their ability to independently confront their world"; they "set goals for themselves and allowed themselves styles of action not condoned by the greater society"; and they had "a certain joie de vivre and often a sense of humor." De Grave suggests that the literary confidence woman emerged in the United States during the decades of transition from the "True Woman," glorified by antebellum gender ideology, to the "New Woman," who had emerged by the early twentieth century. However, the uncanny resemblance between De Grave's antiheroines and Coverly's earlier female protagonist suggests that the origins of the American "confidence woman" may actually be traced to an earlier transition in gender regimes.[52]

III

Various types of evidence suggest that gender norms and roles probably were somewhat less sharply bifurcated in seventeenth-century New England than else-where in the early modern world. In recent years scholars have variously argued that Puritan religious ideology tended to promote the same moral virtues and behaviors in both men and women, that Puritan legal systems functioned in ways that enhanced the relative power of women and undercut traditional British sexual "double standards," and that Puritan men and women often differed sur-prisingly little in their day-to-day conduct, *mis*conduct, and general deport-ment.[53] But that pattern gradually changed over the course of the eighteenth century, with the weakening of New England's early religious establishments and the growing influence of imported British traditions of both genteel womanhood and popular misogyny—traditions that emphasized differences between the sexes. During the turbulent Revolutionary era and its aftermath, gender roles became even more confused and contested, as the social realities of warfare disrupted the sexual division of labor, and as popular ideology alternately lauded female patrio-tism and (allegorically, at least) feminized social and political vice. Indeed, the gender messages of the Revolutionary era were so mixed that a few recent histo-rians have detected an ominous rebirth of "patriarchy" in late eighteenth-century America, where others have discovered the ideological origins of modern feminist claims to public status and civic participation.[54]

The publication of *The Female Marine* took place near the end of that extended Revolutionary period of flux and confusion in gender roles and norms. Within a few years, a new gender ideology—variously designated by modern historians as "domesticity," "separate spheres," and "the cult of True Womanhood"—had been widely popularized by hundreds of published sermons, advice manuals, gift books, and women's magazines. The new ideology, closely linked to the bourgeois values of an emerging middle class, celebrated the divergent natures and roles of the sexes, assigning men to the dangerous "public" spheres of politics and marketplace, while consigning women to the nurturing "private" spheres of home and family. There, as wives and mothers, women were expected to embody the cardinal feminine virtues of piety, purity, submissiveness, and domesticity.[55] While the ideological hegemony of "separate spheres" should not be exaggerated—after all, Female Warrior narratives and other comparably subversive representations of women continued to appear in print throughout the nineteenth century—it did represent a popular and powerful gender standard to which even unconventional authors typically showed deference. For example, after describing the valiant martial exploits of Mademoiselle Appolonia Jagiello, a cross-dressing Polish revolutionary of the 1840s, Civil War veteran and author Loreta Janeta Velazquez quickly assured her readers that Jagiello was "a most womanly woman, and was lacking in nothing that makes true womanhood esteemed by right-thinking people."[56]

Changing gender norms of the eighteenth and nineteenth centuries were reflected not only in new literary prescriptions but also in shifting patterns of sexual activity among young men and women. Although premarital pregnancies had been relatively rare in Puritan New England, rates of prenuptial conception gradually rose over the course of the eighteenth century, peaking in New England (and elsewhere in North America) between about 1780 and 1800, when in some communities about one out of every three brides was pregnant on her wedding day. Historical demographers have linked the increase in premarital pregnancies to a decline in traditional familial and communal controls on sexual activity among the young, and to a broader shift from community-oriented values and behavior toward greater individual assertion and autonomy in a variety of social spheres.[57]

However, the eighteenth-century rise in premarital pregnancies did not mark a permanent trend in American demography. To the contrary, rates of premarital pregnancy fell so rapidly during the first half of the nineteenth century that by 1850 pregnant brides were nearly as uncommon as they had been during the Puritan period. Scholars have attributed that dramatic decline in premarital pregnancies to the religious influence of the Second Great Awakening and to the internalization by young men and women of a new bourgeois ethic of sexual self-control. Of course, in exercising that new restraint, young people had a good deal of literary encouragement. As already described, early American sentimental novels warned against the dire consequences of seduction, while just a few decades later various forms of prescriptive literature celebrated the "purity" required of all True Women. Indeed, *The Female Marine* itself was a playful, arguably tongue-in-cheek contribution to that largely successful campaign to increase sexual continence in America's early republic.[58]

By attributing the rise and fall of premarital pregnancy rates to a breakdown of "traditional" communal controls followed by an internalization of "modern" patterns of self-control, historical demographers have attempted to link changing sexual behavior to the emergence of a new character-type sometimes designated "the modern personality."[59] The modernization model, first formulated by social scientists during the 1960s, posits a fundamentally bipolar view of culture, society, and personality, built upon a contrast between the "traditional" and the "modern." According to Richard D. Brown, the leading exponent of the theory as applied to early American history, traditional peoples tend to be fatalistic: "The prevailing outlook of people in traditional society is one of acceptance or resignation toward life as it is. . . . There is neither the aspiration nor the expectation of spiritual or material improvement for society. . . . Innovation and novelty are viewed with suspicion." Brown describes the modern personality type as the polar opposite of the traditional; it is characterized by individual dynamism, autonomy, cosmopolitanism, flexibility, and a determination to master and manipulate the environment to advantage.[60]

Although modernization theory has become unpopular among many academics in recent years, it nonetheless provides an illuminating perspective on *The Female Marine*.[61] For there can be little doubt as to where "Lucy Brewer" stands in reference to the divide between "traditional" and "modern." The female marine violates traditional norms, exercises autonomy, travels widely, and demonstrates great flexibility in her determination to master her environment. She overcomes the stigma of her premarital seduction and defies conventional gender roles. More broadly, Coverly's pamphlets celebrate a society dominated by the modern impulse toward mastery. In the Third Part of the narrative, Mr. West approvingly describes the reaction of Bostonians to a gale that had uprooted some large elms. Rather than respond fatalistically to an act of God or nature, the Bostonians simply take "block and tackle" and haul the trees back into place. Just as the narrative celebrates the willful rise of a fallen woman, so also does it hail the resourceful raising of some fallen trees. In each case, the behavioral impulse is distinctly modern.[62]

The modernity of *The Female Marine* is even more strikingly illustrated by Mr. West's patriotic disquisition at Plymouth Rock, an oration worthy of being quoted at some length:

> It was (continued he) scarcely 200 years ago [that the Pilgrims landed], and what was the now flourishing States of New-England then!—an almost impenetrable forest, abounding with savages and beasts of prey! . . . But with these

dreary prospects the Pilgrims were not to be disheartened—they landed, and very soon changed the face of New-England; they introduced symmetry by the assistance of all the instruments of art; the impenetrable woods were cleared, and made room for commodious habitations; the wild beasts were driven away, and flocks of domestic animals supplied their place; whilst thorns and briars made way for rich harvests—the coasts were covered with towns, and the bays with ships—and thus the new world like the old became subject to man.[63]

A new world subject to man! It would be hard to imagine a vision of material progress and human mastery more remote from traditional Puritan piety, with its insistence upon the covenanted community's humble dependence on a sovereign God.

Of course, modernization theory has more than its share of detractors; but even its most hostile critics have a hard time denying that some fundamental shift in American society and culture took place between the Revolution and the Civil War. Those scholars have struggled to develop other ways of characterizing that transition, with many resorting to the concepts of republicanism and liberalism. For example, Steven Watts's *The Republic Reborn* argues that the War of 1812 marked a key point of transition between social orders built on eighteenth-century republicanism and nineteenth-century liberalism. In contrast to modernization theorists, who generally imply that modernization is a good thing, Watts suggests that the rise of liberalism was in certain respects a bad one, leading to psychological stress, deep anxieties, neurotic repression, fragmented personalities, and, finally, to the fratricidal bloodbath of the American Civil War. Nathaniel Coverly's *The Female Marine*, it might be argued, conforms to the letter but not the spirit of Watts's thesis. While the War of 1812 did provide Lucy Brewer with her entrée into a world of bourgeois liberalism, that outcome did not lead to stress, anxiety, and repression but to personal autonomy, restored self-confidence, and a happy marriage.[64]

Still, Watts's argument is useful here in reminding us that *The Female Marine* is not simply a generic embodiment of the modern worldview but rather a reflection of cultural attitudes in a particular time and place. That is, it reflects the period of national unity, optimism, and patriotism that followed the Battle of New Orleans in 1815 and climaxed during the early years of the Monroe administration in the so-called Era of Good Feelings—a happy interlude that was abruptly terminated by the financial and sectional crises of 1819. Admittedly, the very concept of an Era of Good Feelings has fallen into disrepute in recent years, even among textbook writers. In *The American Pageant*, for example, Bailey and Kennedy claim that the label is "something of a misnomer." One prominent scholar has gone so far as to dub the period the "Era of *Bad* Feelings." Yet I would argue that an Era of Good Feelings did, in fact, occur—at least in New England—and would offer *The Female Marine* as proof.[65]

While it is, on one level, a cautionary tale of seduction, *The Female Marine* is, on another, a good-humored and optimistic celebration of the patriotic valor of an American woman. In fact, Coverly's changing frontispieces for the pamphlets neatly suggest that the patriotic component of their appeal became increasingly important over time. The original frontispiece of the First Part consists of an upper-torso portrait of the heroine in a low-cut dress that accentuates her breasts; the text beneath the portrait includes a few lines of sentimental verse referring to her seduction—borrowed, in part, from the title page of *Charlotte Temple*. The frontispiece to an edition of the Second Part contains the same portrait but with a military hat crudely added to the figure, the bust more modestly concealed, and the seduction verses removed. The frontispieces of composite editions of *The Female Marine* generally portray a somewhat androgynous woman standing at attention with a musket in her hand and a frigate in the background. A vignette of the great seal of the United States appears on the front wrapper of one of those editions. Finally, the frontispiece of the 1818 edition—the last known—depicts a woman in military dress waving an American flag. Over the course of its publishing history, then, the iconography of the narrative seems to have shifted in emphasis from sentimental seduction to patriotic adventure. In the Era of Good Feelings, even a fallen woman could feel good about herself—and about her country![66]

To recapitulate, the War of 1812 ended in 1815, the year in which the first two parts of Lucy Brewer's narrative were published. At least nineteen printings or editions of the various installments and versions of the narrative were issued, mostly in Boston, during the years 1815 through 1818. The Era of Good Feelings is conventionally considered to have ended the following year, in 1819. Significantly, the actual phrase "Era of Good Feelings" originated in Boston. It was coined in the summer of 1817 in response to the warm reception given by the city's inhabitants to the newly elected president of the United States, the Virginian James Monroe, during a good will tour of formerly hostile New England. The greeting was in many respects reminiscent of that given to Old Ironsides two years earlier, complete with musical band, ringing bells, waving flags, and countless citizens turned out in the streets. It is certainly tempting to speculate that at least some among the throngs that warmly greeted the chief of state owned well-thumbed copies of *The Female Marine*.[67]

LOUISA BAKER,

[A NATIVE OF MASSACHUSETTS.]

Who, in disguise, served Three Years as a MA-
RINE on board an American FRIGATE.

❖

"She was her parents only joy :
They had but one—one darling child,
But ah ! the cruel spoiler came !"

LUCY BREWER,

[A NATIVE OF PLYMOUTH COUNTY, MASSACHUSETTS.]

Who in disguise served Three Years as a MARINE
on board the Frigate CONSTITUTION.

☞ Those who have read the First Part of Miss
BREWER's (alias) BAKER's Adventures, ought
not fail to peruse this.

Iconography of the Female Marine. *Left to right:* (1) Frontispiece of *The Adventures of Louisa Baker* (New York: Luther Wales, [1815]). This is the earliest known image of the female marine. (2) Frontispiece of *The Adventures of Lucy Brewer* (Boston: H. Trumbull, 1815). Note that this is essentially the same portrait as in the "Luther Wales" pamphlet, but with a military hat crudely added to the figure, the bust more modestly concealed, the subject's name changed, and the seduction verses replaced by an advertisement. (3) Frontispiece of *The Female Marine*, "Tenth Edition" ([Boston?]: Printed for the Proprietor [N. Coverly Jr.?], 1816). This is the most common visual image of the female marine. (4) Frontispiece of *The Female Marine*, "Fourth Edition" ([Boston?]: Printed for the Author, 1818). This image is from the last known nineteenth-century edition of *The Female Marine*. Images 1, 2, and 4 courtesy, American Antiquarian Society.

IV

Yet beneath the exuberant good feelings of Boston's citizens may have lurked anxiety, ambivalence, and even guilt. Those darker feelings can also help to explain why so many readers embraced *The Female Marine*. In her recent study of "cross-dressing and cultural anxiety," literary critic Marjorie Garber argues that "one of the most consistent and effective functions of the transvestite in culture is to indicate the place of . . . 'category crisis,' disrupting and calling attention to cultural, social, or aesthetic dissonances." In other words, Garber claims, the appearance of cross-dressing as a cultural motif typically suggests the presence within the culture of some other source of "crisis" or "dissonance," not always directly related to issues of gender and sexuality. In the case of *The Female Marine*, there is certainly no shortage of "crises" or "dissonances" to explore.[68]

In addition to the flux and uncertainty concerning gender roles and sexual norms in post-Revolutionary America (already discussed), another social crisis or dissonance reflected in *The Female Marine* was an increasing anxiety among Bostonians of various social classes concerning the perceived growth of urban vice and disorder during the first decades of the nineteenth century. Between 1790 and 1825, Boston was transformed from a relatively cohesive town of 18,000 inhabitants to a heterogeneous metropolis containing more than three times as many people. As growing population density and fluidity increased the anonymity of city life, traditional social controls weakened and even long-standing social vices assumed new and more threatening forms. At the same time, pious evangelicals (inspired by the Second Great Awakening) and civic-minded business leaders were becoming less and less tolerant of commercialized sex and other perceived manifestations of urban depravity and disorder. That was the context, historian Barbara Hobson explains, in which Bostonians of the 1810s and 1820s first "discovered" prostitution as a serious social problem.[69]

Indeed, it was at precisely the period when Coverly was marketing his pamphlets on the female marine that Boston residents of differing social ranks first mobilized to combat prostitution by a variety of means. In September 1815, just a month after the publication of *The Adventures of Louisa Baker*, a mob of over twenty local laborers and others pulled down a "disorderly house" in Boston, the first of several documented anti-brothel riots to take place in that city between the mid-1810s and mid-1820s.[70] Less than two years later, in 1817, the Boston Female Society for Missionary Purposes, an organization of respectable evangelical women, hired two preachers to spread the gospel in Boston's vice districts of the West End ("Negro Hill") and the North End. At about the same time, civic and evangelical reformers also launched successful campaigns to establish a Penitent

Female's Refuge and a House of Industry for the reform and confinement of prostitutes. Finally, in 1823, Mayor Josiah Quincy of Boston personally spearheaded urban America's first sustained police crackdown on prostitution.[71] It may be impossible to establish a direct causal linkage between Coverly's playful literary exposés of commercialized sex and the subsequent upsurge of serious civic and evangelical efforts to combat it. But there can be little doubt that *The Female Marine* both reflected widespread popular anxiety over urban vice and embodied a wishful fantasy of its defeat through individual exertion and personal moral reform. One wonders whether any of Boston's prostitutes, reportedly prominent among Coverly's regular customers, were inspired by the story to mend their ways.[72]

Another related source of popular anxiety reflected in Coverly's cross-dressing pamphlets stemmed from the increasing visibility of Boston's African American community during the early decades of the nineteenth century—and its perceived association with urban vice. Although many hundreds of African Americans had been living in the capital of Massachusetts since the colonial period (most held in bondage), it was not until after the American Revolution that slavery was abolished in Massachusetts and that Boston blacks were able to establish a somewhat autonomous communal and institutional presence. But unfortunately most African Americans were forced to live in the city's poorest and least reputable residential neighborhoods, particularly in the West End. As early as 1810, more than half of Boston's black population resided on or near "Negro Hill," living by necessity amidst the area's numerous prostitutes and other entrepreneurs of urban vice.[73]

In that context, it is perhaps not surprising that Nathaniel Coverly's "female marine" presents a strikingly ambivalent view of Boston's African American community. On the one hand, the narrator seeks to shock readers by graphically describing the prevalence of interracial sexual liaisons in the West End: "It is not unfrequently that you here see white girls of not more than seventeen years of age throwing their scarified arms around the neck of an ugly looking black, and bringing their ulcerated faces in contact with his!" Yet, on the other hand (and in the very next sentence), the narrator is careful to reassure readers that a "considerable portion" of "the people of colour" on "Negro Hill" are "respectable" and hence "despise" the local prostitutes.[74] The racial anxiety and ambivalence suggested by those passages were arguably typical of Boston's popular press throughout the first half of the nineteenth century. During the 1810s and 1820s, local plebeian publishers issued a series of crudely racist broadsides in satirical African American dialect, including several jocular accounts of anti-black mob violence on "Negro Hill."[75] However, during the decades that followed, Boston emerged as a hotbed of radical abolitionist publishing, while Massachusetts went further than any other northern state in granting full legal and civil rights to African Americans.[76] Coverly's cross-dressing pamphlets thus seem to have anticipated the sharply mixed feelings of white Bostonians of the antebellum period toward the African Americans in their midst.

But, in the final analysis, the most acute source of anxiety embedded in Coverly's cross-dressing pamphlets probably related not to issues of gender, sexuality, or race, but to the region's embarrassing role in the then just-concluded military conflict with Great Britain. To use Garber's terminology, the people of New England, particularly of Federalist port towns like Boston, must have felt an extreme identity "crisis" stemming from the ideological "dissonance" between their region's notorious disloyalty throughout the War of 1812 and their resurgent patriotism at its conclusion in 1815. As Bailey and Kennedy explain: "In a sense America fought two enemies simultaneously: old England and New England. New England gold holders probably lent more dollars to the British than to the federal treasury. New England farmers sent huge quantities of supplies and foodstuffs to Canada, enabling British armies to invade New York. New England governors stubbornly refused to permit their militia to serve outside their own states."[77]

Put simply, for three years many leading New Englanders had been turncoats; but by the spring and summer of 1815, the people of that region desperately wanted to assume the mantle of patriots. The situation must have been particularly poignant for such working-class Bostonians as the sailors who eagerly purchased Coverly's naval broadsides. Many such men undoubtedly supported the war effort, and voted Republican, through the darkest days of the conflict. Yet they may have nonetheless felt implicated—and, as employees of Federalist merchants, may have been practically implicated—in their region's notorious disloyalty. How then did Boston patriots, whether newborn or long-frustrated, resolve their ideological dissonance or identity crisis? Can there be any doubt? They rushed out and purged their collective guilt and anxiety by snapping up copies of *The Female Marine*.[78]

For whether or not Nathaniel Coverly Jr., or his hack writer, or their readers fully understood it, *The Female Marine* is a brilliant allegory for the ideological inconstancy of mercantile New England between 1812 and 1815, an allegory in which the binary categories of male and female—of sexual virtue and sexual vice—represent the polar opposites of patriotism and disloyalty.[79] Just as Lucy Brewer is seduced and prostituted by corrupt companions and commercialized sex, so was New England seduced and prostituted by the lure of British commerce. Just as Lucy Brewer successfully reverses her fall by changing her gender and joining the crew of the frigate *Constitution*, so did New England symbolically annul her treachery by exuberantly embracing the Constitution—embodied both by the actual ship of that name and by the founding father James Monroe. Just as Lucy Brewer affirms her miraculously restored virtue by marrying Mr. West—and that name is a tip-off to the allegory—so did New England, during the Era of Good Feelings, seek to renew her political covenant with the rest of the United States, and especially with the frontier regions that had supported the war all along.[80] In short, *The Female Marine* served to reassure anxious New Englanders that past errors could be corrected and forgiven, that a happy marriage could follow an unhappy seduction, and that New Englanders could feel proud of themselves both as loyal daughters of the Pilgrims and as brave sons of Columbia. It would be hard to imagine a more suitable fantasy for an Era of Good Feelings.

NOTES

1. See, for example, Thomas A. Bailey and David M. Kennedy, *The American Pageant*, 9th ed. (Lexington, MA: Heath, 1991), 212–20; Donald R. Hickey, *The War of 1812: A Forgotten Conflict* (Urbana: Univ. of Illinois Press, 1989), 255–80; Roger H. Brown, *The Republic in Peril: 1812* (1964; rpt., New York: Norton, 1971), 104. On Boston as a Federalist town, note that the Federalist candidate for governor never received less than 62 percent of the Boston vote in any election between 1811 and 1818; see *Columbian Centinel*, Apr. 3, 1811, [2]; Apr. 8, 1812, [2]; Apr. 7, 1813, [2]; Apr. 6, 1814, [2]; Apr. 5, 1815, [2]; Apr. 3, 1816, [2]; Apr. 9, 1817, [2]; Apr. 8, 1818, [2].

2. Hickey, *The War of 1812*, 231. For evidence of the relief and jubilation with which Bostonians received news of the end of the war, see *Columbian Centinel*, Feb. 25, 1815, [1–2]; March 8, 1815, [1].

3. See Tyrone G. Martin, *A Most Fortunate Ship: A Narrative History of "Old Ironsides"* (Chester, CT: Globe Pequot Press, 1980), 124–25, 168; Benjamin W. Labaree, *Patriots and Partisans: The Merchants of Newburyport, 1764–1815* (1962; rpt., New York: Norton, 1975), 187, 191; *Columbian Centinel*, Apr. 12, 1815, [2].

4. *Columbian Centinel*, Apr. 12, 1815, [2]; Apr. 15, 1815, [2]; Apr. 19, 1815, [2]; Apr. 22, 1815, [2]; Apr. 26, 1815, [2]; May 31, 1815, [2–3]; *Daily Advertiser*, Apr. 12, 1815, [2]; May 30, 1815, [2]; *Yankee*, Apr. 14, 1815, [2]; May 12, 1815, [2]; *Independent Chronicle*, June 1, 1815, [2]. On the limited participation of American women in public celebrations during the nineteenth century, see Mary P. Ryan, *Women in Public: Between Banners and Ballots, 1825–1880* (Baltimore: Johns Hopkins Univ. Press, 1990), 19–57.

5. For general information on both Coverlys, see Benjamin Franklin V, ed., *Boston Printers, Publishers, and Booksellers: 1640–1800* (Boston: G. K. Hall, 1980), 76–81. On the precariousness of their livelihood, see the American Antiquarian Society's printers file, which cites newspaper notices indicating that both of the Coverlys had a brush with bankruptcy in 1802; for the actual notices, see *Independent Chronicle*, Nov. 15, 1802; Dec. 20, 1802.

6. See Worthington C. Ford, *The Isaiah Thomas Collection of Ballads* (Worcester, MA: American Antiquarian Society, 1924), 6–11, 19–22, and passim; also see Arthur Schrader, "Broadside Ballads of Boston, 1813: The Isaiah Thomas Collection," *Proceedings of the American Antiquarian Society* 98 (Apr. 1988): 69–111.

7. The Republican vote for governor in Boston between 1812 and 1815 fluctuated between 29 and 32 percent; see citations for the appropriate years from the *Columbian Centinel* in note 1. For a discussion of several patriotic cartoons issued in New England during the War of 1812, see Georgia Brady Barnhill, "Political Cartoons of New England, 1812–61," in Georgia B. Barnhill, ed., *Prints of New England* (Worcester, MA: American Antiquarian Society, 1991), 86–88. On Boston sailors as a prime market for Coverly's ephemeral productions, see the unidentified newspaper clipping, ca. 1866–82, inserted between pages 34 and 35 of Melvin Lord, "Boston Booksellers, 1650–1860," Boston Booksellers Papers 1640–1860, American Antiquarian Society, Worcester, Ma. (cited hereafter as Unidentified Newspaper Clipping). I am very grateful to Ronald and Mary Zboray for bringing that newspaper clipping to my attention.

8. For discussion of one such work, see Daniel A. Cohen, *Pillars of Salt, Monuments of Grace: New England Crime Literature and the Origins of American Popular Culture* (New York: Oxford Univ. Press, 1993), 178–82.

9. See *Boston Patriot*, Aug. 16, 1815, [3]; *The Yankee*, Aug. 18, 1815, [3]; Nov. 17, 1815, [3]; May 3, 1816, [3]. I have found no evidence that "Luther Wales" ever published any other books or pamphlets, and New York City directories of the years from 1813 through 1817 do not list anyone by that name; see the various editions of *Longworth's American Almanac, New-York Register, and City Directory* (New York: David Longworth) for the years 1813 through 1817; also *The Citizens Directory and Strangers Guide* (New York: George Long, 1814). No other publications by "Luther Wales" appear in the American Antiquarian Society's extensive printers file or in the relevant index to Shaw and Shoemaker; see Frances P. Newton, comp., *American Bibliography: A Preliminary Checklist, 1801 to 1819 . . . Printers, Publishers and Booksellers Index* (Metuchen, NJ: Scarecrow Press, 1983), 317. My conclusion is that "Luther Wales" was a pseudonym concocted by Nathaniel Coverly Jr. For the various printings and editions, see below, "Editions of *The Female Marine* and Related Works."

10. Unidentified Newspaper Clipping. It should also be noted that the *The Awful Beacon* includes a copyright notice in Coverly's name, which suggests that it was likely written either by him or by someone in his employ.

11. For basic information and sources on Wright, see the American Antiquarian Society printers file and printers authority cards. He is listed as a "printer" in a number of Boston city directories; see *The Boston Directory* (Boston: E. Cotton, 1813), 270; *The Boston Directory* (Boston: E. Cotton, 1818), 231; *The Boston Directory* (Boston: John H. A. Frost and Charles Stimpson Jr., 1820), 226; *The Boston Directory* (John H. A. Frost and Charles Stimpson Jr., 1821), 259; *The Boston Directory* (Boston: John H. A. Frost and Charles Stimpson Jr., 1822), 256.

12. I am very grateful to Robert A. Gross for generously providing me with this information about Wright's birthplace, family background, and possible apprenticeship. For genealogical information on the Wright family of Concord, see Clarence Almon Torrey, "Edward Wright of Concord, Mass., and Some of His Descendants: A Record of Six Generations" (typescript manuscript, 1943), deposited in the New England Historic Genealogical Society, Boston, Massachusetts (citation provided by R. A. Gross). For evidence concerning Coverly's brief stay in Concord, see William Jones, *An Oration, Pronounced at Concord* (Concord: N. Coverly, 1794), 20; T. Priestley, *The Christian's Looking Glass* (Concord: N. Coverly, 1794), 90.

13. See *American Independence . . . Fourth of July, 1805* ([Boston?: 1805]); also see N. H. Wright, *Ode, Written for the Celebrarion* [sic] *of the Republican Young Men, July 4, 1808* ([Boston?: 1808]).

14. For the approximate date of Wright's marriage, see *Columbian Centinel*, Nov. 18, 1809, [2]; however, also see *A Volume of Records Relating to the Early History of Boston, Containing Boston Marriages, From 1752 to 1809* (Boston: Municipal Printing Office, 1903), 387, which places the marriage nearly a month earlier. For the approximate birthdate of his son (May 27, 1810), see *Vital Records of Newburyport, Massachusetts to the End of the Year 1849*, 2 vols. (Salem, MA: Essex Institute, 1911), I:424.

15. Nathaniel H. Wright, *Monody, On the Death of Brigadier General Zebulon Montgomery Pike, and Other Poems* (Middlebury, VT: Slade & Ferguson, 1814), 25–36; N. H. Wright, *The Fall of Palmyra: and Other Poems* (Middlebury, VT: William Slade, June 1817), 99–108. That Wright, according to the prefaces to those works, seems to have been living in Middlebury, Vermont, in June 1814 and again in December 1816 does present a bit of a problem in trying to link him to Coverly and *The Female Marine;* however, those stays may have been brief or intermittent, and it is clear (from the directories cited in note 11 and the AAS printers file) that he was living in Boston in 1813 and was back there by 1818 at the latest.

16. See Nathaniel H. Wright, *Boston: or A Touch at the Times* (Boston: Hews & Goss, 1819), t.p., 19–20.

17. See ibid., 19–20. For Wright's approximate age, see his obituary: *Columbian Centinel*, May 15, 1824, [2]. For references to his wife and child, see note 14.

18. I am grateful to Elizabeth Young for pointing out this irony to me in her reader's report. Another possible author of Coverly's female-marine pamphlets is Henry Trumbull, a sometimes business associate of Nathaniel Coverly Jr. and the publisher of one of the two earliest editions of *The Adventures of Lucy Brewer* in 1815; see "Editions of *The Female Marine* and Related Works," below. For more discussion of Trumbull's possible authorship of the female-marine pamphlets, see note 63; and *The Female Marine*, Third Part, n. 13, below.

19. Unidentified Newspaper Clipping. On Ann Street as a notorious neighborhood for prostitutes, see Barbara Meil Hobson, *Uneasy Virtue: The Politics of Prostitution and the American Reform Tradition* (New York: Basic Books, 1987), 26.

20. *The Awful Beacon* (Boston: N. Coverly Jr., 1816), t.p.

21. On the prices of the First and Second Parts, see *The Yankee*, Aug. 18, 1815, [3]; Nov. 17, 1815, [3]. According to the Massachusetts Bureau of Statistics of Labor, the "medium" daily wage for a Massachusetts laborer was $.987 in 1815 and $1.07 in 1816; see Carroll D. Wright, *History of Wages and Prices in Massachusetts: 1752–1883* (Boston: Wright & Potter, 1885), 82, 84. The cost of a twelve-and-a-half-cent pamphlet for such a laborer would thus be approximately 12 percent of his daily wage; that would be almost identical (as a percentage of daily wages) to the cost of a $4.95 mass market paperback to an unskilled laborer working an eight-hour day at about $5.00 an hour in 1996. Obviously, that is a somewhat crude measure of affordability, given possible fluctuations in the relative costs of food, lodging, and other necessities.

22. See owners' signatures on American Antiquarian Society copies of *The Adventures of Louisa Baker* (New York: Luther Wales, 1815); *The Female Marine, or Adventures of Miss Lucy Brewer* ([Boston?]: [N. Coverly Jr.?], May 30, 1816); *The Female Marine, or Adventures of Miss Lucy Brewer*, 2nd ed. ([Boston?]: [N. Coverly Jr.?], June 19, 1816); *The Female Marine, or Adventures of Miss Lucy Brewer* (Hartwick, [NY]: L. & B. Todd, [1816?]), from which the inscription is quoted. For locations of surviving copies of the various editions, see Shaw and Shoemaker citations in "Editions of *The Female Marine* and Related Works," below. In only a handful of instances do Shaw and Shoemaker locate more than one copy. The majority of located copies are at the American Antiquarian Society.

23. This paragraph summarizes *The Adventures of Louisa Baker*, or *The Female Marine*, First Part, below. It should be noted that there is an internal contradiction in the first edition of the First Part concerning the timing of Baker's enlistment; although the pamphlet indicates that she enlisted in 1813, it describes her participation in battles that actually took place in 1812.

24. This paragraph summarizes *The Adventures of Lucy Brewer* (Boston: N. Coverly Jr., 1815), or *The Female Marine*, Second Part, below. The narrator explains that she has abandoned her earlier pseudonym, Louisa Baker, and provides her (ostensibly) "*real*" name in order to convince those who "have questioned the truth" of her "real existence" that her writings are actually authentic.

25. This paragraph summarizes *The Awful Beacon, to the Rising Generation of Both Sexes* (Boston: N. Coverly Jr., 1816), or *The Female Marine*, Third Part, below. For the supplementary warnings and moral sketches, see below, 93–97, 118–31.

26. *The Yankee*, June 21, 1816, [3]; Rachel Sperry, *A Brief Reply to the Late Writings of Louisa Baker* (Boston: M. Brewster, 1816). This pamphlet was probably concocted by Nathaniel Coverly in order to enhance the verisimilitude of the earlier female-marine pamphlets; the imprint "M. Brewster" may be yet another pseudonym for Coverly.

27. *The Yankee*, Sept. 6, 1816, [3] (Paul); Oct. 25, 1816, [3], quoted (Clark); *The Surprising Adventures of Almira Paul* (Boston: N. Coverly Jr., 1816), or reprinted text below. The Paul narrative is probably fictional. The Clark narrative is an example of a long Anglo-American tradition of accounts of the pious conversions and deaths of children that originated during the seventeenth century with James Janeway's *A Token*

for Children; see James Janeway, *A Token for Children* [bound with facsimile reprints of other early children's books] (1671–72; rpt., New York: Garland, 1977).

28. See Alexander Medlicott Jr., "The Legend of Lucy Brewer: An Early American Novel," *New England Quarterly* 39 (1966): 465–67; Medlicott, ed., *The Female Marine,* xvii–xxiii. For an example of a twentieth-century author who seems to believe in the reality of Lucy Brewer, see Edward Rowe Snow, *Unsolved Mysteries of Sea and Shore* (London: Alvin Redman, 1964), 111–13.

29. Medlicott, "The Legend of Lucy Brewer," 471. The confusion over sexual identity pervades the text. On the confusion between vice and virtue, see below, 61–62, 66–67; between bravery and cowardice, 85–88; between youth and old age, 95–96, 125–26; between dream and reality, 114; between happiness and sorrow, 116.

30. See Thomas Kent, *Interpretation and Genre: The Role of Generic Perception in the Study of Narrative Texts* (Lewisburg, PA: Bucknell Univ. Press, 1986), 81–101, 124–42, quoted at 126; below, 105–6. To describe Female Warrior ballads and narratives, urban exposés, and sentimental seduction tales as "formulaic genres" does not preclude the possibility—even likelihood—that individual examples would contain creative, idiosyncratic, and unconventional elements. *The Female Marine* is an extreme case in point. For that reason, I am uncomfortable with the designation "automatized texts."

31. See Dianne Dugaw, *Warrior Women and Popular Balladry, 1650–1850,* 1–3, 10, and passim (Cambridge: Cambridge Univ. Press, 1989); Julie Wheelwright, *Amazons and Military Maids: Women Who Dressed as Men in the Pursuit of Life, Liberty and Happiness* (London: Pandora, 1989); Estelle C. Jelinek, "Disguise Autobiographies: Women Masquerading as Men," *Women's Studies International Forum* 10 (1987): 53–62; Simon Shepherd, *Amazons and Warrior Women: Varieties of Feminism in Seventeenth-Century Drama* (New York: St. Martin's Press, 1981); John Ashton, *Eighteenth Century Waifs* (London: Hurst and Blackett, 1887), 177–202; and various other works cited in the notes that follow. Dugaw's work focuses primarily on Female Warriors in *British* popular culture; as discussed and documented below, the Female Warrior motif remained popular in *American* popular literature during the second half of the nineteenth century.

32. See *Female Drummer; The Happy Ship Carpenter; A Lover's Lamentation for the Girl He Left Behind Him; and Her Answer,* all in the Isaiah Thomas ballad collection at the American Antiquarian Society in Worcester; also listed in Ford, *Isaiah Thomas Collection,* nos. 87, 112, 155–56, 253. Also see Dugaw, *Warrior Women,* 87.

33. Aside from the female-marine series on the War of 1812, see, for example, Herman Mann, *The Female Review: Life of Deborah Sampson, the Female Soldier of the War of the Revolution,* ed. John Adams Vinton (1866; rpt., New York: Arno Press, 1972); Ned Buntline [Edward Judson], *The Volunteer; or, The Maid of Monterey* (Boston: F. Gleason, 1847); *The Female Volunteer; or the Life, and Wonderful Adventures of Miss Eliza Allen, A Young Lady of Eastport, Maine* ([Cincinnati: H. M. Rulison, 1851?]); Loreta Janeta Velazquez, *The Woman in Battle: A Narrative of the Exploits,*

Adventures, and Travels, ed. C. J. Worthington (1876; rpt., New York: Arno Press, 1972). For the references to Gannett in *The Female Marine,* see below, 71, 75, 82; Mann, *Female Review.* Gannett served under the name "Robert Shurtleff." For more on Gannett/Shurtleff, see Curtis Carroll Davis, "A 'Gallantress' Gets Her Due: The Earliest Published Notice of Deborah Sampson," *Proceedings of the American Antiquarian Society* 91 (1981): 319–23; Jonathan Katz, *Gay American History: Lesbians and Gay Men in the U.S.A.* (New York: Crowell, 1976), 212–14; Linda Grant De Pauw, *Founding Mothers: Women in America in the Revolutionary Era* (Boston: Houghton Mifflin, 1975), 192–93.

34. See Rudolf M. Dekker and Lotte C. van de Pol, *The Tradition of Female Transvestism in Early Modern Europe* (New York: St. Martin's Press, 1989), 3, 9–10, and passim; Elizabeth Young, "Confederate Counterfeit: The Case of the Cross-Dressed Civil War Soldier," in Elaine K. Ginsberg, ed., *Passing and the Fictions of Identity* (Durham, NC: Duke Univ. Press, 1996), 184, 214–15n7; Richard Hall, *Patriots in Disguise: Women Warriors of the Civil War* (New York: Paragon House, 1993), xi, xiv, 197–202, and passim; Wendy A. King, *Clad in Uniform: Women Soldiers of the Civil War* (Collingswood, NJ: C. W. Historicals, 1992); C. Kay Larson, "Bonny Yank and Ginny Reb Revisited," *Minerva: Quarterly Report on Women and the Military* 10 (Summer 1992): 35–61; Larson, "Bonny Yank and Ginny Reb," *Minerva* 8 (Spring 1990): 33–48, esp. 38–39; J. E. Schultz, "Women at the Front: Gender and Genre in Literature of the American Civil War" (Ph.D. diss., Univ. of Michigan, 1988), 259–346, esp. 272–73, and passim; DePauw, *Founding Mothers,* 191; Mary Elizabeth Massey, *Bonnet Brigades* (New York: Knopf, 1966), 78–85; Mary A. Livermore, *My Story of the War: A Woman's Narrative of Four Years Personal Experience in the Sanitary Service of the Rebellion* (Hartford, CT: A. D. Worthington, 1888), 119–20. For a broader discussion of the various roles of women in connection with early modern armies in Europe, see Barton C. Hacker, "Women and Military Institutions in Early Modern Europe: A Reconnaissance," *Signs* 6 (Summer 1981): 643–71. On women in the military during the American Revolution, see Linda Grant De Pauw, "Women in Combat: The Revolutionary War Experience," *Armed Forces and Society* 7 (Winter 1981): 209–26; also see the citations on Deborah Sampson Gannett in the previous note.

35. See Velazquez, *The Woman in Battle,* 36–37, 41–42, 51, 128; S. Emma E. Edmonds, *Nurse and Spy in the Union Army: Comprising the Adventures and Experiences of a Woman in Hospitals, Camps, and Battlefields* (Hartford, CT: W. S. Williams & Co., 1865); Sylvia G. L. Dannett, *She Rode With the Generals: The True and Incredible Story of Sarah Emma Seelye, Alias Franklin Thompson* (New York: Thomas Nelson and Sons, 1960), esp. 23–25. Velazquez served under the name "Harry T. Buford"; Edmonds adopted the name "Franklin Thompson." For a careful assessment of the social-historical accuracy of the Civil War narratives of Velazquez and Edmonds, see Richard Hall, *Patriots in Disguise.* For references to other cross-dressing Civil War soldiers reportedly inspired by Joan of Arc, see Larson, "Bonny Yank and Ginny Reb Revisited," 39; Schultz, "Women at the Front," 218–19, 268, 288–89; Massey, *Bonnet*

Brigades, 79–80. For bibliographic information on M. M. Ballou's *Fanny Campbell, the Female Pirate Captain*, which went into several editions, see Lyle H. Wright, *American Fiction: 1774–1850*, 2nd rev. ed. (San Marino, CA: Huntington Library, 1969), 35–36. For recent analyses of those Civil War narratives that adopt "literary" or "cultural" approaches, see Young, "Confederate Counterfeit"; Kathleen De Grave, *Swindler, Spy, Rebel: The Confidence Woman in Nineteenth-Century America* (Columbia: Univ. of Missouri Press, 1995), 110–17 and passim. For more on Gannett/Shurtleff, see the works cited above in note 33. For brief but perceptive discussions of the complex interrelationship between the social and cultural (or literary) traditions of the Female Warrior in the European context, see Dekker and van de Pol, *Tradition of Female Transvestism*, 39–40, 101–3.

36. See Dugaw, *Warrior Women*, 143–62. See especially 158–59, where Dugaw rejects that conservative reading of the ballads: "the ballads do not in fact privilege the 'masculine' at all, because at a deeper level they actually subvert not only the privilege of one gender over the other, but the very category of gender itself."

37. See Dugaw, *Warrior Women*, 35, 92–93, 113, 130–31.

38. See Judith Butler, *Gender Trouble: Feminism and the Subversion of Identity* (New York: Routledge, 1990), 24–25, 134–41, and passim. Toward the end of the Third Part of Coverly's trilogy on the female marine, the narrator calls upon his/her readers to consider "that their entrance on the theatre of the world is the commencement of a drama, in which they will be exposed to the view of numerous spectators, who will applaud or censure them according as they perform the parts they have taken—and what is peculiar to these scenes, each one will feel a pleasure or a pain, independent of the applauses or censures of others, from the inward consciousness of the principles of action—because each acts for himself, and does not personate another." Below, 128.

39. See below, 85–88. For a brilliant analysis of gender-based conceptions of virtue in a much earlier period that helped to clarify my thinking on the issue, see Felice Lifshitz, "What Does It Mean for a Woman to have 'Virtue?'" (unpublished paper, Florida International University, 1993); also see Ruth H. Bloch, "The Gendered Meanings of Virtue in Revolutionary America," *Signs* 13 (Autumn 1987): 37–58. For excellent discussions of the dangers faced by women travelling in public in early America, see Patricia Cline Cohen, "Safety and Danger: Women on American Public Transport, 1750–1850," in Dorothy O. Kelly and Susan M. Reverby, *Gendered Domains: Rethinking Public and Private in Women's History* (Ithaca, NY: Cornell Univ. Press, 1992), 109–22; P. C. Cohen, "Women at Large: Travel in Antebellum America," *History Today* 44 (Dec. 1994): 44–50; also see P. C. Cohen, "Ministerial Misdeeds: The Onderdonk Trial and Sexual Harassment in the 1840s," *Journal of Women's History* 7 (Fall 1995): 34–57, passim.

40. Lyle H. Wright, "A Statistical Survey of American Fiction," *Huntington Library Quarterly* 2 (Apr. 1939): 314; Adrienne Siegel, *The Image of the American City in Popular Literature, 1820–1870* (Port Washington, NY: Kennikat Press, 1981), 6 and passim.

41. See below, 66–70, 83–84, 91–92, 94–97, 118–27, passim, quoted at 118; David S. Reynolds, *Beneath the American Renaissance: The Subversive Imagination in the Age of Emerson and Melville* (New York: Knopf, 1988).

42. See below, 64, 111.

43. See below, 142–43.

44. For perceptive studies of public policy toward prostitution in America and England respectively, see Barbara Meil Hobson, *Uneasy Virtue: The Politics of Prostitution and the American Reform Tradition* (New York: Basic Books, 1987) and Judith R. Walkowitz, *Prostitution and Victorian Society: Women, Class, and the State* (Cambridge: Cambridge Univ. Press, 1980).

45. See Cathy N. Davidson, *Revolution and the Word: The Rise of the Novel in America* (New York: Oxford Univ. Press, 1986), 83–150; Leslie A. Fiedler, *Love and Death in the American Novel,* rev. ed. (1966; rpt., New York: Stein and Day, 1982), 74–125 and passim; Herbert Ross Brown, *The Sentimental Novel in America, 1789–1860* (New York: Pageant Books, 1959), 28–51; James D. Hart, *The Popular Book: A History of America's Literary Taste* (New York: Oxford Univ. Press, 1950), 51–57; Frank Luther Mott, *Golden Multitudes: The Story of Best Sellers in the United States* (New York: Macmillan, 1947), 35–40.

46. See Davidson, *Revolution and the Word,* 83–150, passim; for a somewhat similar analysis of a later body of sentimental fiction, see Jane Tompkins, *Sensational Designs: The Cultural Work of American Fiction, 1790–1860* (New York: Oxford Univ. Press, 1985), 122–85. For a somewhat earlier and very different feminist reading of sentimental novels like *Charlotte Temple,* see Wendy Martin, "Profile: Susanna Rowson, Early American Novelist," *Women's Studies* 2 (1974): 1–8; for a more recent critique of Davidson's interpretation, see Klaus P. Hansen, "The Sentimental Novel and Its Feminist Critique," *Early American Literature* 26 (1991): 39–54.

47. Medlicott, "The Legend of Lucy Brewer," 464; below, 61.

48. Below, 76; Susanna Rowson, *Charlotte Temple: A Tale of Truth,* ed. Cathy N. Davidson (New York: Oxford Univ. Press, 1986), 29. Compare a passage in Rowson, *Charlotte Temple,* at page 32 to the nearly identical passage in *The Female Marine,* First Part, below, 66. Compare Rowson's rhetoric in *Charlotte Temple* at pages 28–29 to the attack on the sexual double standard in *The Female Marine,* Third Part, below, 124 (particularly the phrase "Gracious heaven!" and the reference to men as "monsters"). Also see the discussion below on the lines of verse beneath the frontispiece of *The Adventures of Louisa Baker.* On the extraordinary popularity of *Charlotte Temple,* see Davidson's introduction to Rowson, *Charlotte Temple,* xi–xxxiii, passim.

49. See below, 119–21.

50. See Edward H. Friedman, *The Antiheroine's Voice: Narrative Discourse and Transformations of the Picaresque* (Columbia: Univ. of Missouri Press, 1987), xi–118 and passim; Davidson, *Revolution and the Word,* 151–211, quoted at 152, 179, 181, 190. The scholarly literature on picaresque fiction is vast; for citations of many of the more important works, see Friedman's copious endnotes.

51. See Natalie Zemon Davis, *Society and Culture in Early Modern France* (Stanford, CA: Stanford Univ. Press, 1975), 124–51, quoted at 143–44; Davidson, *Revolution and the Word*, 83–150 and passim. On the other hand, a cynic might argue that Coverly's pamphlets are an elaborate ruse to convince the young women of New England to lower their guards on the unrealistic assumption that they would be able to recover as effectively as Lucy Brewer.

52. Kathleen De Grave, *Swindler, Spy, Rebel: The Confidence Woman in Nineteenth-Century America* (Columbia: Univ. of Missouri Press, 1995), 3, 9–10, 19, and passim.

53. On the gender implications of Puritan religious ideology, see Laurel Thatcher Ulrich, "Vertuous Women Found: New England Ministerial Literature, 1668–1735," *American Quarterly* 28 (Spring 1976): 20–40; on Puritan legal systems, see Cornelia Hughes Dayton, *Women before the Bar: Gender, Law, and Society in Connecticut, 1639–1789* (Chapel Hill: Univ. of North Carolina Press, 1995); on the day-to-day conduct of Puritan women, see C. Dallett Hemphill, "Women in Court: Sex-Role Differentiation in Salem, Massachusetts, 1636–1683," *William and Mary Quarterly*, 3rd ser., 39 (Jan. 1982): 164–75. For different interpretations see Mary Beth Norton, *Founding Mothers & Fathers: Gendered Power and the Forming of American Society* (New York: Knopf, 1996), but see 469n81; M. B. Norton, "The Evolution of White Women's Experience in Early America," *American Historical Review* 89 (June 1984): 593–619 (which challenges Hemphill's interpretation at 597n10); Lyle Koehler, *A Search for Power: The "Weaker Sex" in Seventeenth-Century New England* (Urbana: Univ. of Illinois Press, 1980).

54. On the growing influence of British traditions of genteel womanhood and popular misogyny during the eighteenth century, see Ulrich, "Vertuous Women Found," 38–40; Dayton, *Women before the Bar*, 154–55, 228–29, 283–84. On the perceived "rebirth" of "patriarchy," see Susan Juster, *Disorderly Women: Sexual Politics & Evangelicalism in Revolutionary New England* (Ithaca, NY: Cornell Univ. Press, 1994), 117–79, passim; Juster, "Patriarchy Reborn: The Gendering of Authority in the Evangelical Church in Revolutionary New England," *Gender & History* 6 (Apr. 1994): 58–81; Dayton, *Women before the Bar*, 66–68, 156, and passim; but also see Melvin Yazawa, *From Colonies to Commonwealth: Familial Ideology and the Beginnings of the American Republic* (Baltimore, MD: Johns Hopkins Univ. Press, 1985); Jay Fliegelman, *Prodigals and Pilgrims: The American Revolution against Patriarchal Authority, 1750–1800* (Cambridge: Cambridge Univ. Press, 1982). For other important discussions of gender roles and images during the Revolutionary period and thereafter, see Linda K. Kerber, "The Paradox of Women's Citizenship in the Early Republic: The Case of *Martin vs. Massachusetts*, 1805," *American Historical Review* 97 (Apr. 1992): 349–78; Jan Lewis, "The Republican Wife: Virtue and Seduction in the Early Republic," *William and Mary Quarterly*, 3rd ser., 44 (Oct. 1987): 689–721; Bloch, "The Gendered Meanings of Virtue"; Norton, "Evolution of White Women's Experience"; L. K. Kerber, *Women of the Republic: Intellect and Ideology in Revolutionary America* (Chapel Hill: Univ. of North Carolina Press, 1980), 283–88 and passim; M. B. Nor-

ton, *Liberty's Daughters: The Revolutionary Experience of American Women, 1750–1800*
(Boston: Little, Brown, 1980), 242–50 and passim.

55. A few of the key formative works in the vast historiography of antebellum
gender ideology are Carl N. Degler, *At Odds: Women and the Family in America from
the Revolution to the Present* (New York: Oxford Univ. Press, 1980); Nancy F. Cott,
The Bonds of Womanhood: "Woman's Sphere" in New England, 1780–1835 (New Haven:
Yale Univ. Press, 1977); Gerda Lerner, "The Lady and the Mill Girl: Changes in the
Status of Women in the Age of Jackson," *Midcontinent American Studies Journal* 10
(Spring 1969): 5–15; Barbara Welter, "The Cult of True Womanhood, 1820–1860,"
American Quarterly 18 (Summer 1966): 151–75. However, it should be noted that the
dominant paradigm of "separate spheres" has come under increasing attack over the
past dozen or so years on a variety of fronts; see, for example, Ronald J. Zboray and
Mary Saracino Zboray, "Political News and Female Readership in Antebellum
Boston and Its Region," *Journalism History* 22 (Spring 1996): 2–14; Elizabeth R.
Varon, "Tippecanoe and the Ladies, Too: White Women and Party Politics in Ante-
bellum Virginia," *Journal of American History* 82 (Sept. 1995): 494–521; Nancy Isen-
berg, "Second Thoughts on Gender and Women's History," *American Studies* 36
(Spring 1995): 93–103; Laura McCall, "'With All the Wild, Trembling, Rapturous
Feelings of a Lover': Men, Women, and Sexuality in American Literature, 1820–
1860," *Journal of the Early Republic* 14 (Spring 1994): 71–89, esp. 88; Ronald J. Zboray,
A Fictive People: Antebellum Economic Development and the American Reading Public
(New York: Oxford Univ. Press, 1993), 162–69; Ryan, *Women in Public;* Karen Lystra,
Searching the Heart: Women, Men, and Romantic Love in Nineteenth-Century America
(New York: Oxford Univ. Press, 1989), 121–56; Susan Juster, "'In a Different Voice':
Male and Female Narratives of Religious Conversion in Post-Revolutionary Amer-
ica," *American Quarterly* 41 (March 1989): 34–62, esp. 57–58; Linda K. Kerber, "Sepa-
rate Spheres, Female Worlds, Woman's Place: The Rhetoric of Women's History,"
Journal of American History 75 (June 1988): 9–39; and Nancy A. Hewitt, "Beyond the
Search for Sisterhood: American Women's History in the 1980s," *Social History* 10
(Oct. 1985): 299–321.

56. Velazquez, *Woman in Battle,* 35–36. For a very useful discussion of "subversive"
representations of women in popular literature of the antebellum period, see Reynolds, *Beneath the American Renaissance,* 337–67.

57. See Robert V. Wells, "Illegitimacy and Bridal Pregnancy in Colonial America,"
in Peter Laslett, Karla Oosterveen, and Richard M. Smith, eds., *Bastardy and Its
Comparative History* (Cambridge, MA: Harvard Univ. Press, 1980), 353–55; Daniel
Scott Smith, "The Long Cycle in American Illegitimacy and Prenuptial Pregnancy,"
in Laslett, Oosterveen, and R. M. Smith, eds., *Bastardy,* 363–64, 369–70; D. S. Smith
and Michael S. Hindus, "Premarital Pregnancy in America 1640–1971: An Overview
and Interpretation," *Journal of Interdisciplinary History* 5 (Spring 1975): 537–38, 553–57,
561–64, and passim; Edward M. Cook Jr., "Social Behavior and Changing Values in
Dedham, Massachusetts, 1700 to 1775," *William and Mary Quarterly,* 3rd ser., 27 (Oct.

1970): 548–53, 580, and passim; also see Ellen K. Rothman, *Hands and Hearts: A History of Courtship in America* (New York: Basic Books, 1984), 44–51.

58. See Smith, "Long Cycle," 370, 373–75; Smith and Hindus, "Premarital Pregnancy," 537–38, 549–52, and passim; Rothman, *Hands and Hearts,* 50–51; Nancy F. Cott, "Passionlessness: An Interpretation of Victorian Sexual Ideology, 1790–1850," *Signs* 4 (1978): 219–36; Welter, "The Cult of True Womanhood," 154–58 and passim. Ironically, the decline in premarital pregnancy rates among American women during the first half of the nineteenth century coincided in time with a proliferation of prostitutes in American cities; see Alexis de Tocqueville, *Democracy in America,* ed. Phillips Bradley, 2 vols. (New York: Knopf, 1945), II:209–25; Hobson, *Uneasy Virtue;* Timothy J. Gilfoyle, *City of Eros: New York City, Prostitution, and the Commercialization of Sex, 1790–1920* (New York: Norton, 1992); Marilynn Wood Hill, *Their Sisters' Keepers: Prostitution in New York City, 1830–1870* (Berkeley: Univ. of California Press, 1993); and discussion in text below.

59. See, for example, Robert V. Wells, *Revolutions in Americans' Lives: A Demographic Perspective on the History of Americans, Their Families, and Their Society* (Westport, CT: Greenwood Press, 1982), 6–9, 44–45, 65–66, 85–86, and passim; Maris A. Vinovskis, *Fertility in Massachusetts from the Revolution to the Civil War* (New York: Academic Press, 1981), 117–51 and passim; R. V. Wells, "Family History and Demographic Transition," in Michael Gordon, ed., *The American Family in Social-Historical Perspective,* 2d ed. (New York: St. Martin's Press, 1978), 516–32; D. S. Smith and Hindus, "Premarital Pregnancy," 559. For a controversial attempt to link changes in sexual behavior to the broader processes of "modernization" in a comparative (but largely European) context, see Edward Shorter, *The Making of the Modern Family* (New York: Basic Books, 1975). Shorter's thesis, first formulated in a series of articles during the early 1970s, has been challenged in numerous books and articles; for one example, see Louise A. Tilly, Joan W. Scott, and Miriam Cohen, "Women's Work and European Fertility Patterns," *Journal of Interdisciplinary History* 6 (Winter 1976): 447–76.

60. Richard D. Brown, *Modernization: The Transformation of American Life 1600–1865* (New York: Hill and Wang, 1976), 10–15.

61. For an early critique of modernization theory as applied to American history, see James A. Henretta, "'Modernization': Toward a False Synthesis," *Reviews in American History* 5 (Sept. 1977): 445–52.

62. See below, III. For contemporary newspaper accounts of the actual incident, which took place in late September 1815, see *Boston Gazette,* Sept. 25, 1815, [2]; *Independent Chronicle,* Sept. 25, 1815, [2]; *Columbian Centinel,* Sept. 27, 1815, [2]; Oct. 14, 1815, [2]; *The Idiot, or, Invisible Rambler,* Jan. 24, 1818, [3]. The *Gazette* and the *Independent Chronicle* described the gale that uprooted the trees and expressed the hope that they might "be reset in the earth"; the *Columbian Centinel* reported two days later that "the Police had employed persons to raise and replant these tree"; the following month the same newspaper optimistically declared that "all the trees in and

near the Common were again erect, and promise to put forth their verdure the ensuing spring"; however, in January 1818, *The Idiot* (printed by Nathaniel Coverly Jr. and edited by his sometime associate, Henry Trumbull) reported that "the big elms which the tempest prostrated in the Mall, and which they devised a plan to restore again to their late station and life, for the want of *deep roots*, the last season *withered!*" It may be worth noting that the narrator of *The Female Marine* also characterizes her society as "modern" (see below, 103).

63. Below, 112–13. Mr. West's monologue is suggestive of the many orations commemorative of the landing of the Pilgrims at Plymouth Rock that became a staple of patriotic and filiopietistic discourse in New England during the first half of the nineteenth century. For a couple of early examples of that genre, see John Quincy Adams, *An Oration Delivered at Plymouth, December 22, 1802, at the Anniversary Commemoration of the First Landing of our Ancestors, at that Place* (Boston: Russell and Cutler, 1802); James Flint, *A Discourse Delivered at Plymouth, December 22, 1815, at the Anniversary Commemoration of the First Landing of our Ancestors at that Place* (Boston: Lincoln & Edmands, 1816). Parts of West's speech are also similar to passages contained in [Henry Trumbull], *History of the Discovery of America, of the Landing of Our Forefathers, at Plymouth, and of Their Most Remarkable Engagements with the Indians . . .* (Norwich, CT: Published for the Author, 1810), 14–15 and 22. That similarity suggests that Trumbull, who was at times a business associate of Nathaniel Coverly Jr. and who published one of the first two editions of *The Adventures of Lucy Brewer,* may be a viable alternative to Nathaniel Hill Wright (and Coverly himself) as possible author of the female-marine pamphlets. For the relevant passages from Trumbull's *History,* see below, text notes to *The Female Marine,* Third Part, n. 13.

64. See Steven Watts, *The Republic Reborn: War and the Making of Liberal America, 1790–1820* (Baltimore: Johns Hopkins Univ. Press, 1987), 166–72, 271–73, 320–21, and passim. My discussion here obviously oversimplifies Watts's complex and provocative argument; and, as will become clear by the end of this essay, I believe that *The Female Marine* reflected a good deal of society anxiety and psychic stress, placing it more in line with Watts's interpretation than this paragraph might suggest.

65. See Bailey and Kennedy, *American Pageant,* 228; Sean Wilentz, *Major Problems in the Early Republic, 1787–1848* (Lexington, MA: Heath, 1992), 333, emphasis added.

66. *The Adventures of Louisa Baker,* frontispiece; *The Adventures of Lucy Brewer* (Boston: H. Trumbull, 1815), frontispiece; *The Female Marine* ([Boston?]: [N. Coverly Jr.?], June 19, 1816), front cover and frontispiece; *The Female Marine* ([Boston?]: Printed for the Author [by N. Coverly Jr.?], 1818), frontispiece; see illustrations above and below, 4, 26–27. On the verses borrowed from *Charlotte Temple,* see Rowson, *Charlotte Temple,* 17.

67. See *The Yankee,* July 4, 1817, [3]; George Dangerfield, *The Era of Good Feelings* (New York: Harcourt, Brace & World, 1952), 95–96; G. Dangerfield, *The Awakening of American Nationalism, 1815–1828* (New York: Harper & Row, 1965), 3, 33–35;

John M. Blum et al., *The National Experience: A History of the United States,* 7th ed. (New York: Harcourt Brace Jovanovich, 1989), 184.

68. See Marjorie Garber, *Vested Interests: Cross-Dressing & Cultural Anxiety* (New York: Routledge, 1992), 9–17, quoted at 16.

69. See Hobson, *Uneasy Virtue,* 11–14, quoted at 11. For two excellent recent studies of prostitution in another nineteenth-century American city, see Hill, *Their Sisters' Keepers;* Gilfoyle, *City of Eros.*

70. For the mob action of September 1815, see Boston Municipal Court, Record Books, v. 6 (Oct. 1815–Dec. 1816), 5rv, located at the Massachusetts State Archives, Boston; for the identification of the building in question as a "disorderly house," see the same volume, 20v. The term "disorderly house" was a generic designation for business establishments, generally located in private residences, where men and women engaged in such profane recreational activities as drinking, gambling, whoring, blaspheming, and/or carousing. For references to other anti-brothel riots of the mid-1810s through mid-1820s, see William Jenks, Diary, Sept. 23, 1820, Jenks Family Collections, Massachusetts Historical Society, Boston (cited in Hobson, *Uneasy Virtue*); Horatio Woodman, ed., *Reports of Criminal Cases, Tried in the Municipal Court of the City of Boston, Before Peter Oxenbridge Thacher, Judge of that Court from 1823 to 1843* (Boston: Little and Brown, 1845), 107–12, 116–32; Edward H. Savage, *A Chronological History of the Boston Watch and Police from 1631 to 1865* (Boston: Published and Sold by the Author, 1865), 64–66, 107–12; E. H. Savage, comp., *Boston Events. A Brief Mention and the Date of More Than 5,000 Events That Transpired in Boston From 1630 to 1880* (Boston: Tolman & White, 1884), 131; Roger Lane, *Policing the City: Boston, 1822–1885* (New York: Atheneum, 1971), 24–25; Hobson, *Uneasy Virtue,* 23–24, 239. It should be noted that anti-brothel riots did occasionally occur in Boston and other cities during the colonial period; see Carl Bridenbaugh, *Cities in the Wilderness: The First Century of Urban Life in America, 1625–1742* (1938; rpt., New York: Oxford Univ. Press, 1971), 388–89; Bridenbaugh, *Cities in Revolt: Urban Life in America, 1743–1776* (1955; rpt., New York: Oxford Univ. Press, 1971), 316–17.

71. On the activities of the Boston Female Society for Missionary Purposes in Boston's vice districts, see *A Brief Account of the Origin and Progress of the Boston Female Society for Missionary Purposes* (an abridged version of which is reprinted below); Hobson, *Uneasy Virtue,* 20–22. On the campaign to establish institutions for the reformation of prostitutes, see a series of letters to the editor of the *Boston Commercial Gazette:* July 30, 1818, [1]; Aug. 6, 1818, [1]; Aug. 13, 1818, [1]; Aug. 24, 1818, [1]; Sept. 17, 1818, [1]; Oct. 1, 1818, [1] (the last reprinted at the end of *A Brief Account,* below); *Constitution of the Society and Directors of the Penitent Female's Refuge* (Boston: True & Weston, 1819); *Brief Account;* Lane, *Policing the City,* 20; Hobson, *Uneasy Virtue,* 18–21, 118–21. On the police crackdown led by Mayor Josiah Quincy, see Hobson, *Uneasy Virtue,* 11–24, passim; Lane, *Policing the City,* 23–24. Also see David J. Pivar, *Purity Crusade: Sexual Morality and Social Control, 1868–1900* (Westport, CT: Greenwood, 1973), 23–24. For similar efforts to combat prostitution in New

York City during the early nineteenth century, see Carroll Smith Rosenberg, *Religion and the Rise of the American City: The New York City Mission Movement, 1812–1870* (Ithaca, NY: Cornell Univ. Press, 1971), 15–159, passim.

72. For the suggestion that prostitutes figured prominently among Coverly's regular customers, see the reference to "the Ann street population" in Unidentified Newspaper Clipping.

73. For example, the first African American Masonic lodge was organized in Boston in 1787; the African Society, a mutual-aid and charitable organization, was established by Boston blacks in 1796; Boston's first two independent African American churches were founded in 1805 and 1818 respectively; and the Massachusetts General Colored Association, a black abolitionist and civil rights organization, was established in 1826. On African Americans in early-national and antebellum Boston, see George A. Levesque, *Black Boston: African American Life and Culture in Urban America, 1750–1860* (New York: Garland, 1994); Adelaide M. Cromwell, *The Other Brahmins: Boston's Black Upper Class, 1750–1950* (Fayetteville: Univ. of Arkansas Press, 1994), 25–44; Donald M. Jacobs, ed., *Courage and Conscience: Black & White Abolitionists in Boston* (Bloomington: Indiana Univ. Press, 1993); Carol Buchalter Stapp, *Afro-Americans in Antebellum Boston: An Analysis of Probate Records* (New York: Garland, 1993); James Oliver Horton and Lois E. Horton, *Black Bostonians: Family Life and Community Struggle in the Antebellum North* (New York: Holmes & Meier Publishers, 1979). On the concentration of Boston's African American population in the West End, particularly on "Negro Hill," during the early-national and antebellum periods, see Levesque, *Black Boston*, 33–39, 88 (Table I-14), and passim; Horton and Horton, *Black Bostonians*, 2–5; Peter R. Knights, *The Plain People of Boston, 1830–1860: A Study in City Growth* (New York: Oxford Univ. Press, 1971), 30–31.

74. Below, 69. The narrator later ironically contrasts the contempt expressed by a "man of colour" for the corruptions of the neighborhood to the patronage of its brothels by white youths who "claim the appellation of 'young gentlemen'" (below, 92–93). Also see the narrator's implied condemnation of miscegenation (below, 118).

75. Most of the racist broadsides deal either with an anti-black riot on "Negro Hill" or with African American celebrations of the abolition of the slave trade; see, for example, *Dreadful Riot on Negro Hill!* [Boston?]: n.d. [ca. 1816?]); *Grand and Splendid Bobalition of Slavery* ([Boston?]: Sold by the Flying Booksellers, n.d. [ca. 1822?]); *Grand Jubelum!!! Order 12f Annebersary ob Affricum Bobalition* ([Boston?: n.d. [ca. 1827?]); *Copy of a Letter from Phillis, to her Sister in the Country, describing the Riot on Negro Hill* ([Boston?: n.d. [ca. 1828?]); *Hard Scrabble, or Miss Philises Bobalition* ([Boston?]: n.d. [ca. 1820–40?]). Most of the above estimated dates of publications are based on garbled and satirical dates included in the texts of the broadsides (e.g., "Uly 32, 18016" on the first one listed) and hence are not reliable, though all of the broadsides appear to have been published between about 1810 and 1840. I have not been able to determine whether the broadsides describing a riot on "Negro Hill" are referring to one or more specific riots that actually took place, and if so, when. Either the originals or

photocopies of all of the broadsides cited are in the collection of the Library Company of Philadelphia; I am very grateful to James N. Green and Phillip Lapsansky of that institution for kindly providing me with photocopies of those and several similar broadsides. I am also grateful to Daniel G. Siegel of M & S Rare Books (Providence, Rhode Island) for providing me with a photocopy of the first of the broadsides listed.

76. On Boston as a center of radical abolitionist publishing, see Robert L. Hall, "Massachusetts Abolitionists Document the Slave Experience," in Jacobs, ed., *Courage and Conscience,* 75–99; the point is also documented in several of the other excellent pieces in that volume of collected essays; but for an episode of anti-abolitionist mob violence in Boston, see Theodore M. Hammett, "Two Mobs of Jacksonian Boston: Ideology and Interest," *Journal of American History* 62 (March 1976): 845–68. On the achievement by African Americans of many legal and civil rights in Massachusetts during the antebellum period, see Leon F. Litwack, *North of Slavery: The Negro in the Free States, 1790–1860* (Chicago: Univ. of Chicago Press, 1961), 104–111.

77. Bailey and Kennedy, *American Pageant,* 213; see also Dangerfield, *Era of Good Feelings,* 86–87.

78. Recall that Coverly advertised his pamphlets in *Republican* newspapers. On the purchase of Coverly's broadsides by Boston sailors, see Unidentified Newspaper Clipping. On the probability that sailors tended to vote Republican, see James M. Banner Jr., *To the Hartford Convention* (New York: Knopf, 1970), 172n, 193–94. However, it should be remembered that a large majority of Boston men voted Federalist throughout the War of 1812 and even in its aftermath; see note 1. Obviously, ambivalent or aroused patriotism—whether on the part of Federalists or Republicans—would not have motivated *all* purchasers of *The Female Marine;* others were undoubtedly drawn by prurient, sentimental, or romantic interest, or by the appeal of female adventure.

79. For some recent scholarly discussions of the allegorical or metaphorical use of gender images in political discourse during the eighteenth and/or nineteenth centuries, see Young, "Confederate Counterfeit"; Nina Silber, *The Romance of Reunion: Northerners and the South, 1865–1900* (Chapel Hill: Univ. of North Carolina Press, 1993), 13–38, passim; Kathleen Diffley, *Where My Heart Is Turning Ever: Civil War Stories and Constitutional Reform, 1861–1876* (Athens: Univ. of Georgia Press, 1992); Lynn Hunt, *The Family Romance of the French Revolution* (Berkeley: Univ. of California Press, 1992); Ryan, *Women in Public;* Lewis, "The Republican Wife"; Yazawa, *From Colonies to Commonwealth;* Fliegelman, *Prodigals and Pilgrims.*

80. For a classic scholarly discussion of the strong support for the War of 1812 among politicians from frontier regions, see Julius W. Pratt, *Expansionists of 1812* (1925; rpt., Gloucester, MA: Peter Smith, 1957); however, for more recent interpretations, see Watts, *Republic Reborn;* Hickey, *War of 1812,* 29–38; Brown, *Republic in Peril;* George Rogers Taylor, ed., *The War of 1812: Past Justifications and Present Interpretations* (Boston: Heath, 1963); Bradford Perkins, ed., *The Causes of the War of 1812: National Honor or National Interest?* (New York: Holt, Rinehart and Winston, 1962); Reginald Horsman, *The Causes of the War of 1812* (New York: A. S. Barnes, 1962).

EDITIONS OF
THE FEMALE MARINE
and Related Works

This list is based upon American Antiquarian Society holdings; Ralph R. Shaw and Richard H. Shoemaker, comp., *American Bibliography* (New York: Scarecrow Press, 1963); and the *National Union Catalogue*.

1815

The Adventures of Louisa Baker (New York: Luther Wales [actually Boston: N. Coverly Jr.?], [August? 1815]). Shaw and Shoemaker 36517.

The Adventures of Lucy Brewer (Boston: N. Coverly Jr., [November?] 1815). Shaw and Shoemaker 33794 and 36516.

The Adventures of Lucy Brewer (Boston: H. Trumbull, 1815). Shaw and Shoemaker 36515.

An Affecting Narrative of Louisa Baker (New York: Luther Wales; rpt., Boston: Nathaniel Coverly Jr. 1815). Shaw and Shoemaker 33907 and 36518.

An Affecting Narrative of Louisa Baker, "2nd ed." (New York: Luther Wales; rpt., Boston: Nathaniel Coverly Jr. [September?], 1815). Shaw and Shoemaker 36519.

1816

The Adventures of Lucy Brewer (Boston: N. Coverly Jr. 1816). Shaw and Shoemaker 37080.

An Affecting Narrative of Louisa Baker (Boston: Nathaniel Coverly; rpt., New York: John Low, 1816). AAS, not in Shaw and Shoemaker.

An Affecting Narrative of Louisa Baker (New York: 1816). Not in AAS or Shaw and Shoemaker; NUC only.

An Affecting Narrative of Louisa Baker (Portsmouth, NH: Printed for the Purchaser, 1816). Shaw and Shoemaker 36687.

The Awful Beacon (Boston: N. Coverly Jr., [May?] 1816). Shaw and Shoemaker 37081, 39742, and 39784.

The Female Marine ([Boston?]: [N. Coverly Jr.?], Jan. 1, 1816). Shaw and Shoemaker 39743.

The Female Marine ([Boston?]: [N. Coverly Jr.?], May 30, 1816). Shaw and Shoemaker 39744.

The Female Marine ([Boston?]: [N. Coverly Jr.?], June 19, 1816). Shaw and Shoemaker 37745.

The Female Marine, "2nd ed." ([Boston?]: [N. Coverly Jr.?], June 24, 1816). Shaw and Shoemaker 39746 and 39785.

The Female Marine ([Boston?]: Printed for the Publisher [N. Coverly Jr.?], [ca. 1816]). Shaw and Shoemaker 39748.

The Female Marine (Hartwick, [NY]: L. & B. Todd, [ca. 1816]). AAS, not in Shaw and Shoemaker.

The Female Marine, "10th ed." ([Boston?]: Printed for the Proprietor [N. Coverly Jr.?], 1816). Shaw and Shoemaker 39747.

Sperry, Rachel [pseudonym?], *A Brief Reply to the Late Writings of Louisa Baker* (Boston: M. Brewster [actually N. Coverly Jr.?], [June?] 1816). Shaw and Shoemaker 38990.

The Surprising Adventures of Almira Paul (Boston: N. Coverly Jr., [September?] 1816). Shaw and Shoemaker 38563.

1817

The Female Marine, "5th ed." (Boston: Printed for the Purchaser [by N. Coverly Jr.?], 1817). Shaw and Shoemaker 40315 and 42851.

1818

The Female Marine, "4th ed." ([Boston]: Printed for the Author [by N. Coverly Jr.?], 1818). Shaw and Shoemaker 46735.

NOTE ON THE TEXTS
IN THIS EDITION

The text of *The Female Marine* in this volume is based on the "Tenth Edition" of 1816, the most complete of the composite editions of the three-part narrative. However, even the "Tenth Edition" provides only abridged versions of the Second and Third Parts, and also omits bits and pieces of the First Part. In order to produce as complete a text of the narrative as possible, I have tried to interpolate all of the text included in the original three parts but omitted from the "Tenth Edition." Those interpolations range from individual words and brief phrases to more than eighteen pages of continuous text (from the original edition of the Third Part); all such interpolations are marked by double slashes, front-slashes to indicate the beginning of an interpolation and back-slashes to mark the end. Although I have not attempted to indicate every other slight variation in phrasing, typography, or punctuation between the "Tenth Edition" and the original install-ments, I try to mention all such variations of particular interest or significance in the endnotes. Aside from the interpolated words or passages, I have invariably followed the text and punctuation of the "Tenth Edition." In *The Female Marine*, as in the other early-nineteenth-century texts in this volume, British, archaic, internally inconsistent, or otherwise irregular spellings (e.g., centre, connexion, cruize, cloathing, Guerrier/Guerriere/Gurrierre, honour, profane/prophane, un-burthen, unfrequently, visiter) have been retained unaltered and unnoted, with "[*sic*]s" deployed sparingly and only where confusion might otherwise arise; ap-parent printer's errors (or typographical errors) have been corrected but are gener-ally mentioned in the endnotes.

The "Tenth Edition" tends to differ from the original three installments in certain ways that are worth noting. When compared to the original parts, the text of that composite edition seems to have been somewhat softened or moderated—"expurgated" would be too strong a characterization. In some cases, the "soften-ing" is achieved through small changes in punctuation and typography; for exam-ple, there are many fewer italicized words and exclamation points in the "Tenth

Edition." But there are also changes in wording or small omissions of text. For example, a few of the more explicit references to "Negro Hill" are removed in the "Tenth Edition"—in fact, the designation "Negro Hill" does not appear at all in that edition (see below, 68). Also modified are some of the more vituperative or sarcastic characterizations of prostitutes and their customers. Thus the phrase "lewd inhabitants" in the original version of the First Part becomes simply "inhabitants" in the "Tenth Edition"; "miserable stinking cell" becomes "miserable cell"; "misshaped stinkard" becomes "misshapen person" (68, 70).

In a few cases, particularly in the Third Part, the editor of the "Tenth Edition" also seems to have altered the text in subtle ways designed to minimize the seeming impropriety of Lucy Brewer's conduct. For example, in the original version, Brewer expresses regret that she had not preferred the tranquility of her parental home to the "noisy scenes and unlawful indulgences" of her youth; in the "Tenth Edition," the second half of that quoted phrase is omitted, thereby eliminating the heroine's tacit confession to a former preference for "unlawful indulgences" (104). In some cases, it is unclear whether elisions are intended to modify the meaning of certain passages (so as to avoid offending readers and perhaps local officials) or simply to eliminate excess verbiage. For example, the characterization of the prostitutes of "Negro Hill" as "creatures covered with filth and rags, putrid with disease, and devoured with vermin" in the first installment is reduced in the "Tenth Edition" to "creatures covered with rags, and devoured with vermin" (64). Because the practice of interpolating deleted passages of text renders most such changes easily visible in this volume (with other variations discussed in the endnotes), the current edition provides an unusually rich and accessible case study of the processes of editorial revision in the realm of early American plebeian literature.

Concerning the other nineteenth-century texts included in this volume, less needs to be said. In regard to all three of those works, I have followed the same basic editorial procedures outlined above in regard to archaic or otherwise irregular spellings, typographical errors, and so forth. *A Brief Reply to the Late Writings of Louisa Baker* and *The Surprising Adventures of Almira Paul* are both based on the only known editions of those works, each published in 1816, and are both reprinted in their entirety. *A Brief Account of the Origin and Progress of the Boston Female Society for Missionary Purposes* is also based on the original edition of 1818, but has been abridged (by perhaps 25 percent) to eliminate some material of doubtful relevance here, including several purely devotional passages and generic conversion accounts with little or no explicit reference to Boston's vice districts. Although it is not directly linked to the cross-dressing narratives and is written in a very different spirit, the missionary pamphlet does feature nearly contemporaneous descriptions of the same Boston neighborhood of "Negro Hill" that is the setting for much of *The Female Marine*. It also provides a good example of the sort of evangelical discourse concerning urban vice that is alternately echoed and subverted by Coverly's playful narratives.

THE

FEMALE MARINE,

OR THE

ADVENTURES

OF

MISS LUCY BREWER,

Who served three years in disguise on
board the U. S. frigate Constitution ;—
was in the battles with the Guerriere,
Java, &c. and was honourably discharged.   Also, an account of her duel
at Newport with a young and valiant
Midshipman.

To which is added,
An AWFUL BEACON to the rising Generation, containing an account of her
courtship and marriage with Mr. West.

WRITTEN BY HERSELF.

———

TENTH EDITION.

———

Printed for the Proprietor.
1816.

Frontispiece (*opposite*) and title page of the "Tenth Edition" of *The Female Marine* (1816),
the edition that provides the basis for the text in this volume.

THE
FEMALE MARINE,

or the

Adventures of Miss Lucy Brewer

LOUISA BAKER,

[A NATIVE OF MASSACHUSETTS.]

Who, in disguise, served Three Years as a MARINE on board an American FRIGATE.

"She was her parents only joy :
They had but one——one darling child,
But ah ! the cruel spoiler came !"

THE

ADVENTURES

OF

LOUISA BAKER,

[Eliza (Bowen) Webb]

Whose life and character are peculiarly distinguished...Having in early life been shamefully seduced by a pretended suitor, and with her virginity, having lost all hopes of regaining her former state of respectability, became a voluntary victim to *VICE*, and joined a society of *BAWDS*, and for three years lived as a common Prostitute on *NEGRO HILL*, (so termed)....But at length becoming weary of the society of the Sisterhood, she formed the curious project of rendering her services more to the benefit of her country's cause, in her late rupture with Great Britain....she dressed like a male, and under a fictious name, in 1813, entered as a *MARINE* on board an American *FRIGATE* where she performed the duties of her department with punctual exactness, fidelity and honor, without any discovery being made of her sex while on board, from which she was honourably discharged in 1315, when she re-assumed her former dress, and like a true penitent has since returned to her Parents, from whom she has been nearly six years absent.

◆

NEW-YORK....Printed by LUTHER WALES.

[1815]

Frontispiece (*opposite*) and title page of *The Adventures of Louisa Baker* (1815), the first edition of the first of the pamphlets on the female marine. Despite the New York imprint, the pamphlet was probably published by Nathaniel Coverly Jr. in Boston. Note the emphasis in the subtitle on the protagonist's experiences as a prostitute on "Negro Hill." Courtesy, American Antiquarian Society.

ADVERTISEMENT.

Lᴜᴄʏ Bʀᴇᴡᴇʀ, whose life and character are peculiarly distinguished, having been shamefully seduced by a pretended suitor, and lost all hopes of regaining her former state of respectability, became a voluntary victim to vice. But at length growing weary of that manner of life, she formed the curious project of volunteering her services in her country's cause, in the late rupture with Great Britain; she dressed like a male, and under a fictitious name, in 1812, entered as a marine on board an American frigate, where she performed the duties of her department with punctual exactness, fidelity and honour, without any discovery being made of her sex while on board, from which she was honourably discharged in 1815, when she re-assumed her former dress, and, like a true penitent, has since returned to her parents, from whom she had been absent nearly six years.

FIRST PART:

NARRATIVE OF LUCY BREWER.

TO reputable parents who reside in the state of Massachusetts, and within forty miles from its capital, I owe my existence; but the regard which I have for them, (whose feelings have already been too much wrought upon by the rude behaviour of their daughter) forbids that I should disclose their real name, as well as that of the place of my nativity. At the age of sixteen, by the deceptive arts of one whom I could not think capable of a base action, I was shamefully robbed of that which is rightly esteemed of inestimable value to my sex; of that, which, although it did not enrich the monster, made me poor indeed! I was young, and forward to listen to the vows of unfeigned love of a youth (but a few years older than myself) who was the son of a respectable trader residing within a short distance of my father's house. Happy would it have been for me, had I improved by the instruction and wise counsel of those who felt an interest in my welfare; my parents saw my growing attachment to him who afterwards proved my seducer, and trembled for the issue; they admonished me for my credulity, but admonished in vain; already had the solemn declarations of my false friend made too great an impression upon my fickle mind; I felt a due regard for my parents, and believed myself tenderly beloved by them; but, although I blush to acknowledge it, I conceived it impossible that their love and regard for me could be equal to that of my then dear Henry! O love! how powerful is thy influence! how unlimited thy domain!

Happy until the fatal moment was I, no intruding cares disturbed me by day, no busy thoughts interrupted my repose at night; as I can solemnly protest that ere this, no vicious desires ever prompted me to lose my virtue; I was all innocence, and knew no sin, until that fatal period when the vile and insinuating author of my ruin deluded and deceived me; but I have the pleasing reflection that the immoral life which I have since led, brought me early under affliction, and that affliction, I thank Providence, to an early repentance.

I never once reflected that the man who could stoop to seduction, would not hesitate to forsake the wretched object of his passion, whenever his capricious heart grew weary of her tenderness. When he made his solemn vows, I vainly expected him to fulfil his engagements; but was too late convinced he had never intended to make me his wife, or if he had once thought of it, his mind was now altered. I scorned to claim from his humanity what I could not obtain from his love: I was conscious of having forfeited the only gem that could render me respectable in the eyes of the world. I locked my sorrows in my own bosom, and bore my injuries in silence.

Alas! how could I at this melancholy period reveal to my injured parents the important secret! I could not, for a moment, harbour the idea of being myself the bearer of the heart-piercing tidings of an event, of which they had so repeatedly warned me; too well I knew that I could plead nothing in excuse for my conduct; that I loved my seducer was but too true! yet powerful as that passion was, when operating in a young heart glowing with sensibility, it never would have conquered my affection for my beloved parents, had I not been deceived by the specious appearance of my betrayer, and every suspicion lulled asleep by the most solemn promises of marriage; I thought not those promises would be so easily forgotten.

After a series of reflections, I unwisely formed the determination, that if I hazarded my life, my parents and friends should not partake of the shame and disgrace which I was soon to incur; but how was it to be avoided? I was young and inexperienced, without a friend of my own sex with whom I could advise and unburthen my full heart! An hundred different projects filled my head how I ought to proceed in my critical situation; as there was no time to be lost, I at length resolved to elope from my parents and friends, and seek among strangers some hospitable mansion, where I might possibly be permitted to remain until I could with safety return: I had no sooner formed this resolution, than I resolved immediately to put it in execution; accordingly at twelve at night, having privately prepared a few necessaries against my expected confinement, I set off alone and unprotected for Boston, where I flattered myself among the multitude I might be enabled to escape the researches of my friends.

The distance was nearly forty miles from the peaceable mansion of my father, the country thinly inhabited, and the cold so intense, that being from my situation, unable to walk quick, I found myself almost sinking with cold and fatigue before I reached the town. I had now indeed succeeded in reaching the place of my destination, but what was now my situation? a miserable fugitive wanderer among strangers; cold and hungry, and without fortitude to solicit a shelter for the approaching night, I began seriously to relent and reproach myself for my imprudence and folly in deserting my tender parents, thus to expose myself to the cold ingratitude of unpitying strangers: I wept bitterly, and more than once was half resolved to return to my friends, make known to them the cause of my flight, and upon my knees solicit their forgiveness: happy would it have been for me and them had not the dread of shame induced me finally to determine otherwise.

At the close of the day passing down Cambridge-street, a few cents which I possessed obtained me a morsel of cake; it was at a small grocery shop, and as I sat upon a wooden bench partaking of this humble pittance, the grocer's lady entered, who probably very justly judging by my appearance that my situation was not the most enviable, inquired of me if I lived in town, to which I answered in the negative: I told her that I had recently come from the country, to seek a situation as chamber maid in town, as I had been informed that wages were much higher here than in the country: she inquired of me my name and the place of my late residence, to which I gave evasive answers; and when I informed her that I was alone and unattended, and without a friend or an acquaintance in town, I thought, while she surveyed me more minutely and with a degree of suspicion, it was not without an emotion of pity.—Retiring for a few moments, she returned and informed me that she could furnish me with lodgings for the night, if I would accept of such as she could provide: I thanked her, and, as the reader may suppose, was not backward to accept of her kind offer.

With this truly excellent woman, whose kind services to me at this distressing moment time cannot obliterate from my memory, I tarried the night, and was furnished with supper and breakfast, and not a cent exacted therefor. I really lament that my situation is such, that in honor to my dear friend, I cannot here record her name, for the most excellent counsel which she gave me (every word of which I have since by sad experience found to be true, or rather the incidents which she warned me to beware of) was such as would have done honor to the most noble of her sex; I would to God it was recorded upon the tablet of the hearts of all young and inexperienced females, who, like me, should hereafter have occasion (unprotected) to visit the capitals of our country; nor does it less become (as my wicked situation in life has taught me) youths of the male sex, unhackneyed in the vices of the world, to be on their guard! For the benefit of both sexes, I would therefore attempt here to repeat the most excellent advice of this lady, which, should the kind reader pass over with an eye of indifference, and discard the remaining pages of the record of my adventures, I would most humbly conjure him, whoever he may be, carefully to preserve and peruse this, as a just description of not only a class which are ornamental to human nature, but, to the reverse, of a corrupted race, who are prone to wickedness, and are very justly esteemed the pests of society.

After I had partaken of an excellent breakfast, and was preparing for my departure, for what place I knew not, my good lady desiring me to be seated for a few moments, thus addressed me: "Miss Baker, (for that was the name I had assumed) you inform me that you have come to this town for the purpose of procuring for yourself a place as chambermaid, and as you are destitute of acquaintance here, and are apparently young and inexperienced in the world, you will not, I presume, deem it presumption in me, should I give you such advice as may possibly be of advantage to you, in your new situation in life. With this town and its inhabitants I profess to be well acquainted, having been an inhabitant from my infancy; with regard to the former, I believe I may safely say, that there is not a city or a town in any part of the United States, that can boast of a greater proportion of honest, kind and hospitable inhabitants, ever forward to protect the innocent from injury, and to afford assistance to such as require it, and whose course of life has not been such as to debar them from it—it is here, I assure you, that good behaviour will receive its reward, and virtue and innocence be esteemed, even in the humbler walks of life; while vice, in whatever form it may appear, is as justly discountenanced:—Yes, my dear, should you succeed in obtaining a respectable situation, you will not fail, by good behaviour, to gain the applause of such whose friendship may perhaps, prove of essential service to you, destitute as you are of connexions in town. But," continued my worthy friend, "I am sorry to inform you, that such are not the characters of all those who compose the inhabitants of the town: there is indeed another class, whose society I would have you shun as you regard liberty and life; for permit me, my dear, to assure you, that a connexion with these will ultimately cost you one or the other; it is a class composed of such as are by many esteemed the bane of society, while by some few they are viewed as a "necessary evil!" They are a shameful race, whose detestable habits and vices sink them infinitely below the beasts that perish. They are such as abound more or less in all our large cities, and of whom this town has a great proportion: among whom, I blush to say, there are a great portion of our sex! who, by the vilest prostitution, obtain their livelihood. Among these are many of respectable parentage, and yet so young, that you could scarcely suppose them capable of conforming to such shameful vice. These poor deluded wretches, by those older in iniquity than themselves, are by false allurements enticed from their homes, and by contracting their fatal and cursed habits, ruin themselves forever; for of all vices there is none so incurable as this when it is once contracted. Step by step, they descend to the lowest class of prostitutes, with whom all great cities swarm in the midnight hours; creatures covered with //filth and\\ rags, //putrid with disease,\\ and devoured with vermin, there is hardly any vice which entails more complicated miseries upon the unhappy wretches who are subject to it.[1]

Thus, my dear, have I attempted briefly to delineate human life as you will find it here. The picture, I assure you, is not too highly coloured; for while I conceive it impossible to extol or bestow too much praise upon those exemplary characters which first I spoke of, I am confident that we cannot too much execrate the vile deeds which characterise the latter class. You are now, Miss Baker, in their very neighbourhood, and as their pimps are continually in search of new victims, and you young and unattended, beware, my dear girl, I beseech you beware, that you are not deceived, and like thousands allured from the paths of virtue and innocence."

Here my worthy friend concluded, and here, kind reader, permit me humbly to request you for a moment to pause; and blush at the depravity of one of your fellow-creatures, to whom this wise counsel was given, yea, it was really so, lulled in the languors of pleasure, the impression which it made upon my unstable mind, was like the trace of an arrow through the penetrated air, or the path of a keel through furrowed waves.

With a heavy heart, at nine in the morning, I quit the hospitable mansion of my benefactress, in hopes ere the close of another day, to obtain in some capacity or other, a permanent situation in some respectable family, whom in approaching illness I conceived might have the humanity to suffer me to remain with them until such time as my strength would enable me to return to my friends. But whether the appearance of a young and slender female thinly clad, and in a tedious snow storm, with a handkerchief in one hand containing a few articles of clothing, excited their suspicion that all was not right, or whether it was really so as they repeatedly informed me, that they were already supplied with help, I know not, in vain were my supplications for a place at almost every house that I passed. Alas! it is impossible to describe correctly what were my feelings at this moment, night was approaching, the snow, which was already of an unusual depth, was fast descending, my feeble limbs were very sensibly affected by the cold, while the tears which occasionally gushed from my weeping eyes, formed icicles upon my cheeks. Once more did I reproach myself for my folly in deserting a peaceful home and the best of parents, and once more resolved to return penitent to their arms.

The light of day began now to grow more and more invisible, and I yet un-provided with a shelter for the night; it was thus I roamed until the clock struck seven, when cold and hunger forced me in the bar-room of a public inn, situated near the centre of the town, at the bar I made application for a lodging, and was informed that for twenty cents I could be furnished with a bed. Fortunate indeed did I conceive myself, to obtain lodgings for a night so boisterous, and at so late an hour, supperless I retired to rest, and early the ensuing morning again set out in quest of a temporary home; the storm yet continued to rage, and the snow which during the night had astonishingly increased in depth, rendered the roads almost impassable, but the pressing calls of hunger began now to operate so powerfully as to render me careless as to what part of the town I resorted, or to whom I applied for relief.

About noon I unconscionably ascended the heights of West-Boston, where I renewed my applications for a place.—Never could the hydra wish for a better chance for his prey; within the walls of a house, the external appearance of which was spacious, I was welcomed and treated with the attention and with that apparent cordiality, which my depressed spirits at that moment really required.—Never ought I to forget with what feigned kindness I was received by the 'good mother,' who expressed great surprise that the good and pious people of the town could see a young and tender female travelling in so tedious a storm; nor did her daughters, (of which there appeared a considerable throng) appear less disposed to serve the 'poor female wanderer;' by the direction of their good 'ma'am,' tea was early provided, and many restoratives prescribed and kindly administered for the benefit of my health, &c. Although I at that time remarked that there was no visible resemblance in the features of 'ma'am's darling daughters,' whose wan cheeks and sunken eyes were evident marks of their dissipation, yet so completely decoyed was I, that I did not dream of deception; the girls appeared adepts in their business, they apparently strove to out-do each other in their kind offices, nor will the reader be surprised that a heart open to every gentle, generous sentiment, should feel itself warmed by gratitude for those of her sex who professed to feel so much for her.

Here let me stop to remark, that when once a woman has stifled the sense of shame in her own bosom, when once she has lost sight of the basis on which reputation, honour, every thing that should be dear to the female heart, rests; she grows hardened in guilt, and will spare no pains to bring down innocence and beauty to the shocking level with herself: and this proceeds not only from a disposition to reap a reward by the seduction of innocence, but from a diabolical spirit of envy, which repines at seeing another in the full possession of that respect and esteem which she can no longer hope to enjoy.[2]

In the evening the girls having withdrawn each to their apartments, and probably each with a lover, I was left alone with their matron, who, by her ingenious interrogatories, succeeded in drawing from me every particular relative to my situation: at the recital of the difficulties that [I] had encountered since I left my parents, she, letting fall a few hypocritical tears, assured me "that I need now give myself no uneasiness, for until the time that I expected to be confined, and until the time that I should recover my strength to return to my friends, her house should serve me as an asylum, and as for my infant, that she would adopt and rear [it] up to an age that would enable it to provide for itself. She thought me perfectly wise in quitting my parents and friends, as thereby they would probably avoid the shame and disgrace which generally attended such unfortunate cases; no pains, she assured me, should be spared to keep the whole affair from their knowledge."[3]

The reader will probably be surprised that I could so easily be made the dupe to these detestable harlots, yet so ingeniously did they conceal every thing from me that would give rise to suspicion, that I remained totally ignorant of my real situation, until the melancholy period when I brought into the world an innocent victim of my guilt; which, happily for it and its wretched mother, did not survive its birth but a few moments. A few weeks restored me to my former state of health and spirits, when I began to harbour thoughts of returning to my friends, which thoughts I innocently communicated to my pretended benefactress:—Unhappy moment! it was that in which I first suspected that I had been by false friendship decoyed upon those dangerous shoals, which my friend, the grocer's lady, had warned me to beware of. The mask of friendship was now thrown aside, which had been so successfully worn by this perfidious woman, and her accursed votaries. No sooner had I made my intentions known, than a thousand objections were started, and a thousand obstacles thrown in the way; the principal of which was, that my sickness had incurred a debt which ought to be discharged before I quit the house, which, should I presume to do, a suit would ensue, and I should thereby expose myself, not only to my friends, but to the world.

Unfortunately for me, I had too unwisely unbosomed myself to those, who now by threatening exposure, too well knew that they could compel me to conform to almost any thing that they should propose. To conceal from parents and friends the fatal effects of my misplaced confidence, was all that induced me to quit the peaceful roof of the former, and to expose myself, not only to the chilling blasts of winter, but to every misfortune incident to an unhappy female in my situation. If this much I had hazarded to avoid wounding the feelings of my friends, what would I not now sacrifice to prevent it?

This artful woman, and her not less cunning favourites, began now the difficult task of drawing me over by degrees to their nefarious purposes; the former by representing to me the importance of receiving the addresses of the first gentlemen in town, if offered, provided I should wish to rise from the low condition I was in, to a state of affluence; and the latter by suggesting to me the propriety of conforming to the "customs of the town," //(of the HILL, they should have said)\\ which was to act with less reserve, and allow the beaux to take greater liberties than what the bashful country rustics were in the habit of doing: that by their proper management they had each obtained a suitor, and of the first respectability; and that if I would condescend to be dictated by them, they would insure me that I should be not less fortunate.[4]

Such was the language and such the means used by my conscientious benefactress, and her arch pupils to fit me for their market. Alas! how justly shall I be reprobated by my readers when they learn from me, that I at length became less inflexible in my determination to support my chastity. From this unhappy period of my life, ought my iniquities to receive their date. Modesty forbids that I should state every particular, relative to my sinful career: let it suffice to say, that I, after receiving the proper lessons from my tutoress, became perfected in those fascinating powers which seldom fail to decoy the amorous youth to practise vices perhaps before unthought of, and then leave him to deplore his thoughtless credulity. Could those young fellows who devote too great a portion of their time at the midnight revel, but once reflect what a complication of disease and wretchedness they heap upon themselves, and that it is their money alone that gains them admittance, I am certain they would cease to visit those houses of ill fame.

My long residence in one of those brothels will enable me to describe to such of my readers who have too much delicacy, even to gratify a curiosity, ever to visit this modern Sodom, the seat of riot and dissipation, a continual round of vice and wickedness which mark a considerable portion of its //lewd\\ inhabitants; in performing this, all immodest expressions will be carefully avoided, as it is my object to record such incidents only as may be perused by the most virtuous of my sex, without putting modesty to the blush.[5]

This corrupted spot, which fortunately for the town comprises but a few acres, appears to have been a department allotted to the people of colour, as most of the inhabitants are of this description: //hence it receives the vulgar appellation of "Negro Hill"—\\ the tenements erected thereon, like its wretched inhabitants, are of every description, from the comfortable dwelling to the most miserable //stinking\\ cell, apparently erected and propped up for a temporary purpose only.[6] In those of the first class the ladies, strumpets of distinction claim a residence, while the latter are inhabited by a lower order, apparently composed of the worst of creation.[7] If there can be reasonably any distinction made in grades of harlotry, the former ought to receive the preference as being generally supported as private misses, who expose themselves less in public, go more decently clad, and make use of less indecent expressions. They have generally at the head of their mess, a matron, who receives from all the appellation of "ma'am," and passes for the mother of all who reside under her roof, and who seem to regard her as their tutoress.[8] With her they regularly board at an exorbitant price, and each are provided with ready furnished apartments. The old Beldam is generally too a retailer of wines, sweet meats, &c. which she keeps merely for the accommodation of gentlemen lodgers; from whom, with the aid of her fair pupils, she seldom fails to sponge a round sum therefor. I have known many bottles of wine privately upset by these arch girls, that had been called and paid for, that their cullies might apply to their "good ma'am" for more. It is by their expertness in playing at such games that their conscientious governess appreciates their worth and knowledge of the world. If they prove themselves adepts in their business, they are sure to receive "ma'am's" caresses; but, if to the reverse, they prove themselves unprofitable servants in the vineyard, it is then this guardian angel becomes their infuriated enemy, taxes them with the crime of departing from the precepts and examples set them, and loads them with the most opprobrious epithets.[9] These arch hags value nothing but money, and value not how they obtain it. They are very civil to strangers, who visit them with well lined pockets, and will contrive many plans to put them fairly out of the way for the lucre of their cargo; and many have been made rich by such windfalls.

The girls seldom quit their beds till noon, when they hobble down stairs and refresh themselves with bitters, toast and coffee; at three they commence the arduous task of dressing themselves for their evening revels. Their object is to disguise themselves as much as possible from what they really are! which they so effectually do, with the aid of paint, patches, false teeth and hair, that a stranger, to view them by candle light, would suppose some modern Solomon had been collecting beauties from the four corners of the world; but could he but have a peep at these bewitching girls in their dishabille, their awkward gestures, their blotched faces, their crimsoned eyes, their rotten teeth and stenchified breath, would, I think, effectually wean him from every thing like an amorous assault.

Such are the characters who compose the higher grade of false fair //who inhabit the Hill\\.[10] There is still another, who, if possible, are not only far more disgusting to the sight, but whose actions may well be said to vie in wickedness with the evil one; an impudent air being the only charms of their countenance, and a lewd carriage the studied grace of their deportment.—Swearing, drinking and obscenity are their principal qualifications; and she that wants a perfection in those admirable acquirements, is as much ridiculed by her associates for her modesty, as a plain dealing man among a gang of knaves for his honesty.[11] These are the creatures who inhabit those wretched brothel houses of the second class: they are of every age and complexion; but black is [by] far the most respectable colour among them![12] It is not unfrequently that you here see white girls of not more than seventeen years of age throwing their scarified arms around the neck of an ugly looking black, and bringing their ulcerated faces in contact with his! The respectable part of the people of colour, however, of whom there is a considerable portion who reside in the vicinity, as much despise and avoid the company of these filthy strumpets, as the real gentleman does that of a convicted jail bird! Their companions are principally composed of sailors of the lowest grade and straggling mulattoes and blacks, and who generally are never without those unpleasant proofs of their imprudence and folly in forming so dangerous a connexion. There are but few of these girls, however young, but can boast of having been half a dozen times under the hands of a doctor, as many times in prison, and probably three or four times an inhabitant of the almshouse.[13]

As soon as the day closes, these filthy hags, like the vermin that burrow in the earth, creep from their rotten cells, or mud holes, in search of their nocturnal prey. Then the grand revel commences: six or eight filthy hovels, which they term "dancing-halls," are resorted to by tag, rag and bobtail, and shoals of those pretty misses, who with their artificial faces and sweet perfumes never fail to grace the //respectable\\ assemblage, and who like the dancing girls of Egypt, strive to please by their obscene gestures: they are not over scrupulous in the choice of their beaux, as it frequently happens that the most contemptible misshapen person bears off the prize, provided he has cash to pave the way; but few of these creatures are called by their proper names, having assumed fictitious ones, are almost all "Ann Eliza's," "Ann Maria's," "Melissa Matilda's," &c.[14]

The terrific and perpetual yell of these nocturnal disturbers of the public repose, ever attended by the howlings of their affrighted dogs, is not perhaps equalled by those of the numerous hordes of the wild inhabitants of the Ganges: this continues with little intermission from the setting until the rising of the sun. The unsuspecting stranger who accidentally becomes a spectator of these midnight scenes is not only filled with disgust, but trembles for his personal safety.

It was even here, sad to relate, the narrator spent three years of her youthful days. Alas! may Sterne's recording angel drop a tear of pity, and obliterate her faults.[15]

In 1812, forming an acquaintance with a young man, the first lieutenant of a privateer then lying in a neighbouring port, who, in the course of an evening's conversation humorously observing that had he been a female, his disposition would have been the same to rove about and see the world, I suggested to him the difficulties that must attend him, exposed as he must be to the insults of such who conceived it no dishonourable action to insult a female, who would presume thus to venture abroad alone and unprotected; to which he replied, "were I a female and disposed to travel, I would assume a different dress from that usually worn by your sex, which I am confident would rather expose me to injury than afford me protection: I would garb myself as a male, and for such pass among all those with whom I might have occasion to associate; this I am confident I could effect, and travel abroad by sea and land, with proper precaution, without exposing my sex. That a female can do this, and from the knowledge of her most intimate acquaintance conceal her situation, history furnishes us with many instances.—Here my friend referred to the remarkable instance of Miss Sampson, who during the revolutionary war disguised like a male by the name of Robert Shurtliff, and as such, by the most scrupulous concealment of her sex, served her country as a private soldier, and performed her duty without a stain on her virtue and honour.

From this moment I became dissatisfied with my situation in life: for three years I had trod the detestable rounds of dissipation, it was enough: those vicious scenes in which I had taken so distinguished a part I now began to view in their proper light; new projects occupied my mind: ashamed to return to my abused parents, whom I had so long deserted, I felt now no other disposition than in disguise to visit other parts of the country, and to pursue a course of life less immoral and destructive to my peace and happiness //in this life\\.[16]

Fortunately for me, the inadvertent remarks of my friend impressed my mind with new ideas relative to my situation, and with the possibility of my escaping by stratagem from the clutches of my shepherdess, for had I publicly attempted to have strayed from the flock, prosecution, and probably a jail, would have been my deserts; I was positive that I now saw my way clear, for by garbing myself in the habiliments of a male, I should be enabled to escape their vigilance.

Having provided every thing necessary for my entrance in a new character on the stage of life, I seized upon a favourable opportunity early one morning to equip myself therefor; being garbed complete in a sailor's suit, I quit unnoticed my lodgings and passed into the public street. From my awkward appearance in attempting to assume the character of a male, I was not without my fears that I should be suspected, nor were my apprehensions relieved until passing through Court-street, I ventured to accost one of my own sex, who answering with a ready 'yes sir,' strengthened my confidence that I should pass for a male!

I bent my course toward the old Market, where entering a victualing cellar, I procured breakfast—the remainder of the day I spent in rambling about the town, highly pleased in being enabled to visit public places, where females (if known) would not have been admitted. Lodging I obtained without difficulty, and the next morning sought a passage for the southward—this was difficult to obtain at this time, as the harbour being closely blockaded by the enemy, no vessel would venture abroad, and for the want of funds not being able to travel by land, was compelled reluctantly to give up the idea of a southern excursion.

Passing through Fish-street, I entered a house where was a public rendezvous for the enlistment of men to go on board one of the United States' frigates then lying in the harbour, and shortly bound on a cruize.

Encouraged by the active part which one of my sex had taken in the late American war, without exposing her sex, I viewed this as a favourable opportunity to try my fortune in the public service of my country, provided I could avoid the search which new recruits must generally undergo—this I succeeded in doing by an artful stratagem, and entered as a marine, received my advance and clothing, and the next day was taken on board!

New scenes now opened to my view—pains were now taken by the officer of marines to instruct me in the manual exercise, of which I had no necessity of pleading ignorance; I had taken the precaution to provide myself with a tight pair of under draws, which I had never shifted but with the greatest precaution, which, together with a close waistcoat or bandage about my breasts, effectually concealed my sex from all on board. My good fortune in having for my commander one of the most humane and experienced officers in the American navy, was much in my favour, as the respect entertained for him and //the\\ under officers caused the utmost harmony to prevail among the ship's crew.[17]

In August we set sail with a fair wind and in good spirits; we first stood an easterly course, in hopes of falling in with a British frigate cruizing in that direction. I suffered a little confinement by sea sickness, (so peculiar to fresh hands) which was all the illness I experienced during the whole cruise. In the use of my arms I made great proficiency, which I soon learnt to load and discharge with an expertness not surpassed by any in my corps.

We passed near the isle of Sables, and took a station off the Gulph of St. Lawrence, near Cape Race, to intercept vessels bound either to or from Canada.—While cruizing off this station, we captured two merchant vessels. Having received information, that the British squadron were off the Grand Bank, and not far distant, our brave commander determined to change his cruizing ground; he accordingly stood to the southward. On the 17th, he was informed by the commander of an American privateer, that a British ship of war had been seen the day before, standing to the southeast, and that she could not be far off. Our intrepid commander immediately made sail, intending, if possible, to fall in with her.

On the 19th, at 2 P. M. a vessel was discovered at the southward; our ship instantly gave chase, and soon gained on her. At 3 P. M. it could plainly be perceived that she was a ship, under easy sail, close hauled to the wind; soon after she was ascertained to be a frigate; our ship continued the chase. //At about three miles distance, our commander ordered the light sails to be taken in, the courses to be hauled up, and the ship to be cleared for action.\\ The chase now backed her main top sail, and waited for our ship to come down.[18]

It is frequently observed by those who have been in battle, that at the commencement of an engagement, the most resolute feel daunted, in some degree: but I can solemnly declare, that I never felt more composed; as every person on board, even to the youngest lad, are on such occasions anxious to distinguish themselves at their post, so I felt an extreme desire to render myself conspicuous, and to perform that which woman never before achieved. Stationed in the tops, I waited only with impatience for the battle to commence.

As soon as our ship was ready for action, she bore down, intending to bring immediately to close action the British frigate, which about this time had hoisted her ensign. As soon as our ship came within gun shot, the British //frigate\\ fired her broadside, then filled away, wore, and gave a broadside on the other tack.— They, however, produced no effect; her shot fell short. The British frigate man-œuvred and wore several times for about three quarters of an hour, in order to take a raking position. But not succeeding in this, //she\\ bore up under her top sails and jib, with the wind on the quarter. Our brave commander immediately made sail to bring his ship up with her. At 5 minutes before 6 P. M. our ship got along side, within pistol shot, he ordered a brisk firing to be commenced from all her guns, which were double shotted [*sic*] with round and grape shot; and so well directed, and so warmly kept up was our fire, that in fifteen minutes the mizen mast of the British frigate went by the board, her hull was much injured; and her rigging and sails torn to pieces. I was at this time busily employed in the top plying my faithful musket with the best success, whenever the smoke would permit me to see a blue jacket of the enemy; in the heat of the action a grape shot striking and splintering the butt of my musket, it was noticed by one of my comrades who stood within a few feet from me, who, patting me upon the shoulder, exclaimed, "never mind it, George, you have already won laurels sufficient to recommend you to the pretty girls, when you return to port!"[19]

The grape shot and small arms of our ship completely swept the decks of the British frigate; thirty minutes after the commencement of the action the main-mast and foremast of the British frigate went by the board, taking with them every spar except the bowsprit; she then struck her colours, and as soon as her crew could be removed, and in consequence of her sinking condition, was set fire to and blew up a quarter past three. She had fifteen men killed and sixty-one wounded; while our loss amounted to no more than seven killed, and eight or ten wounded.[20]

Soon after this noble achievement our gallant ship returned to port, where she remained for some time, undergoing necessary repairs. While here, I had frequent opportunities to go on shore, and in more than one instance was actually in company with girls who were late my associates, but who did not identify my person, so artfully did I disguise myself; I felt no disposition to re-assume my former dress, or to return to that wicked course of life which I now more than ever detested. It was from some of my old acquaintance that I learnt, that as soon as it was discovered that I had fled, the "blood hounds" were unkennelled and sent in every direction after me! I conversed familiarly with many, who, in my late situation knew me well, but to whom I was now a stranger, as I did not disclose the important secret. Curiosity alone induced me to visit a place at which I had already spent too great a portion of my miserable life. It was here I resorted for an evening's amusement with my shipmates, where, over the cheerful glass, we could boast of the //superior\\ skill and judgment of our officers, and of the superior sailing of our ship.[21]

As soon as refitted, our ship was ordered upon another cruize; during which I had another opportunity to assist my brethren in revenging their injuries. In December, while cruizing along the coast of South America, two strange vessels were discovered on our weather bow. At ten they were discovered to be ships.— One of them stood in for the land, the other stood off shore towards our ship. //At 10 our commander tacked to the southward and eastward, hauled up the main sail, and took in the royals.\\[22]

At quarter past one, the ship in sight proving to be an English frigate, and being sufficiently distant from land, our commander ordered the main sails and royals to be taken in, to tack ship and stand for the enemy, who soon bore down with an intention of raking our ship, which we avoided by wearing. A general action now commenced with round and grape shot. Both vessels, for some time, manœuvred to obtain a position that would enable them to rake, or avoid being raked. About three o'clock, the head of the British vessel's bowsprit and jib boom were shot away; and in the space of an hour, her foremast was shot away by the board, her main top mast just above the cap, &c.

About four o'clock, the fire of the British vessel being completely silenced, and her colours in the main rigging being down, she was supposed to have struck, but her flag was soon after discovered to be still flying. About a quarter of an hour after, the main mast of the British vessel went by the board. About three quarters of an hour after four, our ship got into a very good position for raking, when the enemy prudently struck her flag, being then almost a wreck. She was a frigate mounting forty-nine guns, with a compliment of four hundred men, of which sixty were killed, and about one hundred and fifty wounded. Our loss was comparatively small.[23]

In this engagement I did not attempt to signalize myself less than in the former. From the ship's top I discharged my piece nineteen times, which, as I had now learnt to take pretty exact aim, must, I think, have done some execution. An accident soon after the conclusion of the engagement occurred, which was near betraying my sex to the whole crew of the ship: attempting to go below, I made a misstep, and fell from the shrouds overboard; not knowing how to swim, I sunk immediately; a boat was sent to my relief, but before they could recover me and get me on board, life had become nearly extinct. As soon as they succeeded in getting me on deck, (as I had not strength to do it myself) some of my shipmates were ordered to strip off my clothes and to furnish me with a dry suit, and they had nearly divested me of my out dress, when I mustered sufficient strength to beg of them to desist, as I then felt able to effect it myself.

Not long after our late engagement we returned to the United States, where our brave officers and whole ship's crew were received by our countrymen with every demonstration of joy and esteem, for our late gallant exploit.

So closely were all our harbours blockaded at this time by large ships of the enemy, that it was thought imprudent for us to attempt then to get out: we consequently lay a long while in port, during which the time for which I had entered expired; but I again immediately re-entered, and before the conclusion of peace made two more successful cruizes—at the expiration of which, I received a regular discharge.

Thus for nearly three years had I passed for and performed the duty of a marine, on board a frigate the most calibreous [*sic*] of any in the American navy; during which time I have been in three severe engagements, and never absented myself from my post in time of danger.—I have like others of the ship's crew, freely associated with my shipmates, both at sea and on shore; and yet, as extraordinary as it may appear, I have not the most distant idea that a single soul on board ever had the least suspicion of my sex.[24] I had thoroughly studied the memoirs of Miss Sampson, and by a strict adherence to the precautionary means by which she was enabled to avoid an exposure of her sex, I was too enabled to conceal mine.

I now more than ever felt a disposition to return to my parents, from whom I had been nearly six years absent.[25] Having received my prize money and wages, I now determined once more to reassume the female character, and clad myself accordingly; to furnish myself with a few necessary articles of clothing, I went (as the ladies term it) "shopping," and having made a purchase of a suit entire in Cornhill, with the assistance of a mantua-maker and milliner, was enabled once more to appear in my original character.

As I was under some apprehension that some one might possibly recognize my person in one of the two characters in which I had appeared, I did not think it advisable to continue long in Boston. I therefore a few days after set out for ——, my native home, which place I reached the succeeding day with safety.

I entered my parents' house at noon day—They were at dinner; I smiled, they gazed, but knew me not. By my mother I was invited to partake with them, and not until I had thrown out hints relative to some past affairs of the family, did they recognize in me their long lost child. Happy meeting! It was the return of the prodigal, penitent to her afflicted parents.

My friends soon after my departure traced me to Boston, but could never there obtain any further information of me: they listened with attention to the sorrowful tale of my adventures, while the tears trickled down the cheeks of my parents, at the recital of my adversities.

It was first my determination never to make public the unpleasant traits of my character; but I have since been persuaded to disclose so much as is contained in the foregoing //pages\\, by a friend in whom I could confide.[26] Every circumstance, however trivial, which could possibly lead to a discovery of my real name, that of my parents, or of the place of my nativity, will be withheld; as a disclosure can profit the reader nothing, but may do me essential injury. If what I have exposed to public view is sufficient to induce youths of my sex never to listen to the voice of love, unless sanctioned by paternal approbation, and to resist the impulse of inclination, when it runs counter to the precepts of religion and virtue, then, indeed, have I not written in vain.[27]

LUCY BREWER,

[A NATIVE OF PLYMOUTH COUNTY, MASSACHUSETTS.]

Who in disguise served Three Years as a MARINE
on board the Frigate CONSTITUTION.

☞ Those who have read the First Part of Miss
BREWER's (alias) BAKER's Adventures, ought
not fail to peruse this.

THE ADVENTURES OF

LUCY BREWER,

(ALIAS) [Eliza(Bowen) Webb]

LOUISA BAKER,

[A NATIVE OF PLYMOUTH COUNTY, MASSACHUSETTS.]

Who after living three years a distinguished member of an *immoral Society* of her *Sex*, in BOSTON,
became disgusted with the Sisterhood, and garbed as a *Male*, entered as a MARINE on board
the Frigate CONSTITUTION, where she faithfully served in that capacity during three years
of our late contest with Great Britain, and from
which she was honourably discharged without a
discovery of her sex being made.

BEING,

☞ A continuation of Miss BREWER's Adventures
from the time of her discharge to the present day
—comprising a journal of a tour to New York,
and a recent visit to Boston, garbed in her male
habiliments.

To which is added her serious address to the

YOUTHS OF BOSTON,

and such as are in the habit of visiting the town
from the country.

☞ " *To vindicate the principles of* VIRTUE *and*
MORALITY——IS MY OBJECT."

BOSTON—Printed by *H. TRUMBULL*, 1815.

Frontispiece (*opposite*) and title page of an early edition of *The Adventures of Lucy Brewer* (1815), the Second Part of the female-marine trilogy. Courtesy, American Antiquarian Society.

SECOND PART:
CONTINUATION OF THE NARRATIVE OF LUCY BREWER.

It was indeed with extreme reluctance, that I a few months since yielded to the persuasion of one of my most confidential friends, to furnish the public (under a fictitious name,) with a detail of the most remarkable traits of the last six years of my life:—the contents of my little book was hastily sketched, and esteemed as almost unworthy of public notice by its compiler. But, contrary to all expectation, so great has been its circulation, and so great the avidity with which it has been sought after and perused by even the most moral and exemplary characters among us, that I have, contrary to my determination, even again consented to become my own biographer—and in continuation of my adventures already made public, to furnish the reader with the particulars relative to my not less curious proceedings, since my discharge from public service, as well as many important incidents of my life, which were omitted in my late work. In thus again exciting public curiosity, I have a two-fold object in view—first, if by painting to public view, those horrible scenes of midnight, which disgust and fill with awe the virtuous mind, we can avert the dreadful evil and fatal consequence contracted by the unheeding YOUTH, in this particular a principal object will be effected—secondly, as some few have questioned the truth of my real existence, and the authenticity of my late work—some, because I gave not my real but a fictitious name, and concealed the place of my nativity—//while\\ others have doubted the truth of my story, upon no other grounds than that of //the improbability of\\ a *female's* being enabled to endure the hardships peculiar to a mariner's life, for so long a period, and that too without a discovery of her sex!—to the former I would reply, that their doubts ought now to be removed, as I now condescend to give my *real* name, as well as that of the county within which I drew my first breath—while to the latter I would observe, that had I in my late narrative represented myself as having gone directly from the happy abode of my parents, on board of a public vessel (unhackneyed in vice and a stranger to hardships as I then might have been) and in disguise performed the duty of a marine, I must confess they then might with more propriety have doubted;—but, ought not such to consider, that a three years residence in a common brothel, among a race of beings the most corrupted and detestable on earth, would fit even a *female* for the performance of the most desperate enterprise! As a further proof of the possibility of a female being enabled to perform military duty, and yet without a discovery of her sex being made, I would refer the reader to the case of Miss Sampson, who, garbed as a male, for seven years performed the duty of a private soldier.[1]

//I was born in a small town in the county of Plymouth in the State of Massachusetts—my real name is LUCY BREWER—at the age of sixteen I unfortunately became acquainted with a youth of respectable parentage, who resided within a short distance of my father's house—he at first pretended to harbour a very great share of love for me, solemnly declaring that I should one day become his wife—my parents were suspicious of his real views and admonished me for my credulity—but the artful tales of the vile and insinuating deceiver had made too great an impression—he saw my growing attachment for him, and by the most solemn promise of marriage, having lulled every suspicion asleep, obtained the forfeiture of the only gem that could render me respectable in the eyes of the world!—My vile seducer now threw off his mask of pretended affection for me, and in an exulting tone, declared that he had never really intended to make me his wife, and that I must never presume to trouble him with the fruits of my misplaced confidence!—thus after adding insult to injury, the wretch deserted me, and I never saw him from that time until since my return to my parents.—I now too late began to repent of my folly in not adhering to the good advice of my parents and friends, as I was now likely soon to incur a disgrace, that would too very materially effect them, should it come to their knowledge—as the only means to avoid which, I formed the resolution to seek an assylum abroad, among strangers, where I might be permitted to remain until I could return with safety to my unsuspecting friends;—it was in the dead of a cold winter's night, that I accordingly (furnished with a small bundle of cloathing) quit the peaceful abode of my tender parents, and alone and unprotected, bent my course for Boston, where I arrived the succeeding day almost famished with cold and hunger!—my object was now to obtain a situation as chamber or kitchen maid, in some respectable family, and made application accordingly to many persons in the course of the afternoon, but without success—I very fortunately obtained lodging for the night, and supper and breakfast at the house of a gentleman in Cambridge Street: whose lady was very kind to me, and before I left her house in the morning, gave me most excellent advice how I should conduct myself, provided I should succeed in obtaining a place in town—she particularly warned me to beware of a class of miserable and detestable beings of my own sex, who by the vilest prostitution obtained their livelihood!—At half past 9 (taking leave of my hospitable friend, who had so kindly treated me) I again set out in search of a place—the day proved cold and stormy, and the snow was of considerable depth on the ground, yet notwithstanding I passed through almost every street in town, applying in vain for a place—at the close of the day, cold, hungry and without the prospect of a shelter for the dreary night, I burst into tears, and began seriously to repent of my folly in quitting my parents house—unexpectedly I obtained lodgings for the night at a public house in Elm street, and in the morning early again set out in quest of a place—I passed up through Hanover to Tremont street, and from thence up Beacon street, and at about 12 o'clock unconsciously ascended the heights of West Boston.[2] Here I continued my application for a place and at 3 in the afternoon on the west side of the hill was so fortunate (as I then thought) to find the asylum sought for!—the good old lady (or rather nefarious witch) of the house, pretended to have great pity for me!—her darling daughters were requested to spare no pains to afford relief to the "poor female wanderer!"—warm tea and toast was served me, and every restorative administered. In the evening marm's "spotless flock" having withdrawn, the old beldam succeeded in drawing from me every particular relative to my situation, the reason of my deserting my parents, &c.—the old hag letting fall a few hypocritical tears, assured me that I might now consider my troubles at an end, that I should find her a *mother* and her house an assylum until such time as I could with safety return to my friends—indeed so artfully did this "old fowl and her chickens" conceal from me every thing that could give rise to suspicion, that not until after my confinement, had I the most distant idea of the manner in which these vile harlots obtained their livelihood!—my infant not surviving its birth, and having obtained sufficient strength to return to my parents, from whom I now had been five months absent, I was making preparation to bid adieu to the hospitable mansion of my "good marm" when this old deceiver threw off the mask of pretended friendship, and by threatening me with exposure, and prosecution if I should presume to leave her house without discharging a debt which my sickness had incurred, compelled me to give up the idea of an immediate return.

From this moment this antiquated hag, and her not less cunning pupils began by degrees to unfold to me the important secret, which they had never before thought proper to disclose—no pains were spared to decoy me from the paths of virtue and innocence, and to fit me for their market! and O! must I add, to my everlasting shame, that they at length fully succeeded in their nefarious schemes, and rendered me the object they so much desired. I was soon pronounced a forward scholar by my arch preceptress, by whom I was taught—

"How to entrap the armourous [*sic*] youth,
And to send him pennyless from my bed!"

For three years I continued an associate of the detestable harlots who inhabit those vile brothel-houses which the Hill contains—in which time no one could have had a better chance to become acquainted with their dispositions, their habits, and their wicked and deep concerted plans to decoy the unheeding youth, who too frequently resort there to witness their midnight revel—many of these scenes I shall in course record, and to *youth* impart that advice which I hope may prove to their advantage—

"For I will disclose their hidden vices,
"Acts of black night, abominable deeds,
"Complots of mischief and villanies
"Ruthful to hear."—

After a three years residence with these vile prostitutes, I became disgusted with their wretched habits, and was resolved to quit them at all hazards—accordingly, a short time after, a favourable opportunity offering, I, clad in a male suit, escaped from my "fair Shepherdess" unsuspected.

I walked through many public streets in Boston, and finding that no one had the least suspicion of my sex, I resorted to a public rendezvous in Fish-Street—here, agreeable to a former notion, I formed the desperate resolution of entering as a Marine on board the Frigate CONSTITUTION—by a stratagem I escaped the usual search, and with a number of new recruits I went on board without the least suspicion of my sex—I was furnished with a uniform and musket and made great proficiency in learning the manual exercise.—I was on board this frigate, three years, in which time I made four cruizes and have been in three severe engagements—and in the whole time succeeded in concealing my sex from all on board. A few months since I received an honourable discharge, when, re-assuming my female garb, I returned to my parents, from whom I had been six years absent! They did not at first recognize me, as they had supposed me long since dead; when they became convinced that I was indeed their daughter, my mother wept bitterly;—to my parents I now related the most remarkable incidents that had attended me for the six years, but my father would not credit the account of my sea adventures until I produced my discharge, my military suit &c.\\³

In conformity to the earnest request of my parents, and agreeable to my own resolve, I now felt determined to quit the complicated scenes of busy life for rural retirement, and to exchange the musket for the distaff and spinning wheel. For the first week I entertained myself in rambling over my father's farm, and in viewing the little arbours, where, in the days of my youth, I had spent so many agreeable hours; and as my father owned an excellent fowling-piece, I occasionally amused myself in destroying the birds that were in the habit of visiting his corn-fields. But to one who had for six years mingled with the busy world, a secluded life and these rural scenes soon became less amusing. I now felt a strong inclination to visit the Southern States, and begged of my parents to consent to my contemplated tour, with a solemn promise that on my return I would endeavour to reconcile myself to domestic scenes, and think no more of leaving tender parents and a peaceful home.[4] My parents with some reluctance consented, and I accordingly in July last took a seat in the mail stage for Newport. For particular purposes I again assumed my male habiliments. There were four passengers beside myself, three men and a female; one of the former, (a monkey-faced stripling) was garbed like a midshipman; another I judged to be a sea captain, and the third was a venerable old gentleman who resided in or near Providence; and the female, a modest young miss, apparently about seventeen years of age. For the first ten miles the company proved civil and agreeable, while we were entertained by the old gentleman with an account of the great improvements that had been made in the country through which we were passing, since his remembrance.

At a public inn we stopped to dine, where the captain and midshipman, as if more thirsty than hungry, quaffed so immoderate a quantity of wine and brandy, as to render their company far less agreeable. As they supposed the young lady the only female among them, they treated her in a rude and unmanly manner; making use of language the most indecent, without regard to female delicacy. For my own part I sat in silence, though somewhat nettled at the unbecoming behaviour of these two men (for they deserve not the appellation of gentlemen.) The good old gentleman, who indeed appeared to merit better company, in the most inoffensive manner possible attempted a gentle reproof; but he was repaid by the valiant young knight of the *dirk* with a dastardly rebuff.

The old gentleman now remained silent, while the swinish brace continued to crack their unmannerly jokes upon the harmless young lady.[5] I had until now sat speechless, and apparently regardless of the conversation going on, when the low billingsgate abuse bestowed upon my sex, aroused me to a sense of my duty. I now in turn rebuked the green *dirkman*, but in language a little more severe than that made use of by my aged friend. The flame caught—the pretty features of the eagle buttoned stripling were now distorted with rage. Dangling the little weapon that hung by his side, that it should not escape my notice, he broadly hinted that I probably mistook him; that he had more than once *bravely* withstood the attack of a formidable foe upon the ocean, and more than once assisted in compelling a superior force to yield; and that I therefore ought not to suppose that he was to be easily intimidated by man;—that he considered himself injured by the observations I had made, and that he never would put up with an insult with impunity; that I must now either make an acknowledgment (in other words, beg his pardon) or consent to place myself in a situation which would enable him to obtain the satisfaction demanded!

To the vain boastings and threats of Master Braggadocio, I made no other reply than that whatever honour he might have acquired by former conquests, I conceived that his rude and unwarrantable attack upon venerable old age and an inoffensive female was rather a proof of a mean and cowardly disposition, than of that undaunted bravery with which he had characterized himself; that I had been even myself favoured with a view of the enemy upon the ocean, with whom I had exchanged some shots, but that I must leave it with my officers to say whether I had done my part in compelling a superior force to yield; to conclude, that I had been taught by my ship's noble commander a lesson which I hoped never to forget, viz. never to give up the ship, or lower the peak, unless compelled to do so by very superior force;—I was therefore under the necessity of declaring to him that I would not make any acknowledgement whatever; that as to placing myself in a situation that would enable him to obtain the satisfaction demanded, though averse to the dis-honourable practice of duelling, yet, if he persisted in his demand, I could not consistently refuse to gratify him, as the affair might so soon be settled, we being then within a very short distance of Rhode-Island.

Lest my forwardness to accept of the challenge of the little gentleman to murder or be murdered, should excite the surprise of my readers, it may be necessary here to state, that I had ever marked it as an invariable fact, that he who was so unprincipled as to offer insult to old age, or to use a female ill, so far from delighting in the smell of gunpowder, would even betray a want of manly courage by the simple display of a shot bag or powder flask. Hence I was confident that my little antagonist could never muster courage sufficient to meet me agreeable to his own proposal—and I conceived it would amount to no more than afford me an opportunity to extort the humble confession from him, which he was imperiously demanding of me.

We were now within a few miles of New-port, when some part of the iron-work of our carriage gave way, and we were compelled to resort to a public inn in the neighbourhood to await the necessary repairs. The sea captain here took a private carriage for New-Bedford. The landlord proving to be a jolly good natured man, I felt disposed, with his assistance, to have a little diversion at the expense of my noble duellist! I related every thing privately to the landlord with regard to the altercations and the challenge that had ensued, begging the loan of a pair of unloaded pistols and the use of a private chamber for a few moments, assuring him that it was a farce only and not a tragedy I was about to act. The landlord receiving confirmation of my story from the old gentleman and the young lady, the pistols were produced, with which I retired to the chamber.

After making a little necessary preparation by placing a table in the centre of the room, upon which I laid the pistols, I dispatched a message for the brave youth who was not [to] be "intimidated by man!"[6] The lad, probably supposing that I had repented, and was now willing to make the acknowledgment required, did not hesitate to comply with my request.[7] As he entered the room, espying the instruments of death, he appeared to wilt considerably, and walked less erect than these men of buckram generally do on 'Change, or through Broadway. After desiring him to be seated, and taking care to secure the door, I addressed him as follows: "You conceived yourself insulted a few hours since by the observations which I made in defence of the young lady whom you treated so ill—you have demanded satisfaction, which I am now prepared to give in the very manner you proposed; the pistols you see we have at hand; seconds we want none: //although you will be doubly armed, pledge me your honor that you will take no advantage, and I will be satisfied\\—the pistols are equally loaded, take your choice, and the length of the room shall be our distance."[8]

Had I the ability of Hogarth, I might in some measure picture to view the appearance of my affrighted antagonist at this moment; who, with a trembling voice, in reply, observed, that "he was sensible that he had given the challenge, but was averse to fighting without seconds; that if I would postpone the business until our arrival at Newport (where his friend resided) he would meet me with pleasure!"[9] In reply, I assured him that the affair had become of too serious a nature to trifle with, and taking up one of the pistols, with a stern countenance assured him that I should not agree to any postponement //whatever\\; that before we left the room the business must be settled.[10] The trembling youth now attempted to expostulate, signifying his wish to settle the business in some other way!! I replied, that there were but two ways in which it could be terminated—he had proposed one, and I should take the liberty to mention the other,—which was, that he made a suitable acknowledgment to the old gentleman and young lady. This was a bitter pill indeed for the youth to swallow, who had assisted in compelling a superior force to yield; but observing me with a cocked pistol, sternly demanding of him to conclude without delay, and not doubting my sincerity, he reluctantly yielded.[11] I now sent the landlord (who was not far off) for the old gentleman and young lady, to whom the young man made a humble and satisfactory acknowledgment! Thus terminated the affair: and thus was this promising young officer, who had vainly boasted that he had been in too many engagements to be intimidated by man, compelled humbly to yield to the dictates of a woman!

The carriage being now ready, we again took our seats, and in an hour after were safely landed at the coffee-house in Newport; the coach door was no sooner thrown open, than my humbled duellist (like a bird liberated from its wiry prison) flitted away, and I have not seen him since. The old gentleman took an affectionate leave of me: shaking me by the hand, he jocundly observed, that "he was seventy-three years of age, had taken an active part in two or three different wars, and had seen much hard fighting; but that there was never a victory obtained (in which much blood was spilt, and tons of ammunition expended) that gave him half so much satisfaction as the one I had achieved by me [*sic*], with the aid of a pair of empty pistols!" The young lady too, on taking leave of me, very politely thanked me for the protection which I had afforded her, inviting me to call on her uncle, where she proposed to visit, if I tarried long in town.

I took lodgings at the coffee-house, and at ten the ensuing morning took passage on board the sloop Huntress, for New-York; the packets which sail from this port, for beauty and convenience are exceeded by few or none in America. //I was still garbed as a male, and passed for one without any suspicion of my sex—\\I experienced but one inconvenience on the passage by //thus\\ personating the character of a male; there was an uncommon number of passengers, male and female—the forward apartment of the cabin was allotted to the gentlemen, which contained but half their number of births; two were therefore obliged to occupy one birth, or sleep on a trunk, or the floor; while in the ladies' apartment there were several spare births. Rather than run the risk of exposing myself, I wrapped myself in my great coat, and enjoyed a tolerable nap on a chest; the wind was favourable, and we had a pleasant passage of twenty-four hours. I was now safely landed in the great city of New-York, of which I had heard much, and which, for commercial business, may be termed the capital of America.[12]

I had yet left a principal part of my prize money and wages, in addition to which the sale of the first edition of my adventures had added something to my funds; I therefore calculated while I remained in the city not to deprive myself of any reasonable enjoyment, as it was probably the last excursion of the kind I should ever make. //To avoid all possibility of detection, by a complete disguise of my person, and\\ [t]he better to effect this, I made a purchase of an officer's uniform complete, not even omitting the epaulet and broad military hat.[13] Thus garbed, I resorted to all parts of the city, and to every place of innocent amusement, without the least apprehension of exposing myself to detection. I took lodgings at a very respectable house in Pearl-street, kept by a Mrs. Van Ness, with whom a number of very reputable gentlemen boarded, and by whom I was treated with the greatest politeness, and respected as an officer of no mean grade.

About three weeks after my arrival in the city, taking my usual afternoon's walk in the bowery, I was not a little surprised to meet with the young lady of whom I //have so frequently\\ made mention in the preceding pages, //the same\\ in whose defence I had consented to exchange shots with my fellow traveller, the famous little knight of the dirk! In my new uniform she did not at first recognise me; but after introducing myself by some //trivial\\ hints of the humorous transaction, she seemed highly pleased with the unexpected meeting. To a young gentleman who accompanied her, and who proved to be her brother, I was introduced as the *gentleman* who had so honourably resented the abusive treatment which she received from the "cowardly puppy," the particulars of which she had made known to her friends.[14]

From the young gentleman and his sister I now received a polite invitation to accompany them to their father's house, in Pine-street. Unprepared for an interview so unexpected, I attempted to excuse myself by engaging //to do myself the honor\\ to call on them in the afternoon of the day ensuing; but excuses availed nothing;—they insisted that I must then favour them with my company, as in the evening they expected the company of a large circle of young ladies, to whom they had related the particulars of my late affray with the cowardly midshipman, and that they would now unquestionably be pleased with the company of a gentleman, who had manifested so noble and generous a disposition to protect the unguarded of their sex![15]

Finding all excuses unavailing I at length consented to accompany them, and was conducted to a spacious house in Pine-Street; here I was introduced by the young lady to her father, mother, &c. The old gentleman bid me welcome to his house, and thrice thanked me for the protection of his daughter, while travelling unaccompanied by any acquaintance. The family were wealthy, and lived in fashion//—in the evening I was invited to tea, and at 11 o'clock was furnished with an excellent cold supper\\. At seven we were honoured with the company of a circle of fashionable young ladies, with whom I spent an agreeable evening, and by whom it was more than once hinted to me that as the war was at an end, I was now probably on a matrimonial excursion, in search of an agreeable companion, with whom they wished me much domestic happiness! With this agreeable family I tarried the night; //and after partaking of an excellent breakfast\\ in the morning, I was invited by the old gentleman's son (a very polite young man) to accompany him to Greenwich, a pleasant ride of about three miles from the city; we passed the State Prison of New-York, which on our return my friend gained me permission with himself to pass through.—This massy block of buildings is commodiously constructed, and encompassed a spacious yard for the convenience of the unhappy convicts; but, O! it was indeed a melancholy spectacle to view five hundred of our most wretched fellow mortals, of both sexes, and of every age, thus shut up from the world, and for their bad deeds, doomed to spin out a life of miserable existence![16]

As my friend had learned that my only object in visiting the city was to witness the curiosities and to partake of the innocent amusements of the place, he seemed to take unwearied pains in pointing out //to me\\ every thing calculated to excite my curiosity. In the course of the day, among other public buildings, we went to view the Alms-House. Here were supported at public expense a large number of miserable dependents; some of whom probably by unavoidable misfortune, and a great proportion by their extravagance and intemperance, had reduced themselves to a state of penury and want.—Here I was not a little surprised to see an old acquaintance, a girl of pleasure, with whom I had formed some acquaintance the first year of my residence on West-Boston Hill, of which she too was an inhabitant, and was there known by the name of Maria Murray, but by the sailors was //more\\ commonly called "Scotch Maria." Her emaciated form exhibited the appearance of a walking skeleton; she was indeed now an object too miserable for human eyes to behold! Such has been the fate of thousands, and such inevitably will be the fate of those who now by vile prostitution gain their bread, unless preserved by a seasonable reformation.[17]

I continued in New-York until the 28th of August, when taking an affectionate leave of my friend and his connexions, by whom I had been treated with so much civility, I took passage on board of a Providence packet, with an intention of returning from thence immediately home—having privately exchanged my new uniform for a dress more convenient for the passage: as I did not feel disposed again to take up lodgings on a chest, or to be deprived of conveniences enjoyed by lady passengers. We had a fine run from New-York, and were all safely //landed\\ in Providence on the morning of the 30th. From Providence finding it difficult to obtain a direct conveyance home, I took a seat in the stage for Boston, where I proposed to spend a few days incog [*sic*].[18]

//To guard myself well against every possibility of a detection, in a place where I had been so well known to many,\\ I now took extra pains to disguise myself in every possible way. In my new military coat and pantaloons, with a chapeau cocked on one side, and with an epaulette attached to my right shoulder, I repaired to a barber's shop, where my hair received a fashionable crop, and my head and shoulders a plentiful shower of powder. Thus equipped, with a small rattan in my hand, I took a walk upon 'Change, where, although surveyed by many from head to foot, no one, I am conscious, had the least suspicion of my sex. I several times passed through Cornhill, and many of the most public streets, and frequently met persons whom I well knew, but they did not appear to recognize me.[19]

In the evening I resorted to the Hill, to take a final leave of this infamous seat of riot and dissipation, which I never calculate to visit more, whatever may be the character I may hereafter assume.—The terrific yells of the blacks—the vile imprecations of the sailors, and their intoxicated strumpets—the discordant and jarring sounds of violins, clarionets and tambourines, issuing from their stenchified "dancing halls,"—and the perpetual howlings of their affrighted dogs, as I ascended Garden and passed Buttolf-streets, could not fail to remind me of days when I took myself an active part in these nocturnal revels.

I now felt an inclination to try my skill at deception, by hazarding a visit to the very house where I had been taught my first lessons of vice—its occupiers were nearly the same, I had been informed, as when I fortunately succeeded in making my escape from the clutches of the old Beldam. Confident that I should succeed, I //incautiously\\ approached the house and tapped at the door—it was opened by ma'am! who dropping a low curtsey, bid me walk in.[20] I was conducted to the parlour, in which there was fortunately no other person but my old tutoress, and a little girl, of 10 or 12 years of age, who probably had been kidnapped from her friends and home by this unprincipled old hag, and who was intended for a future market!

I took a seat near the window, and calling for a small quantity of wine, I displayed all the pomposity possible, which undoubtedly was construed by "ma'am" as a proof of high rank and noble blood. Our conversation at first was rather of a political nature, as the old lady concluding by the badge upon my shoulder, that I must be an officer 'direct from the wars,' did not fail to bestow the highest encomiums on the bravery of the American officers. For my own part, it was a satisfaction to me to know that I was now so completely deceiving this vile old deceiver, who once so fatally deceived me! The old hag, probably mistaking the real object of my visit, took an opportunity to hint //to me\\ that the *girls* had gone to take an evening's ride, but would return before 10. Being confident that the old witch was completely deceived as to my person, I thought this a favourable opportunity to introduce the subject of Miss *Baker*, of whom I inquired of "ma'am" if she had any knowledge, as it was reported she had been for three years an inhabitant of the Hill, but that I had concluded the whole story a fabrication. "No!" exclaimed the old woman rather confused, "the story is not altogether fictitious; I suppose myself to be the person with whom she boarded, and the one whom the *dirty slut* has so basely calumniated. Having conducted herself in a shameful manner she was obliged to desert her parents and friends, and came to this town pennyless and almost destitute of cloathing, in an inclement season of the year. It was in the afternoon of a bitter cold day when she first called at my house inquiring for a situation as a kitchen or chamber maid; judging by her appearance that she was not in a situation to endure hardship, I took her in, and out of pure *charity*, consented to board her until she should sufficiently recover from her expected illness, to return to her friends. But how disposed was this ungrateful *jilt* to repay me for my *kindness!* After residing nearly five months with me, for which I had not received a single cent, she would have absconded, had I not received timely notice of her intentions to prevent it. As I carried on the mantua-making business, and had a number of young misses as apprentices, I hinted to the ungrateful girl that the least she could do was to tarry a short time longer with me and assist the girls in their sewing-work!—This she with some reluctance consented to do, and after being employed in her new business for a short time, she apparently became so pleased with her situation, and so great was the love and friendship that existed between her and my apprentices, that she continued with me perfectly contented for three years: nor had I the least suspicion of any disposition on her part to quit my employ, until the day she absconded.—Fearing that she might have been enticed off to some of the bad houses in the neighbourhood, I made diligent search after her, but she was not to be found, nor did I gain any information of her until one of her books was a short time since put into my hands. Such, Major, is the true statement of the whole business; and I will leave it with you, Sir, to decide whether I have not been unjustly censured by the base creature!"[21]

The old Bawd had indeed told a plausible story, and had unmercifully lashed me, without my daring to utter a syllable in vindication of myself, or in confirmation of what I had published to the world. It was pleasing to me, however, to see how completely she was now deceived in my person, and how innocently she honoured the "ungrateful jilt" with the title of "Major." As the evening was now far spent, and the hour approaching in which my immaculate "ma'am" looked for the return of her fair "apprentices," I judged it most wise for the "Major" to be off, lest these false fair ones, better skilled in physiognomy, might discover the deception.

I retired immediately from the Hill to an inn in Marlborough-street, where I took lodgings for the night. In the morning, observing that my boots had received a plentiful coat of the white coloured clay, peculiar to the Hill, I took them to a boot black in the neighbourhood. Pompey, whose occupation it appeared had taught him to determine with some accuracy the places of resort of his customers, by the state of their boots, in a jocular manner observed to me, that "if master had not the appearance of a gentleman of too much delicacy, he should judge by the appearance of my boots that I had recently visited a part of the town not the most respectable." Here I could not but remark, that while this man of colour spoke most contemptuously of this corrupted place, yet it was actually the favourite place of resort of many youths who claim the appellation of "young gentlemen!"[22]

I now repaired to the house of a confidential friend in Middle-street, where my trunk was deposited. Here I exchanged my uniform for that worn by me on board the ship, and //thus garbed, I\\ went in search of some of my old shipmates, in order to take a final leave of them. I found but two of them at a boarding-house in Fish-street; they had both entered as seamen on board a ship bound to Europe, which was shortly to sail. They both urged me to accompany them, and engaged to procure me an easy birth; but I thought proper to decline. From them I learnt that there were but a few of the Constitution's crew remaining in Boston; many had accompanied the expedition up the Mediterranean, some had gone on board of merchantmen, and others to the southward to procure births. After taking a glass or two with my shipmates, and wishing each other prosperity through life, we parted, never probably to see each other again.[23]

I now once more took leave of Boston, and fully satisfied with the ludicrous part that I had acted, and the new scenes I had witnessed in my late excursion, I returned to the peaceful abode of my fond parents, who were very impatiently awaiting my return. Here I have since agreeably passed my time in assisting my aged mother in performing the domestic work of the family, in perusing some entertaining and valuable works which compose my father's library, and in sketching for the press this imperfect narrative of my late adventures. It only now remains that I impart that advice to the youth of Boston, &c. which I in the former part of this little work proposed to do; which, should it have its desired effect, I should, in some measure, consider myself rewarded for the complication of miseries which have attended me for the last six years.

I am aware, that in thus attempting to warn youth of the fatal effects of an immoral life, I shall expose myself to the censure and ridicule of such as yet may have doubts of my sincere repentance, and question the propriety of my admonishing youth to beware of vices which I, for six years, industriously practised myself!—For the satisfaction of such, I now most solemnly declare, that I do feel that I have been thoroughly awakened to a due sense of my shameful career, while an inhabitant of the Hill—and if a prodigal could ever return penitent to her friends, I so returned to my afflicted parents, sincerely repenting of the evil of my ways;—let the doubts of all such therefore be removed, and as prevention is ever of more value than the most perfect cure, let them rather consider this as an affectionate effort to preserve the honour of those who yet possess it, to serve the honest fame of those who enjoy a good reputation, and to secure the peace of mind of all those who are yet unconscious of offence. To all these, an early warning is most precious. Timely advice may be to them a rescue from destruction. Those, who preserve the innocent from falling into guilt, deserve well indeed of their fellow creatures; and if any one can presume to such desert, he merits the favour of heaven.

Unheeding youth, enter not the bowers of ease, nor repose in the shades of security. Here the heart softens, and vigilance subsides; we are then willing to inquire, whether another advance cannot be made, and whether we may not at least turn our eyes upon the garden of pleasure. We approach them with scruple and hesitation; we enter them, but enter timorous and trembling, and always hope to pass through them without losing the road of virtue, which we for a while keep in our sight, and to which we propose to return. But temptation succeeds temptation, and one unlawful indulgence prepares us for another; we, in time, lose the happiness of innocence, and solace our disquiet with sensual gratifications. It is then our highest wisdom to tread the paths of virtue in the morning of our days, that the evening may terminate with a smiling serenity.

Many indeed are the fatal effects of an unlawful intercourse with the vile harlots of the Hill, which came within my own personal knowledge while a resident there—but the following instances, I trust, will prove //of a nature\\ sufficient to deter reflecting youth from yielding to the false allurements of these detestable off-scourings of the human race.[24]

The first I shall mention, is the melancholy case of a youth bred in the country, and at the age of sixteen apprenticed to a //respectable\\ merchant in town.[25] He was of respectable parents, of an amiable disposition, and the picture of health and innocence. Reared under the watchful eye of tender parents, until this unhappy period of his life, he was probably a stranger to vice, and supposed all as innocent as himself. But a few months had he been in town, when a curiosity peculiar to too many in the situation of himself, induced him one fatal night to resort to this seat of perpetual riot and dissipation. As he ascended the filthy hill, the discordant sounds of the musical instruments unconsciously drew him to the entrance of one of their dancing cabins; he entered, and mingled with the haggard crew. But the unsuspecting youth did not long remain an idle spectator; from one of "ma'am's" most forward pupils (who probably had already marked him as her victim) he received a pressing invitation to join in their dance. The youth probably unaccustomed to decline //the acceptance of\\ so polite an invitation from a young lady, did not hesitate to comply. From the "Hall" he was conducted by this arch girl to her lodgings; here the credulous youth was taught to believe, that the "good lady" of the house was entitled to a dollar for a pint of wine, from all young gentlemen, on their first introduction!—It was at twelve at night when this now debauched youth was discharged pennyless from the apartment of this filthy prostitute; who, in the morning exultingly boasted of her good fortune, in meeting with a youth who had engaged to be her constant and she presumed a profitable customer. In this the thoughtless young man proved too faithful to his promise—young and inexperienced, and a perfect stranger to the deceptive arts of harlotry, he became enamoured with the false colourings of this //arch\\ hag. Isabilla (for that was the name which this daughter of evil had assumed) would indeed pass for a girl of seventeen—but, strip the creature of her false embellishments, and there would nothing more of the original remain than an emaciated carcase, ulcerated with disease!—she was indeed thirty-four years of age, had been twice lawfully married, was the mother of five children, was two years a kept miss, and had now been four years a common prostitute on the Hill! Such was this "fair Dulcinea" whose charms had captivated a youth of seventeen![26]

The thoughtless youth now became constant in his visits, nor dare he (like the unfortunate Barnwell) approach the habitation of his mistress, without well lined pockets, or a store of rich presents—which no doubt were purloined from his unsuspecting master![27] But a day of dreadful retribution at length arrived, in which life itself was the forfeiture of his unwise indulgences!—a disease, the effects of an unlawful intercourse, rendered incurable by concealment, now threatened the unhappy youth with instant dissolution! Medical aid was administered, but in vain; the grim tyrant had already marked the young man, yet in the morning of his days, as his own! who, after enduring the most excruciating torture of body and mind, closed his eyes on this world and its transitory scenes for ever! It so happened, that at the very hour in which the mortal remains of the unfortunate youth were to be consigned to their mother earth, that the detestable Isabilla, (the //base\\ author of his untimely exit) in company with myself and three other females, passed the house (in a carriage) from which the funeral was to be attended; the neighbours had already gathered, and the coffin, shrouded with the gloomy pall, was placed upon the hearse![28] Every eye in the carriage at this instant was cast upon the heedless Isabilla, who, so far from appearing to be affected by a view of the melancholy spectacle, exultingly wagging her head, observed, that 'she believed poor William had gone aloft!'

O! my dear youths, may the fate of this unfortunate young man, who so early fell a victim to his own imprudent indulgences, serve as a beacon to warn you of the danger of resorting to those vile haunts of disease, robbery, and murder! Beware that you are not allured by external embellishments; permit one, who has been an eye witness of the act, to assure you, that those *artificial decorations* cover a form, which, could you but see in its natural state, could not fail to fill you with the utmost disgust. Reflect for a moment, that the shortest period of unlawful indulgence, may cause you years of pain! As a proof of this, permit me to refer you to the wretched lot of many of the miserable inhabitants of our alms-houses and hospitals; in them see the fatal effects of debauchery and dissipation! although yet in the morning of their days, they have the appearance of labouring under the infirmities of old age![29]

I have yet another instance of youthful imprudence to record, which should be a caution to such as are in the habit of visiting the town from the country; it is an instance of robbery, committed upon a young man whose business was that of bringing considerable quantities of pork from an interior part of the state to Boston market, and for which he generally received cash to a considerable amount.— Like the other unfortunate youth //whose case we have just mentioned\\, he too became the dupe of one of "ma'am's fair apprentices," (for each had her cully.) As frequently as his business called him to town, he never failed to spend a night with his 'lovely Charlotte,' who, although she was not permitted to fathom his pockets, had made such discoveries as to satisfy her that they were well lined; but all her attempts //(in a clandestine manner)\\ to get possession of their valuable contents had been in vain. At midnight every pocket of his garments had been thoroughly searched, but were found empty; it was apparent that he was in the habit of privately secreting his valuable effects somewhere, previous to his retiring to bed; to ascertain the fact, two of the girls were stationed in an adjoining room, where, through a crevice in the wall, they were to watch the motions of the young man; they had not been long here, when the wished for discovery was made; the youth was perceived to slip his watch and pocket-book into one of his boots! A report was immediately made to the old Bawd, who found no difficulty in devising a plan that would put them into possession of the property, and without subjecting themselves to suspicion. The plan was this, that at midnight the room should be privately entered and rifled of its most valuable contents, including all the wearing apparel, not forgetting the garments of their profitable lodger, his boots, &c.; the doors were then to be thrown open, the lock to be wrenched from the street door, and the hue and cry of "robbery!" to be raised by the old woman. This plan in every particular was carried into effect; the clothing of the stupid youth, together with the valuable contents of the boot, were buried in the cellar! By break of day "ma'am" rushing into the chamber where the artful Charlotte and her unsuspecting cully lodged, awakened them with her cries, that "she was ruined!" that "her house had been broken into, and pillaged of its most valuable effects!" The youth rallying, and finding himself bereaved of his clothing, joined too in the cry, that "the villain had not left him a single garment!" while Charlotte at this moment (as she was requested to do) proclaimed her loss of the "little property she possessed, the fruits of a year's *industry!*" A few old clothes were now procured for the really unfortunate youth; who, either so stupid as to suppose that burglary and robbery had really been committed, or aware that a public proclamation of his loss would be productive of nothing but the frowns and natural observation of the more wise, that "*he should keep off the Hill!*" departed without making further ado! His clothing, &c. were now taken from their earthly deposit, and the contents of the pocket book examined, which was found to contain 112 dollars in bank notes! one half of which, together with the watch, 'ma'am' claimed as her portion; the residue was divided among her "apprentices!"[30]

Such, my young friends, are the effects of too free an intercourse with these vile unprincipled prostitutes; whom, if you regard property, reputation, and health, you will shun—as an unlawful connection with them will ultimately cost you one or the other.

Look around you, my dear youths, and behold many a promising young person plunged into wretchedness, whose ruin is to be ascribed to too great a love of pleasure: who has given way to the inclination, and precipitated himself into the habit of dissipation, till he has become deaf to all good advice, proof against admonition, entreaty, and persuasion, and is now among the ruins of human nature. //Let these instances warn you of your danger, and persuade you to devote some part of that time, which is spent in pursuit of unlawful pleasures, to reflection and consideration.\\[31]

Seriously consider, that you are born to die; that you will die, but to live again; live for ever in the unexplored regions of futurity, to inherit the consequences of your present conduct! Remember, immortal! though thou mayst now whirl in the giddy round of dissipating pleasures, and wantonly burst the bonds of reason and religion, and without regard to counsel and instruction //to the contrary\\—"walk in the ways of thine own heart, and in the sight of thine own eyes," that thou art accountable to thy Maker for thy whole conduct, and that, "for all these things, he will call thee into judgment."[32]

FRONTISPIECE

MR. and Mrs WEST, Viewing the Rock on which our Fore-Father's Landed at Plymouth.

THE
AWFUL BEACON,

TO THE RISING GENERATION OF BOTH SEXES.

OR

A FAREWELL ADDRESS TO THE YOUTHS OF, AND FINAL ADIEU TO THE STATE OF MASSACHUSETTS.

By Mrs. LUCY WEST,
[Late Miss *LUCY BREWER*,]   (Eliza Bowen)
A Native of Plymouth County, Massachusetts.

Who in disguise served Three Years, as a MARINE on board the Frigate CONSTITUTION.

☞ This Part (which being the Third and Last) will be found to be still more interesting to the public than the two preceding ones. It is recommended as worthy the perusal of young persons of both sexes, and of all classes, as to promote their temporal and spiritual good, is a principal object of its compiler.

" *Learn to do well by others harm, and you will do full well*,"   BARNWELL.

BOSTON—Printed for N. COVERLY, jr.—1816.

Frontispiece (*opposite*) and title page of *The Awful Beacon* (1816), the Third Part of the female-marine trilogy. Courtesy, American Antiquarian Society.

AN
AWFUL BEACON
TO THE
RISING GENERATION
OF
BOTH SEXES.

———

BY Mrs. LUCY WEST.

———

"Learn to do well by others' harm, and you will do full well."

ADVERTISEMENT.

This Part, being the third and last, will be found to be still more interesting than the two preceding ones. It is recommended as worthy the perusal of young persons of both sexes, and of all classes, as to promote their temporal and spiritual good is a principal object of its compiler.

THIRD PART:

AN AWFUL BEACON.

An unexpected occurrence, since the close of the last biographical sketch of my life, induces me once to address you upon a subject, which, as it regards your future welfare, you must consider of inconceivable importance to you all. In the modern state of the world, the moralist will agree with me, that additional guards are necessary for the innocent, the young, and the thoughtless, to prevent their being led into the numerous //and diversified\\ temptations which surround them.[1] The situation of the dissipated and voluptuous is rendered still more dangerous; and persons who have unhappily begun to deviate from an honest conduct, are too often entered, in fact, on the road to ruin. To all these an early warning is most precious. Timely advice may be to them a rescue from destruction. Beauty will always be the lot of some; but highly as it may be valued, it may be the fatal cause of seductions, which will lead to all the crimes that disgrace and ruin a wretched individual. To warn such of you, therefore, as are yet so happy as to enjoy a good reputation, and to secure the peace of mind of those who are yet unconscious of offence, is a principal object which I have in view in presenting you with my farewel address.

Before I enter upon my monitory address to the dear youths of my native state, to whom I //am\\ now about to bid a final adieu, it may be proper that I should so far satisfy public curiosity, as //(in continuation of my adventures from my Second Book)\\ to relate the particulars of the unexpected circumstance which has changed my name and condition in life//—an event indeed then quite unexpected\\.[2] And as this little work will unquestionably fall into the hands of some of my own sex, some few particulars of my first introduction to the man who has since become my husband, our courtship, marriage, &c. will not, it is presumed, be displeasing to them.

Having returned to the peaceful abode of my parents, with a full determination there to spend the remainder of my days, employed in the pleasing task of assisting my aged mother in managing the domestic concerns of the family, I became now more than ever reconciled to a country life, where my time was not suffered to lag heavily along for the want of amusements. Soon after my return I formed an acquaintance with a large circle of young ladies of respectable families, whose agreeable visits rendered my situation still more pleasing. Indeed, these pleasing scenes made me now more than ever regret, with heartfelt anguish, my having ever been forced to leave the peaceful abode of my parents. After what I had for the last six years experienced from the duplicity of mankind, the vicissitudes of fortune, and the pangs inseparable from the pleasures of the gay world, I regretted //with sorrow\\ that I had not preferred the //certain\\ tranquillity to be found here, to those noisy scenes //and unlawful indulgences,\\ with which I had been in early life too much diverted![3]

Thus I continued to spend my time agreeably at the rural abode of my parents for several months after my return, in which time there was no remarkable occurrence as regarded myself, of sufficient importance to record—it may not however be unnecessary here to mention, that in my evening excursions with my fair associates, I was not unfrequently honoured with the company of a young gentleman, of about my own age, and who was the only son of a respectable tradesman of our village. The seeming partiality which the youth by his polite attention manifested for me, I at first imagined proceeded only from friendship, but becoming more constant in his visits, he one evening, when my parents were absent, took an opportunity to address me as follows:—"Lucy, I have never yet disclosed to you the hope I have entertained of making you mine by the most endearing connection, nor should I at this time have mentioned it, our acquaintance having been of so short a period, were I not under the disagreeable necessity of leaving you for a few weeks—I leave you free; I will not even ask you to engage yourself to me—your happiness will be mine, and should any other man fix his soul upon you, as I have, and should you find you could be happier with him than with me, I will not presume to say I should oppose the measures you might then adopt. But you may be assured it has been, since my //first\\ acquaintance with you, my highest wish to call you mine, and though you may never perhaps be sensible how great my affection is for you, yet you may be assured it can never admit of a change."[4]

I listened with attention. "Your generosity," said I, "pleases me; the affection you profess I cannot doubt, when I reflect on the many instances of it you have shown me." I could not proceed, and continued silent with my eyes fixed on the floor—I felt at that time, that I had said too much, but it was past, and I could not recal it. William (the name which I have chosen to designate the youth) observing me silent, thus continued to address me—"You are all goodness, Lucy, but I have yet another favour to request, a favour that I fear you will not grant:—I shall write to you, and may I hope that you will sometimes condescend to soften and enliven the tedious hours of absence, by writing to me?" I hesitated, and was preparing to evade his request; but he continued, "Do not refuse me this; it is all the consolation I can have while absent from you." I could not refuse him, and not without reluctance, however, promised to answer some of his letters. The remainder of the evening passed in an interesting conversation relative to my sea adventures, &c. with the novelty of which he seemed much pleased. He bade me an affectionate farewell, but with apparent regret that business compelled him to be absent for a few weeks.

It is a truth which I am not ashamed to acknowledge, that I from this moment felt a peculiar esteem for this generous hearted youth, and that his amiable manners, and exalted sense, had, in a great measure, secured my affections. He had been absent nearly a fortnight, when my father informed me that in the newspaper, there was in the list of letters therein published, one announced for me, as remaining in the post office of P——. Presuming it to be from no other person than him who had so urgently pressed me to grant him the privilege of writing to me, I with this fond expectation, without a moment's delay, obtained the letter; but on breaking the seal, my surprize may be better imagined than described on finding its contents as follows:—

"NEW-YORK, DEC. 2, 1815.

"Miss Brewer,

"A few days since a small pamphlet was put into my hands by my sister, entitled, "The Adventures of Lucy Brewer," &c. recounting the recent achievements of a young lady of Plymouth county, in Massachusetts, who in disguise had served three years in the capacity of a marine on board the U. S. frigate CONSTITUTION; and the particulars of a recent excursion to this city, clad in //her\\ male habiliments, &c &c. which so exactly corresponds with similar circumstances //(as therein recorded)\\ which attended my sister, on a visit to her friends in Massachusetts the last summer, that our whole family have been led to conclude that *we* were the dupes whom the authoress mentions as having given so many thanks for the protection which had been //so kindly\\ afforded one of its members! Yes, Miss Brewer, I am confident that you must either, by some invisible means, have been privy to every circumstance which attended the visit of that person, whom //garbed in military uniform\\ we supposed to be an officer of the army, and with whose company we were honoured the last summer; or you, indeed, as you have mentioned, are the identical person who //thus garbed\\ so completely deceived us. If such should prove the case, I must indeed pronounce you one of the greatest adepts at deception which the whole country can produce, of either sex. My sister declares your statement of the treatment she received from the "eagle-buttoned stripling," and which so justly excited your indignation, in no way exaggerated—she too confirms the particulars of the challenge, the empty pistols, and the humble confession you //so\\ nobly extorted from your faint-hearted antagonist; but cannot be persuaded that she could possibly be so much deceived as to your person—if in this she is mistaken, and you really have been enabled so far to disguise yourself, as to pass, unsuspected, for the character which you so ingeniously assumed, while at my father's house, do immediately acknowledge the receipt of this, and be so good as to name the town in which you at present reside; as I propose in a few weeks hence a tour through the eastern states, should you be pleased to favour me with the information solicited, and your place of residence prove within forty miles of my rout, distance, I assure you, shall not prevent another personal interview with one, to whom (male or female) I shall ever consider myself under the greatest obligations for the protection afforded my sister from the insults of a dastardly coxcomb, while travelling unattended by an acquaintance.[5]

"I am, with the greatest respect,

"Your sincere well-wisher,

"CHARLES WEST."

Nothing could cause me more surprise than the receipt of this letter, from one whom (although I had received proofs of friendship, and in whose company I had spent many agreeable hours) I never calculated when I left the hospitable mansion of his father, to see again. It was my first conclusion to remain silent, and not to subject myself to further exposure by complying with the request of Mr. W. in acknowledging the receipt of his polite though unexpected favour. Contrary to this determination, I was however, persuaded by my parents, to acknowledge its receipt by the following short epistle:—

"———, Plymouth Co Jan. 5, 1816.

"DEAR SIR,

"Your favour of the 2d ult. was duly received; and in answer, am happy that I have it in my power to assure you, that I am indeed the identical person who passed for Major B. and who enjoyed the agreeable company of your friends, at your father's house, the last summer—and the same to whom your amiable sister politely acknowledged herself indebted, for protection while travelling from Boston to Rhode-Island, the last spring. My present place of abode is at my father's house in the town of ———, county of Plymouth, Massachusetts. I must conclude, Sir, by assuring you that I know of no family for whom I have a greater regard than yours, and the agreeable hours that we have spent together, cannot be equalled, unless they are repeated.

"I am yours, affectionately,

"LUCY BREWER."

The letter of which the foregoing is an exact copy, with a single exception (the original specifying the town in which I then resided) I lodged at the post office, but not with the most distant idea of ever being honoured with a visit from the person to whom it was directed. The period of the absence of William, agreeable to his own calculations, had now nearly expired, and for whose return I began really to feel a degree of impatience. In compliance with a modest request of his, I had during his absence almost entirely secluded myself from the society of my new formed acquaintance, I amused myself by wandering through the now barren and lonely fields, or along the broken shores of the briny ocean, on which my father's farm bordered—frequently resorting in pleasant weather, to a point of the beach where stood a large rock, whose base was washed by every tide. On this rock I would not unfrequently seat myself, and enjoy the splendors of the scene—the drapery of nature—the small islands within the bay were discernable, and appeared dimly to float among the waves, where skiffs and sails of various descriptions were passing and repassing,—the cheering voices of the hardy seamen, homeward bound, elated with the prospect of reaching their destined port, and joining their friends in a few hours, were not unfrequently heard—while on the land, the light gales whispered among the leafless branches of the lofty oaks, thinly scattered upon the banks of the sea-beaten shore, or waved the tops of the distant forest, with majestic grandeur. Hills piled on hills, receding, faded from the pursuing eye mingling with the blue mist which hovered around the extreme verge of the horizon—such were the romantic scenes to be viewed from the chosen seat of my father, the abode of my youthful days.

As I was one afternoon deeply engaged in admiring the romantic prospect before me, the ratling of a carriage which halted at the door of my father's house, roused me from my reverie;—I hastened homeward to ascertain who our unexpected visiter might be—whom, to my inexpressible surprize, I found to be no other than my friend Mr. West!—who, as I entered the door, gracefully bowing accosted me with "Your most obedient, Major B——" Never on any occasion could my surprize be greater; indeed I for the first few moments felt so much embarrassed as to be unable to return the compliment; nor do I believe that I could have //for many minutes after,\\ mustered courage sufficient to have treated the young gentleman with the politeness that he really merited, had not he, rightly judging of my confused sensations which my countenance must have betrayed at his unexpected appearance, //smiling, advanced toward me,\\ taken me by the hand, and thus addressed me: "Ah, my lovely heroine! why do you appear so much surprised at the appearance of one, who only comes humbly to acknowledge himself your dupe?" This gave me time to recover so far as to desire him to be seated, and endeavouring to assume an air of more confidence, attempted to apologize for the seeming embarrassment which his sudden and unexpected appearance had caused me. "My situation, sir," said I//, smiling\\, "compels me quietly to submit to become the subject of your diversion—I acknowledge that I have played the deceptive part, and a little deceived you; but//, sir (continued I)\\ I cannot but flatter myself, when I declare to you that I was actuated by motives that were innocent, you will have the goodness to pardon me." Here Mr. West interrupted me with a hearty laugh, assuring me that I had nothing to apprehend—that as for himself, he must declare that he was very agreeably disappointed; but having by my polite attention to his sister, completely secured her affections, the discovery might make a different impression upon *her* mind.[6]

I now introduced my new visiter to my parents, as the young gentleman from whom I had received so much polite attention, while a visitant at his father's house in New-York. The old gentleman shaking Mr. West by the hand, bid him welcome, jocundly observing at the same time, that "as heaven had never blessed him with a son, his daughter seemed ludicrously disposed to make up for the deficiency, by sometimes personating that character." Here a more minute detail of my almost incredible adventures were given by my aged father, //from the time that I first left home,\\ which, having been already published to the world, it would have been folly to have attempted to conceal from //the knowledge of\\ Mr. W. who observed, that "as a reformation had happily taken place, and I with true penitence and a due sense of my error, had returned to my afflicted parents, he should never think ill of me for what could never reasonably be considered as a voluntary transgression, having been allured by a perfidious woman from the paths of virtue and innocence."[7]

Mr. West, in compliance with a particular request of my father, tarried with us until the morning ensuing, when he pursued his journey for Boston, but with assurances that on his return he would favour us with another visit. The //abilities and\\ amiable disposition of this young gentleman was such as could not fail to render his company agreeable, and with which my father seemed highly pleased—indeed, except to the one to whom I was partially engaged, I knew of no man to whom I should have less objection to be united. But the regard which I then entertained for my absent friend was such as no earthly consideration could have diminished, and whose affection for me, I had every reason to suppose, was too great to render him capable of resigning me to another with any degree of fortitude.[8]

But, alas! at the very moment that I had been impatiently looking for the return of this youth (the //time\\ of his absence having expired) I was, to my inexpressible grief, informed by his afflicted parents of his melancholy fate. Alarmed at his long stay, they had forwarded letters to Hudson, where business had called him, and received for answer that their unfortunate son had left that place for home nearly three weeks previous—that he arrived safe at New-York, where it was ascertained that he took passage on board a Portsmouth packet, which unfortunately foundered within a few miles of Boston Light.//—my readers will recollect the accounts published a few months since in the Boston papers of the sad disaster!\\ Thus was it rendered certain that this amiable youth, in the flower of his days, and probably just anticipating with delight his return to his friends, had found a watery grave.[9]

For the future fate of the unfortunate William I have a well grounded hope, which precludes anxiety. The innocence of his life, and the purity of his sentiments and morals, and an assurance of his being a real christian, leave me no reason to doubt of his being in a state of happiness. The same goodness of heart, and amiableness of manners, which rendered him dear to me while living, now afforded me the greatest consolation. I mourned indeed, but not like those who are without hope. Had he been of a different turn of mind, the sudden manner in which he left the world, would have been far more terrible and shocking.—Since we cannot know how soon, nor how suddenly we may be called from life, it is highly necessary that we should often reflect on that important and interesting period, and prepare to meet its approach without terror; yet the number is comparatively few of those who could perceive the approach of death without distressing apprehensions. Religion is frequently considered, by the young and gay, as a gloomy thing, unfit to be introduced among sprightly people. They imagine it banishes amusement and gaiety, and renders those who feel its influence morose and unsocial. But their ideas are wrong. Religion, indeed, forbids vicious indulgences, but it is not an enemy to any kind of innocent enjoyment—it does not encourage levity and dissipation, yet it is not an enemy to mirth at proper times. It would be highly improper to appear sad and disconsolate at a wedding, but still more so, to be gay and merry at a funeral; we may at all times be cheerful, and yet innocent. There are many people who pay such a scrupulous attention to the rules of politeness, as never to receive the smallest benefit from another, without returning thanks, who ridicule the idea of prayer //or\\ praise to the Almighty, notwithstanding he is continually showering innumerable blessings around them, and is the source from whence all their pleasures flow.[10] This appears highly inconsistent, but though it is a disgrace to those who openly profane the sacred name which the christian reveres, we must own the truth of the assertion. True religion not only increases our pleasures, and opens to us continually new sources of enjoyment, but renders the pangs of adversity less distressing. It is a subject of regret that it is so little practised; in this country especially, where we enjoy so many blessings, it is strange that our citizens should be unmindful of the power who protected them, and their rights, and placed them in the possession of peace, liberty and independence. No nation, perhaps, had ever more to induce them to be grateful and virtuous than this—yet we are too apt to forget the hand who bestows our felicity, while we enjoy it without interruption.

But to return. The melancholy tidings of the untimely exit of the dear, hapless youth, to whom there was every probability of my being united for life, caused for many days an unusual depression of spirits. Alas! how perverse is fate! Many of the dispensations of providence at first view, appear as destructive to our happiness, but are finally productive of events, that will teach us that we are incapable of judging for ourselves.

> "In all his ways confess the Almighty just,
> And where you can't unriddle, learn to trust."

The christian religion furnishes its believers with abundant consolation, in every affliction. Sensible that an allwise Creator will do them no injustice, they can look up to him as a father, a friend: and though they feel severely the blow that wounds their peace, yet they can say "thy will be done." It is often essential to our peace, that our most ardent wishes should remain ungratified. Could we be allowed to choose our own fortune, or to direct the events of our lives ourselves, it is highly probable that we should be rendered miserable. Some good purpose of which we are at the time ignorant, is undoubtedly to be answered by every event we term unfortunate. Hence, as regarded my much expected union with the beloved but unfortunate WILLIAM, providence appears to have ordained otherwise—to have designed me for the companion of another.

Nearly three months had now passed since the departure of Mr. WEST for Boston, whose long tarry had led us to conclude that he must either by indisposition be detained, or that he had (notwithstanding his engagements to favour us with another visit) returned home by the way of Dedham, Hartford, &c. But in this we were all happily disappointed by his safe arrival one evening as we were sitting down to tea. I could not but remark, that at his entrance, an unusual degree of satisfaction beamed on the countenance of my parents, who had already formed the most exalted opinion of the merits of their welcomed visitant.

The evening passed most agreeably. We were entertained by Mr. WEST with the adventures of his recent excursion to the capital of New-England, where he had spent his time in a manner quite pleasing to himself—he represented the town, for pleasantness, &c. far surpassing his expectations, while upon its inhabitants, for their natural good humour and polite attention to strangers, he bestowed the highest encomiums—he said that he had (like most of the Yorkers) been inclined to cherish rather an unfavourable opinion of the "yankees," but from what he had now seen of them, he was satisfied that they would not in any point of view suffer in a comparison with the most learned characters of the middle or southern States. He had visited almost every public place in town, calculated to excite curiosity, or to afford amusement and instruction—the many excellent bridges which connect the neighbouring villages with the town, for convenience and beauty of structure, be represented as far surpassing any that he had ever before seen—the State-House, for beauty, &c. he thought equal, and far more pleasantly situated than the City Hall of New-York, nor did he conceive the Bowery of that city half so pleasant as the justly admired Mall of Boston. That "Boston folks are full of notions," he had frequently heard observed, but he had not but in one instance discovered a proof of their being peculiarly so more than the inhabitants of any other town—the tremendous gale of September having greatly diminished the beauty of the Mall, by demolishing a great proportion of the sturdy elms with which it was ornamented, many of which were of an uncommon size, and some partly decayed with age, which the wind had surprisingly prostrated, while the earth for some rods from their trunks was ploughed up by their wide spreading roots—the Bostonians, who at first no doubt conceived the beauty of their late admired Mall in a great measure destroyed, at length hit upon the curious expedient of replacing with "block and tackle" those sturdy elms, which their fathers had probably a century ago placed there for the convenience of the succeeding generation!—which, (continued Mr. W.) in their endeavours to preserve, should those now sapless trunks be found to yield to the art of man, and again take root, the world will owe much to the "notions of Boston folks" for a discovery that must prove of great importance.[11]

Mr. WEST (agreeable to the solicitations of my father) consented to spend a few days with us—"I cannot, (said he, smiling,) fail to spend my time agreeably in the company of Major B——, beside, a short residence in the country may improve my health." He appeared highly pleased with the romantic appearance of the country, and during his stay with us more than once accompanied me to my favourite place of resort, the rock bordering upon the sea coast, of which mention is made in the preceding pages. To view a part of the country which had never before been visited by him, and to acquaint himself with the customs and manners of its inhabitants, appeared to be the principal object of Mr. WEST's tour through the eastern states—nothing therefore worthy of notice, escaped his observation, and such incidents or objects as he considered of sufficient importance, he did not fail to minute in his memorandum;—having heard much of the celebrated Rock, at Plymouth, on which our forefathers were said first to have landed, he expressed an anxious wish to view it, although he was assured there was nothing peculiar in its appearance, different from any other rock of equal size. With this he was not however satisfied, and earnestly requested me to accompany him //thither\\ the succeeding morning, which, with the leave of my parents (the distance being but short) I consented to do.[12]

Early in the morning ensuing Mr. W. did not fail to remind me of my engagements, and we accordingly, soon after breakfast, proceeded in quest of the first landing place of the Pilgrims. An obliging inhabitant of the town pointed out to us the detached parts of the celebrated Rock, which for the accommodation of the commercial interest of the town had been separated, a part of which formed a corner stone of a rough built well in front of the court-house. There was indeed nothing extraordinary in the appearance of this grey coloured stone, which, remaining in its natural state, I viewed but with an eye of indifference. But Mr. WEST, who was indeed much more of an antiquary, appeared to view it with a degree of philosophic satisfaction. After expressing his surprise that it should be suffered to remain without the least inscription by which it might be distinguished from any other, (placing his hand thereupon) he thus addressed me:—"This rock, Lucy, in the appearance of which you may indeed perceive nothing very peculiar, and which you may conceive //as\\ unworthy the notice of the passing stranger, I do indeed view, and contemplate the event which gave rise to its celebrity, with inexpressible satisfaction. It was the first firm foundation on which the worthy pilgrims set their feet in this now thickly inhabited quarter of the new world!//— It was (continued he) scarcely 200 years ago, and what was the now flourishing States of New-England then!—an almost impenetrable forest, abounding with savages and beasts of prey!—the vast trees that grew up to the clouds, were so encumbered with plants that they could scarcely be got at—the wild beasts made those woods still more inaccessible—the human race, cloathed with the skins of those monsters, fled from each other, or pursued only with intent to destroy—the earth seemed useless to man, and its powers were not exerted so much for his support, as in the breeding of animals, more obedient to the laws of nature—the earth produced every thing at pleasure, without assistance, and without direction; it yielded all its bounties with uncontrolled profusion for the benefit of all—the spring was restored from the spoils of autumn—the leaves dried and rotted at the foot of trees, supplied them with fresh sap to enable them to shoot out new blossoms.

Such Lucy (continued my friend) was the situation of the surrounding country, when first visited by those who sought here a retreat from foreign persecution—\\It was upon this very rock that this little band of Puritans first landed—here they no doubt with one heart and mind united in returning thanks to an Almighty God, for bringing them safe to a land even of so unpropitious an aspect. With what Christian like patience did they endure the difficulties that attended them, before they succeeded in effecting a peaceable settlement; //—the country was not only overspread with thick woods, but\\ the caprices of a savage race were to be soothed—their jealousies of new settlers to be removed, or their power to be opposed; and when all these difficulties should be surmounted, the pious emigrants must continue subject to the //first\\ condemnatory sentence denounced on the human race, "by the sweat of their brow to earn their bread." But with these dreary prospects the pilgrims were not to be disheartened—they landed, and very soon changed the face of New-England; they introduced symmetry by the assistance of all the instruments of art; the impenetrable woods were cleared, and made room for commodious habitations; the wild beasts were driven away, and flocks of domestic animals supplied their place; //whilst thorns and briars made way for rich harvests—\\the coasts were covered with towns, and the bays with ships—and thus the new world like the old became subject to man." Mr. West concluded with observing that these were events worthy of commemoration, and ought to have been perpetuated by a suitable inscription upon the rock.[13]

//My friend, as if anxious to view every part of this ancient settlement, solicited me to accompany him to a rise of ground near the burying-place, from which we had a fair prospect of the town and harbour—the day was now drawing to a close—the sun was sunk behind the western hills, which cast their sombre shades over the valley, while the retiring beams of day adorned the distant eastern eminences with yellow lustre—we now took a circuitous route around the hill and moved towards home—"This pleasant ride (observed Mr. W.) reminds me of our agreeable excursion to Greenwich, which I think, Lucy, you must not have forgotten,"—I assured him that I had not—"To-morrow morning (continued he) I must make arrangements for my return to my native State, there I once enjoyed your agreeable company, and what unbounded pleasure, Lucy, would it afford me could I prevail upon you to accompany me there now!"—I startled at the observations of Mr. W. and it was sometime before I could sufficiently collect myself to assure him, that in this, there would be a great impropriety—observing me not a little confused at the proposition, Mr. W. proceeded thus to explain—"Lucy you mistake my meaning—do not think so disrespectful of me as to suppose that I would presume to solicit your company in your present situation—rather permit me to assure you, Miss Brewer, that it is my sincere wish to convince you of my esteem and affection for you, an affection which I have for some weeks indulged, and I will presume to say, not without hope of a return. Your happiness is far dearer to me than my own, it is in your power to make me completely happy, by consenting to become mine by the most endearing connexion in life. I should not thus early have disclosed my intention to you, did not my business require my immediate return to New-York." The brilliant tear trembled in his eye, he pressed my hand and entreated me to forgive him if he had presumed too far. "You have indeed," said I, "called for my attention in an affair of a serious nature"—I could not proceed, and he continued— "It is indeed important—I do not wish you to enter into an engagement with me, till you have had sufficient time for reflection, and have obtained the consent of your friends—if it should meet your own and their approbation, I will protract my stay a fortnight longer, as I could spend that time with my relatives at Newport, and it would enable you to make such preparation as you might deem necessary—I shall take the liberty before my departure to morrow [*sic*] morning, to hint to your parents what my wishes are with regard to you, provided you do not yourself object to the union which I have proposed." I answered him with as much ease as possible, and he insensibly led me from one subject to another, till I found we had discussed almost every topic relative to my future situation.\\[14]

We reached home late in the evening, and having tarried much longer than we proposed, my parents had become alarmed for our personal safety. The evening, as usual, was passed with agreeable conversation. The morning ensuing, Mr. West having//, as he proposed,\\ taken an opportunity to exchange a few words with my father relative to our proposed union, took his departure for Newport.[15]

I had so long been accustomed to sorrow and anxiety, that I could scarcely persuade myself that all that passed was not a dream. I had now unequivocal evidence that the partiality Mr. West had shown toward me, and which I imagined proceeded only from friendship, arose from love. I was certain that he had held some conversation with my father, indicative of his attachment for me, but what was their final conclusion I knew not, nor had I any knowledge thereof until nearly a week afterward, when my parents requesting my company alone for a few moments, my father addressed me as follows:—

"My dear child, //from the principles of that education which you have received, I doubt not but you must be convinced that it is my duty to promote your interest as far as I am able, and how far my conduct as a father has been consistent with that rule, I appeal to yourself: Your own conscience will witness, whether (before you unwisely left me, and since your return) I have not at all times studied to promote your interest, and it is with pleasure that I now say, that (since your happy return to your afflicted parents) your filial duty has been equal to my highest wishes,—\\I have now to inform you, that your friend Mr. West (//a few moments\\ previous to his departure) with assurances of his love and regard for you, solicited my consent to your forming an important union with him. As the proposal was important, and somewhat unexpected, I informed him that I could not with propriety give him an immediate answer; but after a few days consideration, if I concluded favourably, he might depend on receiving a few lines from me, expressive of my approbation. I have now concluded, //(continued my father)\\ and have penned a few lines to send to Mr. West by to-morrow's post.—I have no objection to your complying with the young gentleman's request, as I believe it will be for your mutual happiness.//—Indeed, I had some suspicion of it while he was with us; but, being well convinced of his merit, I was almost assured no step of that nature would be taken without my consent. That consent you now have, and even my approbation.\\ May you both be as happy as I wish! I desire no more." //Here my honoured father stopped, tears hindered him from proceeding, and me from making a reply.\\[16]

The following is a copy of the letter which my father the day succeeding forwarded to Mr. West, whose consent I have obtained, as well as that of the writer, to make public, for the satisfaction of my readers:—

"———, March 20, 1816.

"My dear young friend,

"Ever since I had the pleasure of your acquaintance, I have considered you as a young gentleman of real merit, //who would not be guilty of an ungenerous action,\\ and to that was owing not only the respect with which I always treated you, but also the common indulgence to converse freely with my daughter. //My dear sir, if you ever live to be a father, you will know what I feel on the present occasion: A willingness to give her to you, from a firm persuasion of your merit; and anxiety for her preservation, from a conviction in my own mind, that there is nothing permanent in this world. However, sir,\\ [y]ou have my free consent to marry my child, my only child, and may the Divine Providence be your guide in the whole of your progress through this life! My ill state of health serves as a monitor to inform me, that my time in this world will be but short; and there is nothing would give me greater pleasure than to see my dear child happily settled, before I go hence, and be no more. How great, sir, is the charge which I commit to your care—an only child, and the hope of my declining years! I have not the least doubt of her conjugal fidelity, and your felicity in acting conformably to the character of a husband. Upon that supposition you have now my consent, according to your professed wishes. I shall therefore expect to see you at this place, as soon as you can make it convenient, to receive from my hands what is most dear to me in this world.[17]

"I am, sir, yours sincerely,
BENJAMIN BREWER."

This letter //(of which the foregoing is a true copy)\\ was forwarded by Wednesday's mail, and on the Sunday following Mr. West favoured us with another visit. It was towards evening when he arrived. I was sitting by the window when he entered, and to whom, after the usual compliments, I observed, that as the evening was pleasant, I had just been thinking of a walk to my favourite rock, but had no one to attend me, and was happy that he had come in season to perform that duty. Mr. West //bowing,\\ said he would accompany me with the greatest pleasure. We took a winding path which led along pleasant fields through a little grove to the seashore, and we sat down on the bank. I reflected on the contrast between my situation at that moment, and that in which I was a fugitive wanderer among the most abandoned of the human race.—Tears of gratitude and joy, in spite of all my efforts to prevent them, flowed from my eyes. I wiped them hastily away.—"What is the matter?" inquired Mr. W. with eagerness. "Nothing," said I. "Pardon me, Lucy," said he; "if I say these tears cannot proceed from nothing; am I not your friend? Tell me what sorrow—" "It is not sorrow," I replied smiling; "the remembrance of the many hours I have passed in this retreat will ever be dear to me, and some of them having passed in the company of friends now absent, produce a recollection—" "I understand you perfectly, Lucy," was the reply; "but let us now bid adieu to care and every unpleasing reflection, and only look forward to the bright prospect now opening to our view. Since you have given me the hope of your becoming mine, why should the ceremony be delayed? //Your mind is too dignified to permit you to pay an attention to too scrupulous forms.\\ Why is it necessary to protract the time of courtship to a tedious length, when the choice of both parties is fixed?" "I do not wish to pay too much attention to forms," I replied; "yet I cannot consent at present to pay no regard to them." Here Mr. West represented his business at New-York of such a nature as required his immediate presence, and that he must calculate on a speedy return; and having thrice assured me that the study of his life should be to promote my happiness, he at length persuaded me to be his the Thursday following.[18]

On our return home //late\\ in the evening, I acquainted my parents with our decision, and of the appointment of the day on which the nuptial ceremonies were to be performed, to which they consented.—The important day arrived—and I was, in presence of my loving parents, and a number of my friends and acquaintance, united to the man in whom all my affection is centered![19]

Our dispositions are similar, our love is mutual, and I am happy to add, that there is a prospect of our being as happy as this life of imperfection will admit of. Where there is a want of reciprocal affection, a married couple cannot be happy, even though they may possess the best of tempers, and every convenience of life. If either of them are attached to another object, the anxiety of their minds will banish happiness //and mutual confidence\\. Happiness dwells with content, and there cannot be content when the mind is continually in pursuit of a favourite wish it can never obtain. True friendship is the most noble, exalted, and generous sentiment that ever actuated the human mind. //But how few are there who are capable of enjoying it in its original purity. How few are to be found who do not mingle selfishness, avarice, pride and ambition, with this most delicate refinement of the soul. It is by this, that friendship becomes no more than

> ——————————————*"A name,*
> *A charm that lulls to sleep,*
> *A shade, that follows wealth or fame,*
> *But leaves the wretch to weep."*

How often do we see people while in prosperity, followed, courted, caressed and admired; friends surround them on every side, and every face salutes them with a flattering smile. But the moment the scene is changed, those "summer friends" forsake them, and by their altered behaviour, the shafts of adversity are acuminated, and their situation rendered still more wretched.\\ A companion in life, who is a real friend, is one of the greatest blessings we can enjoy. How truly wretched must that person be, who has no one to whom he can give the endearing appellation of friend, no one, in whose generous breast he can confide his secrets, and repose his cares! The world, in such a situation, must appear a wilderness, and mankind as savages, from whom he has every thing to dread, and nothing to hope. Who would wish for existence without a friend? Not all the wealth of the Indies could afford one real joy, unless we could share it with those for whom we felt a particular affection.[20]

> "Our joys when extended, will always increase,
> "Our griefs when divided, are hush'd into peace."

A Farewell Address to the Youths
of my native State.

Having//, as I proposed, \\ furnished my female readers with the particulars of my introduction to the man with whom I have formed an important union in life—our courtship, marriage, &c. I shall now //attempt to\\ impart a few words of advice to the dear Youth of my native state, to which I am now about to bid a final adieu. That I have been in a situation to witness the many deceptive arts practised by the lewd and profligate, to ensnare the innocent, none will deny; to our large sea-port towns these miserable offscourings of the human race resort from every part of the country—there, leagued together, they concert plans to allure the unsuspecting stranger from the paths of innocence and virtue; they obtain their bread by the vilest prostitution, and are continually on the search for new victims, whom they delight to render as miserable as themselves. Of these vile wretches, the capital of New-England may perhaps boast of a greater proportion than any //other\\ town of equal size in the Union. Persons whom curiosity has induced to visit these vile haunts of debauchery and riot, declare that "West-Boston Hill" has not its equal. Here the 'foul deeds of midnight' are not alone confined to persons of a particular description—to the reverse, here black and white, young and old, mingle as if they were of one and the same family. Alas, the depravity of human nature! What a shocking spectacle it is for public view, to behold so great a portion of that class whom the world have honoured with the appellation of the "Fair Sex," thus degrading themselves to a degree beneath the brute creation! To see not only those who are apparently so young, as to make us charitably suppose them incapable of such abominable deeds, but even those whose ages are more than three-score years!—mothers there are, who encourage, nay, *compel* their daughters to follow their wicked examples!—O shame, where is thy blush?[21]

Kind reader, charge not the authoress with presenting you with a picture too deeply coloured: permit me rather to declare to you that it is correctly delineated—I state nothing but what I could substantiate by the most positive proof, to which I have myself been a witness. To the world I have declared that among these wretched creatures I even spent three years of *my* early life—and to the world I have declared, that I too, like thousands, was //unconsciously\\ decoyed by the deceptive arts of a perfidious, an abandoned wretch of my own sex! and shall these three years of wretchedness profit me nothing? may not good come out of evil? Yes, if my youthful friends//, who are yet unconscious of offence, \\ are deterred from practising vices against which I warn them by the friendly advice I now give, then indeed do I reap a great profit, then shall I be satisfied that I have not erred for nought.[22]

O! my dear Youths! were you but made acquainted with the horrible transactions of midnight, of which I have been an unwilling spectator, you would shudder at the recital—they are many of them of a nature too abominable thus publicly to describe—let a disclosure of acts less shocking to the feelings of humanity, suffice.

There have I viewed Youths of unblemished characters, and in blooming health, allured by the deceptive arts of harlotry, robbed of their wealth, diseased and driven from the loathsome cells of the authors of their wretchedness, unpitied, and to spin out a life of wretched infirmity. I have known many instances of young girls of not more than twelve years of age, of respectable families, enticed from their parents, by the detestable Beldams of the Hill, and by them devoted to a state of wretchedness. By the proprietresses of those vile brothels, apprentices are enticed from their masters, children from their parents, and parents from their children—they are too, in many instances, the principal instigators of forgery, robbery and murder! For money, they are ever willing and ready to perpetrate deeds of the deepest die!—their wealth is the reward of the vile prostitution of those miserable beings whom they harbour for the purpose. Such, indeed, is the true character of those unprincipled women, to whose thirst for gain may be imputed the destruction of youth, beauty, and innocence, which these priestesses of Satan daily offer up as sacrifices to their infernal master![23]

That they are not unfrequently the means of destroying conjugal happiness, of plunging the best of women into a state of wretchedness and despair, by enticing from them their husbands, it will not be doubted—should any doubt the fact, the melancholy instance which I am about to state, and of which I have personal knowledge, as occurring within my native village, will suffice to convince them. The particulars I shall state as I received them from a peculiar friend and an associate of the unfortunate MARIA, who indeed presents us with a picture highly, although I can assure them, not falsely coloured.[24] Her affecting account follows:—

MARIA D——, was among the fairest and sweetest girls that I have ever known. If the love of the fondest and best of parents—if the most enchanting grace and beauty—if the pure spirit and disposition of a seraph could have saved her from misery, Maria had been saved. My heart bleeds at the recollection of her. Indeed it is with difficulty that I can command myself while I attempt to tell this tale of joy turned into sorrow; of the fairest hopes reversed and blasted; of the brightest lustre and beauty extinguished forever.

Her parents were not rich, but they were good. Although they had lived much in the world, they retained a simplicity of character which is now rarely encountered except in the description of poets. //Their benevolent breasts were fraught with a tenderness of feeling whose luxury is known only to the poor and humble. The rich and the prosperous know it only by name.\\ Their simplicity, their benevolence, their sensibility, were concentrated in the bosom of the young MARIA. They gave an emphasis to her opening beauty—suffused her cheek with a richer hue—and rode, in triumph on the beams of her eyes, through the heart of every beholder. I remember MARIA at her first appearance in the ball room. She was then about fourteen years of age. The inquiry ran—"what rose bud of beauty is this!" The epithet was applied with peculiar propriety: it depicted in one word, her youth, her beauty, her innocence and sweetness. It was easy to read in the countenance of this gay and artless young creature, the exulting expectations with which she was entering in life. Her childhood had passed away amid the blandishments and caresses of her fond parents; all had been ease, indulgence and gratification; admired, applauded and beloved by every body who saw or knew her, every day, every hour, every minute had been filled with animation, joy and rapture. As yet she had frolicked only on "life's velvet lawn," covered with a canopy of blooming amaranth; and her young fancy was teeming with visions of bliss in bright and boundless prospects. Alas! poor MARIA: How soon was the serene and joyous morning to be overcast! A lover presented himself. Like Maria, he was in the bloom of youth, and had every advantage of person and address; but his breast was not, like Maria's, the residence of pure and exalted virtue. He loved her indeed; or rather he was infatuated by her beauty; but he was incapable of forming a correct estimate of the treasure which was lodged in her bosom; of that heart whose purity, //delicacy,\\ fidelity//, generosity\\ and sensibility, an angel might have avowed without a blush. The dupe, however, of fervent and pathetic professions, she accepted this man; and Maria, who was formed to crown the happiness of a sensible and virtuous man, became the miserable wife of a weak, vicious and debauched man. Although he once professed to prize his lawfully wedded wife above all other women, yet too soon did he (regardless of his marriage vows) desert this lovely but unfortunate woman, to sport with detestable harlots! Those vile brothels, which have ever been a disgrace to the capital of New-England, became his favorite resort!—Here, among the most filthy and miserable of the human race, did this thoughtless, cruel man make a willing sacrifice of all that can render mankind respectable![25]

Merciful God! Must I remember the contrast which I so often witnessed, in agony? //Poor Maria! Her velvet lawn was exchanged for a wilderness of briars and brambles; her amaranthine canopy for the keen cutting blasts of a winter's sky.\\ I have seen Maria in the thronged assembly room when every eye was fixed upon her with delight, and followed her in speechless admiration through the mazes of the graceful dance; and I have seen the same Maria far removed from the world's society, and even yet in the bloom of youth, all lonely and drooping like a wounded flower! I have seen the lovely girl, presiding, like a bright, propitious planet, at her father's hospitable board; and I have seen her the solitary and menial drudge of her own gloomy and forsaken household. I have beheld her the animating soul of the polished circle, dispensing light and life by her smiles; and my own soul has sunk within me, to see her insulated from the world, and piercing and languishing under the neglect of her once ardent and assiduous husband. She had seen the time when every transitory dejection of countenance had been watched by him, its cause //[as]siduously\\ explored, and consolation administered with a tenderness which could not fail of its effect. But now, without a single inquiry, without one touch of pity, he could see her face pale with sorrow, and her once radiant eyes dim with weeping. At such a moment, instead of bending before her as he once had done, and pressing her hand to his sympathetic bosom, he would cast on her a look so cold and chilling as to freeze the vital stream of life even in its fountain, flying out of his house with contempt and disgust, and lavish on the vicious and impure those affectionate attentions which he had solemnly vowed to her alone. He might have been happy; and might have realized to his beauteous wife all those dreams of conjugal innocence and bliss with which her youthful fancy was wont to regale her. But instead of these pure and calm joys, whose recollection might have gilded even the moment of death, he chose riot, debauchery and guilt; //to his own virtuous and celestial bed, he preferred habitual imourity [*sic*] and prostitution;\\ and instead of the perpetual spring which she had fondly anticipated, poor Maria experienced only perpetual winter. She is gone; and, with her sister angels, she has found that peace which her unfeeling husband refused to her on earth. Her death stunned him into his senses. In vain he endeavoured to recal her fleeting breath; in vain he promised and avowed if she could be restored to him, to atone for his past neglect by future tenderness. To him the resolution of amendment came too late.—May it come in time to a portion of my readers.[26]

The foregoing affecting account of the effects of inconstancy is but one of a thousand which might be herein recorded, and which might be imputed to an unlawful intercourse with those vile prostitutes who are the avowed enemies of conjugal peace and happiness. //I must beg the patience of my readers while I record another instance, not less affecting than the one with which we have just presented them, and of the truth of which they may rely, having been myself an eye witness to almost every circumstance which attended it—the particulars were these:—About five years since a Mrs. GREY (the wife of a very honest and respectable farmer of New-Hampshire) without assigning any reasons therefor, or acquainting her husband with her intentions, deserted her family and came to Boston—what her real object was in thus leaving a kind and an obliging husband, and three lovely children, and of whom she appeared excessively fond, could never be determined—whether it was, however, for a criminal purpose or not, it is certain that she had been but a short time in town, before she was discovered and picked up by one of those infamous characters, whom the old Bawds of the Hill have constantly in their employ—a set of indolent and unprincipled men, who make it their business to go about in search of custom, and of such unfortunate females as venture abroad unprotected, and whose credulity, by their accursed insinuating arts, they may be enabled to impose upon—(OF SUCH MONSTERS, MY DEAR YOUTH, BEWARE!)—By one of these wretches was this poor deluded woman first conveyed to the Hill, and by him introduced to the Sisterhood, as his wife, to whom he had been recently married!—but not long did he as such retain her before she became the property of another, and another, and at length became the adopted wife of a proprietor or keeper of a "dancing-hall"—here she was at length discovered by one who had been her near neighbour in New-Hampshire, who was the first to convey to her disconsolate husband, information of her miserable situation—as Mr. G. and his wife had from their marriage day, until that of her unaccountable disappearance, ever lived peaceably and harmoniously together, no tongue can express his surprize on learning the miserable fate of a once beloved wife on whom he doated, and of whom he had long before concluded that some fatal casuality [*sic*] had deprived him forever.—Without a moment's delay he hurried to Boston to satisfy himself of what appeared to him an almost incredible circumstance, altho derived from a respectable source—I was in the Hall when he entered, attended by two of his neighbours—his wife at the instant was within the bar serving out liquor to customers, and did not notice her husband until she was accosted by him with "madam, do you know my face!"— what answer he received I could not distinctly hear, it was such however as was accompanied with a frightful screech—the keeper of the hall appeared, between whom and Mr. G. an altercation now ensued, each claiming marm as his lawful wedded wife!—the spectators however (who were chiefly sailors) receiving from the friends of Mr. G. satisfactory proof of his prior claim, threatened the hall keeper with severe flagellation if he did not immediately surrender madam to her rightful claimant, who, finding himself opposed by all present, thought it prudent to acquiece.—Mr. G. now retiring to a corner of the room with Mrs. G. addressed her in a manner the most affecting—after expressing to her his surprize at finding her, after so long an absence, in the woeful situation she then was, he represented to her the distress and anguish which her sudden disappearance had caused himself and family—and the disgrace to which she would, by her abominable conduct, subject him and her innocent children—"oft (said Mr. G.) have their pitiful cries for their lost mother pierced my heart, their surprize that you could leave them who so tenderly loved you, and their prayers for your safety, and speedy return, they have not ceased to utter!"—the poor man could proceed no farther, grief insupportable forbid him utterance—he wept bitterly—his wretched wife, like one petrified with horror, remained speechless—Mr. G. having a little composed himself, informed her, that as he had ever treated her with that love and regard which he conceived himself bound to do, by the most solemn vows of the marriage contract, and as she had betrayed a want of conjugal and parental affection, by deserting, and ruining forever the peace and happiness of an innocent family, he must now leave her to her destiny, to spend the remainder of her wretched days in the vile brothel, which she had prefered to the once happy abode of her family!— upon saying which, Mr. G. and his companions departed.[27]

It would be doing injustice to this wretched woman, to say that she did not appear for many months after, very sensibly effected with the distress to which she had subjected her friends, as represented by her husband. However ready the world may appear to condemn Mrs. GREY, and to pronounce her conduct of the most contemptible nature, yet had it not been for the nefarious schemes of one of those vile monsters, who go about seeking whom they may devour, she yet would have remained innocent—she had imprudently hazarded a visit to Boston (where she had a sister residing) without the consent or knowledge of her husband—it was late in the evening when she arrived, by enquiry she was attempting to find her way to her sister's dwelling—but, alas, by her enquiry she proved herself a stranger—to one of those execrable monsters ever in search of prey, this was enough—with the guile of a serpent, he proffered his services to conduct the unfortunate stranger to her sister's house, which were imprudently accepted, and she was unconsciously conveyed to one of those vile haunts of iniquity, where by every infernal means, that the inventive faculties of her execrable seducers could give birth to, she was compelled to make a sacrifice of all that could render her respectable in the eyes of the world!—to return now to an injured husband, she dare not—for her poor children she was sure that her affection had not diminished, but that she was no longer worthy the name of mother—her mind was continually harrowed with the heart piercing reflection of having been the means of destroying the peace of those, whom, as a parent, she was bound to protect—her repose at night was disturbed by frightful dreams—in short, as life had now become a burthen to her, she formed the dreadful resolution of putting an end to her own existence, which she doubtless would have effected, had I not prevented it;—she one night between ten and eleven o'clock left the house where she lodged, and proceeded, unobserved as she supposed, for Cambridge bridge—having reached it, she descended some steps near the toll house, and seating herself on the lowest, she ardently recommended her spirit to that God she was thus going to offend, by not bearing patiently what he was pleased she should suffer—she took off her bonnet and shawl, and laid them beside her, and then partly rising to take the fatal plunge, I caught her in my arms, and after making use of the most persuasive argument possible, to deter her from the execution of her desperate design, at length succeeded in persuading her to return home with me.[28]

Gracious Heaven! since it is the opinion of so great a portion of the world, that one false step forever blasts the fame of a woman; when she has once forfeited the title of virtuous, all is lost, why should those vile monsters be suffered to proceed in their licentiousness unpunished!—ought not they to be viewed with as much detestation and abhorrence, as the robber and assassin!—Such men are the pests of society; families, as well as individuals, are robbed of their peace by them. Where is the heart so hard that will not bleed when an innocent unsuspecting female, is enticed from her parents, and disposed of to the highest bidder!—horror and remorse, ever attendant on conscious guilt, rends her heart—hope cannot soothe her sorrows; if she looks toward the future, she must shrink dismayed at the gloomy prospect; nothing but disgrace, contempt, and reproaches await her.[29] If she takes a retrospective view of past scenes, the hours of innocence, the contrast only serves to heighten her distress. An injured husband beholds his wife, or parents with keenest anguish, behold their darling child, in whom they fondly placed their hopes of future happiness, declining in health, their honour gone, a prey to unutterable misery! And who are the authors of their misery? those vile wretches whom we have described, who are nocturnally prowling for innocent prey!—that a number of these vile out-casts are constantly employed, fed and cloathed, by the shameless bawds of the Hill, is a fact with which I have too much knowledge—wretches, who for the lucre of a few base pence, would sacrifice their nearest relatives!—ought not the names of such detestable scoundrels to be branded with eternal shame![30]

My dear Youth—as you will hear from me no more, and as I intend this as a

BEACON, to warn you of the dreadful consequences to which you will expose yourselves, should you suffer yourselves to be decoyed by the deceptive arts of these insinuating villians [*sic*]—permit one who by sad experience is well acquainted with their vile machinations, to impart to you that FRIENDLY ADVICE, which, if seasonably attended to, may prevent your eternal ruin!—I would conjure you, my dear friends, as you regard health, reputation and life, to avoid those dangerous shoals, those foul harbours, where thousands have suffered shipwreck!—while steering the course of safety, which leads to the haven of happiness, beware that you are not deceived by the false-lights of harlotry!—the sweet sounding musical instruments—those boards sumptuously spread with danties [*sic*]— the sparkling liquor—and those "artificial beauties" clad in drapery and drenched with perfume—are intended only to decoy the unsuspecting stranger, as false lights are displayed upon a savage coast, to deceive the unwary mariner!—and when these false allurements fail them, then do those vile "moon-cursers" those kidnappers of innocence, dispatch their runners in search of victims, whom with the pretence of conducting in safety to their friends, convey to those filthy brothels, and commit them to the charge of their keepers, by whom they are either persuaded or compelled to become proselytes to vice!

My young friends, I am sensible that I present you with a frightful picture, but I declare to you that it is drawn with the pencil of truth—for such as I describe to you, is the filthy part of West Boston Hill, such the contemptible characters who inhabit it, and such the detestable schemes which they practice to beguile innocent youth!—I state nothing but what I have been an eye witness to—and were I to state minutely every vile transaction which came within my observation while an inhabitant of the Hill, I should intrude perhaps too much upon the patience of my readers.—However low the depravity of the human race is sunk in what we have already recorded, yet as one who has undertaken to give council, I conceive it an indispensable duty to expose vice that it may be avoided—nor have I recorded those alarming instances of human depravity, without the sincere hope that it may contribute to rescue many a young innocent from similar wretchedness, and prevent some of riper years from experiencing a similar fate of the unfortunate Mrs. GREY. It ought certainly to be considered as one of the most weighty arguments against the practice of such vice, that frequently tender and venerable relations, connexions and friends, are involved in the agitations, afflictions, and disgrace, which fall upon its detested authors.

My dear Youth, I have yet another picture to exhibit to your view—it is indeed a mancholly one, but it is delineated from life. But view for a single moment, yonder sprightly Youth—in the bloom of life and health—the picture of innocence, and a stranger to vice—in his person, all that the glowing fancy of the poet could picture as elegant and graceful, while the gentleness of his manners, and the sweetness of his disposition, renders him an object of universal admiration. And who may this beloved youth be?—the darling son, the only child of respectable, kind and indulging parents—who are flattered with the fond expectation, that by his strict adherence to the good council, and the moral preceipts, with which they have endeavoured to improve his youthful mind, he will not fail in riper years to obtain from his fellow creatures, the respect which is due only to those whose lives are examplery. But, my youthful readers, indulge me with your attention a little while longer, while I picture to your imaginations another object, not less worthy of your serious contemplation. Behold yonder frightful emaciated figure! hobbling through the public streets with the aid of a crutch! whose tattered garments are covered with filth and vermin, and whose trembling limbs, and death-like countenance, betoken the deprivation of youthful vigour and health, and the inheritance of wasting disease! Behold him now shunned, unpitied and despised by those who were late the respectable companions of his youth, to whom he acknowledges his penury and want, while he reproaches himself for his prodigality in lavishing upon the vile and profligate, what he now so much stands in need of.[31] And who may this wretched object be? No other, kind reader, than the one whom we have just described to you—the same modest, blooming youth, who but yesterday, was so justly esteemed and admired for his many manly virtues—the promising youth, in whom were centered the fondest expectations of kind and indulging parents!

Methinks my readers will be hear [*sic*] ready to exclaim with astonishment—"How sudden the transition!"—and to enquire—"whence this rapid change, from a state of health, vigour and respectability, to that of wretched debility, misery and want!" Kind readers, once more I solicit your attention for a few moments—I have yet another and far more disgusting picture to present you—a minute inspection of which, will satisfy you whence this sudden and awful change, from a state of ease, affluence and respectability, to that of the most woeful wretchedness.—

View yonder HILL—the chosen seat of debauchery and riot!—the nursery of vice!—the source of every evil that is calculated to render the heedless youth, the miserable object which I have just described to you!—contemplate, seriously contemplate for a few moments, the disgusting scenes which this infamous Hill continually presents—and if you regard decency, you will turn from the frightful picture with disgust, and with the virtuous exclaim—"alas! the depravity of human nature!"—Behold those filthy, half clad, miserable female objects, issuing by dozens from their wretched habitations, linked arm in arm, and reeling through mud and mire from brothel to brothel!—Tell me ye thoughtless sons of folly, who seek pleasure in the midnight revel, what is there so attracting in these detestable harlots, for whose sake you make a voluntary sacrifice of health, wealth and reputation!—is it their lewdness, their wanton obscenity, their intemperance, and the vile imprecations which they never cease to utter?—or is it their apparent regard for wretches of the lowest order, without respect to colour!—Alas, whatever it may be, it is a serious fact that numbers (like the unfortunate youth, whose melancholly case we have just mentioned) are allured from the paths of virtue and innocence, and plunged into a state of unutterable dispair!—O! my dear Youth! if your hopes of future greatness, rests upon the acquirement and support of an unblemished reputation—beware, I beseech you, of those shameless wretches, who from step to step, urge you on to the commission of the most atrocious crimes, and then leave you to deplore your thoughtless credulity.

My dear young friends—that you may never (like myself) by sad experience learn the fatal effects of departing in youth from the paths of virtue and innocence, is my sincere wish—but if you will now condescend to receive advice from a true Penitent, permit me to conjure you to cherish virtue. Virtue is of intrinsic value and good desert, and of indispensible obligation; not the creature of will, but necessary and immutable; not local and temporary, but of equal extent and antiquity with the divine mind; not a mode of sensation, but everlasting truth; not dependent on power, but the guide of all power. Virtue is the foundation of honor and esteem, and the source of all beauty, order, and happiness in nature. It is what confers value on all the other endowments and qualities of a reasonable being, to which he ought to be absolutely subservient, and without which, the more hideous deformities, and the greater curses, they become.

The use of it is not confined to any one stage of our existence, or to any particular situation we can be in; but reaches through all the periods and circumstances of our being. Many of the endowments and talents which we now possess, and of which we are too apt to be proud, will cease entirely with the present state; but this will be our ornament and dignity, in every future state to which we may be removed. Beauty and wit will die, learning will vanish away, and all the arts of life be soon forgot; but virtue will remain forever. This unites us to the whole rational creation, and fits us for conversing with any order of superior natures. It procures us the approbation and love of all wise and good beings, and renders them our allies and friends. But what is of unspeakably greater consequence is, that it makes God our friend, assimilates and unites our minds to him, and engages his almighty power in our defence. Superior beings, of all ranks, are bound by it no less than ourselves. It has the same authority in all worlds that it has in this. The further any being is advanced in excellence and perfection, the greater is his attachment to it, and the more is he under its influence. To say no more; 'Tis the law of the whole universe; it stands first in the estimation of the deity; its original is his nature; and it is the very object that makes him lovely.

Such is the importance of virtue.—Of what consequence, therefore is it, my dear Youth, that we practise it! There is no argument or motive, in any respect fitted to influence a reasonable mind, which does not call us to this. One virtuous disposition of soul, is preferable to the greatest natural accomplishments and abilities, and of more value than all the treasures of the world. If you are wise, then study virtue and contemn every thing that come in competition with it. Remember, that nothing else deserves one anxious thought or wish. Remember, that this alone is honor, glory, wealth, and happiness. Secure this and you secure every thing. Lose this and all is lost.

My dear young friends—let not the season of youth be barren of improvements in virtue, so essential to your future felicity and honour.—Now is the seed time of life; and according to *what you sow you shall reap.*—Your character is now, under divine assistance, of your own forming; your fate is, in some measure, put into your own hands.—Whatever impulse you now give to your desires and passions, the direction is likely to continue.—It will form the channel in which your life is to run; nay, it may determine its everlasting issue.—Consider then the employment of this important period, as the highest trust which shall ever be committed to you; as in a great measure decisive of your happiness, in time, and in eternity.—As in the succession of the seasons, each, by the invariable laws of nature, affects the productions of what is next in course; so in human life, every period of our age, according as it is well or ill spent, influences the happiness of that which is to follow.—Virtuous youth gradually brings forward accomplished and flourishing manhood; and such manhood passes of itself, without uneasiness, into respectable and tranquil old age.—But when nature is turned out of its regular course, disorder takes place in the moral, just as in the vegetable world.—If the Spring put forth no blossom, in Summer there will be no beauty, and in Autumn there will be no fruit.—So, if youth be trifled away without improvement, manhood will be contemptible, and old age miserable.—If the beginnings of life have been *vanity*, its latter end can be no other than *vexation of spirit.*"

Happy would it be for young people if they would consider their period of life as a most important era in their existence—that their entrance on the theatre of the world is the commencement of a drama, in which they will be exposed to the view of numerous spectators, who will applaud or censure them according as they perform the parts they have taken—and what is peculiar to these scenes, each one will feel a pleasure or a pain, independent of the applauses or censures of others, from the inward consciousness of the principles of action—because each acts for himself, and does not personate another.

Youth is an entrance on a journey long and various—through an untried path, where are many dangers and difficulties.—They should therefore look well to the steps they are about to take, and use the precaution of travellers in a strange land— should inquire whether the way they are in is right or wrong—whether it is the path of honor and pleasure, or of disgrace and pain.

Were we frequently to attend to the flight of time, and consider its end; to examine on what our hope of future bliss is founded, and anticipate that day of discovery and decision which is hastening upon us, it would excite diligence, and weaken our attachment to inferior objects. To a mind conscious of its native dignity and immortality, this employment cannot be either unpleasing or unprofitable. It is the highest proof of wisdom so to act in our present situation, that when removed to another, the change may be as happy as it will be lasting. We need not fear that this will diminish in the least our present happiness. The Gracious Being who formed us requires no service at our hands, but will tend to promote our present good. "Godliness is profitable to all things;" by living in conformity to its rules, we escape many evils, and are preserved in virtue and innocence. We enjoy every gratification that can give delight to a reasonable mind. Were mankind generally influenced by this noble principle, how happy would be the state of human society! The voice of discord would be no more heard. The various ranks and classes of men would be connected in the strongest and most pleasing band of union. The present state of existence would be only a happy prelude to one still more exalted and glorious in the realms of eternal day.

However visionary or puritanical these reflections may be deemed by the gay, the inconsiderate, and the licentious, a time is approaching when such will discover and own them to be the language of truth.

When the dream of folly is ended, their life will appear a barren waste, and every pursuit, which terminates with it, unprofitable. But those who have early applied their hearts unto wisdom, and made her precepts the governing rule of action, will possess that substantial treasure which can never fail. They will approach the confines of the grave with a hope that is full of immortality, and in the last "hour of adversity be joyful."

My dear Youth—impress your minds with reverence for all that is sacred, let no wantonness of youthful spirits, no compliance with the intemperate mirth of others, ever betray you into prophane sallies. Besides the guilt which is hereby incurred, nothing gives a more odious appearance of presumption to youth, than the affectation of treating religion with levity. Instead of being an evidence of superior understanding, it discovers a pert and shallow mind; which, vain of the first smatterings of knowledge, presumes to make light of what the rest of mankind revere. At the same time, you are not to imagine that when exhorted to be religious, you are called upon to become more formal and solemn in your manners than others of the same years; or to erect yourselves into supercilious reproves [*sic*] of those around you: The spirit of true religion breathes gentleness and affability. It gives a native unaffected ease to the behaviour. It is social, kind and cheerful; far removed from that gloomy and illiberal superstition which clouds the brow, sharpens the temper, dejects the spirit, and teaches men to fit themselves for *another* world by neglecting the concerns of *this*. Let your religion, on the contrary, connect preparations for Heaven with an honourable discharge of the duties of active life. Of such religion discover on every proper occasion, that you are not ashamed; but avoid making any unnecessary ostentation of it before the world.

To what do the constraints of religion, and the councils of age with respect to pleasure, amount? They may all be comprised in a few words—not to hurt yourselves, and not to hurt others, by your pursuits of pleasure.—Within these bounds pleasure is lawful; beyond them it becomes criminal, because it is ruinous. And are these restraints more than a wise man would choose to impose on himself? We call you not to renounce pleasure, but to enjoy it in safety. Instead of abridging it, we exhort you to pursue it on an extensive plan. We propose measures for securing its possession, and for prolonging its duration.

To conclude, my dear Youth, it is our highest wisdom to tread the paths of virtue in the morning of our days, that the evening may terminate with a smiling serenity, and, when the struggles of reluctant nature are over, the soul may securely wing its way to the settled regions of unmolested security.

It is a preposterous resolution of some people to defer being virtuous till they grow old, imagining that wisdom is the natural consequence of old age—people easily pardon, in youth, the common irregularities of the senses; but they do not forgive the least vice of the heart. The heart never grows better by age—and can we think that, when the purest and sprightliest part of life has been prostituted to vice, the dregs are an offering fit for our Maker? And can we think, that he will accept of such a sacrifice?\\32

Thus, my dear respected Youth, have I //as I proposed,\\ hastily thrown together, as they occurred, a few moral reflections, which, if they are not productive of the good really intended, I shall feel a consciousness of having performed my duty. As I am about to leave my native state, //and\\ perhaps never again to return, I have conceived it to be an important duty to warn you to beware of the vile and deceptive arts of those who are prone to wickedness—wretches, with which our large cities, &c. abound. May the few instances which I have herein recorded of their detestable //round of\\ iniquity, serve as an AWFUL BEACON to warn you of the danger to which you will expose all that can render you respectable in this world, by forming even the slightest acquaintance with them.[33]

My dear friends, I must now bid you //all\\ an affectionate and final FARE-WELL![34] May God direct you in every thing for the best, which is the sincere prayer of

Your real friend,
LUCY WEST.

//ADVERTISEMENT.

☞ Those who purchase and peruse the present Third and Last Part of Mrs. WEST's Adventures, (and who have not read the First and Second Parts) should not fail to obtain them, as they are so inseparably connected that by perusing a detached part only, the reader remains ignorant of those important incidents of her life, which, as they regard her birth—her elopement from her Parents, and her six years residence on West-Boston Hill—her Sea Adventures &c. &c.—will not prove less amusing and interesting than the contents of the present and last Part.

☞ The First and Second Parts of the Adventures of Mrs. WEST (late Miss BREWER, alias, BAKER) may be had by the gross, dozen or single, at the Book Store of N. COVERLY, jun. Milk-Street—BOSTON.\ \35

A BRIEF REPLY

to the

Late Writings of Louisa Baker,
[Alias] Lucy Brewer

Mrs. RACHEL SPERRY,

[An inhabitant of West-Boston Hill,]

A

BRIEF REPLY

TO THE LATE WRITINGS OF

LOUISA BAKER,

[*ALIAS*]

LUCY BREWER,

[late an inhabitant of West-Boston Hill—and who
in disguise served Three Years on board the
Frigate CONSTITUTION.]

———

By Mrs. Rachel Sperry,

[now an inhabitant of West-Boston Hill.]

———

Miss BAKER—

Since you impute your immoral life to me !
The world shall now know who and what you *be* ;
We all have our failings —faults to which we're prone,
But e're you *proclaim them, examine well your* own.

———

BOSTON—Printed for M. BREWSTER.—1816.

Frontispiece (*opposite*) and title page of *A Brief Reply to the Late Writings of Louisa Baker*
(1816), probably fabricated by Nathaniel Coverly Jr. or his hack, in order to cash in further
on the popularity of his other pamphlets on the female marine.

A BRIEF REPLY, &c.

THE public have been amused for the year past, by the writings of a young woman, who assumed the name of LOUISA BAKER, since LUCY BREWER, and now Mrs. WEST!—but whose *real* name, is neither *Baker, Brewer* nor *West!*—No, while this "Penitent" young miss, wishes to acquaint the world with the surprising circumstances of her life, that she may preserve her character from reproach, she would do it under a fictitious name!—while she unmercifully lashes others, she herself escapes flagellation, by a species of deception peculiar to herself. She has palmed upon the public what she terms "a biographical sketch of her life"—a surprizing record, indeed, of juvenile transgressions, irresistable temptations and timely repentance!—she relates many plausible things of herself, and to one, not well acquainted with her, they might appear as deserving of credit—but, we can assure the public, that she has presented them with a mis-representation of facts. Miss *Bowen* (for such indeed was her *real* name) has an undoubted right to publish biographical sketches of her life, to blow her own trumpet, and sound her own praise—but she must not do it too much at the expence of others. Agreeable to her own declarations, her character is marked with many unpleasant traits, which I should forbear to expose, had she not taken the liberty to impute to me, deeds of the deepest die!—I am sensible that I am not without my failings, that I am, indeed, an inhabitant of West Boston Hill, where I have perhaps too much conformed to the fashions of the place, in encouraging girls of pleasure, in their plans to beguile youth, that I might obtain my fee—but, as the saying is—"*the devil is entitled to his due*"—I can no longer withstand the abuse of one, who I am confident has taken as active a part as myself, and who now is pleased to apply to me such approbious [*sic*] epithets, as "old Bawd!" "old Hag!" "old Beldam!" &c. &c.—I am determined therefore no longer to keep the secrets of "madam WEST" (as she now terms herself) but will disclose to the public such facts, as shall convince them that not the one half has been told them.—

In the spring of 1806, I had the misfortune to lose my husband, who was unfortunately drowned, by the upsetting of a boat near Boston light—I was left with three small children, and with nothing wherewith to support them—as they were too young to labour for their bread, none were found willing to be taxed with the expence of their maintenance. In this dreadful dilemma was I placed, when I was advised by an acquaintance to remove upon the Hill, and to open a house for the accommodation of such persons, as were generally willing to pay a liberal price for board.—As the Hill had always been represented to me as a very vile place, I could not at first think of adopting the plan of my friend, although the starving condition of myself and family, demanded that something should be immediately done;—I did not, however, yield to the persuasion of my acquaintance, until it appeared the only alternative, to preserve me and my young family from a state of misery and want.

Under these disagreeable circumstances, I consented to become an inhabitant of the Hill—where I opened a house for the reception of such as were tolerable decent—they were, I must confess, comprised principally of females—but each had their chamber, and whatever company they might have had in the evening, it was such as never disturbed my repose, or interfered with my personal concerns—altercations, and riotous proceedings, of whatever nature or kind, were strictly forbidden by me—in the day time, my female boarders were generally so obliging as to assist me in my sewing work, of which I had always a great share.

Sometime in the fall or winter of 1809, at the close of the day, and in the midst of a severe snow storm, a female (apparently about 17 years of age) in the most wretched condition, called at my house, and offered her services in the capacity of kitchen or chamber-maid—I was not in want of either, but I could not refuse one of my sex, in the wretched condition in which I saw her, a shelter for the night—I gave her a welcome reception, and administered every thing to her relief that my house afforded—nor were my boarders, (whom I had taught "to feel for another's woes,") less backward to perform the kindest offices for the poor fugitive wanderer.

In the evening (the girls having retired to their different apartments) I, without making use of any compulsatory means, requested her to inform me of the cause of her being thus in her wretched condition, and at that inclement season of the year, destitute of a place—when she related to me every circumstance, as recorded in the first pages of her book; stating, that she had confided too much in the declarations of pretended friendship of a false young man—who having succeeded in depriving her of all that could render her respectable in the eyes of the world, had added insult to injury, by declaring that he would neither marry her, nor provide for the fruits of her misplaced confidence!—that thus deserted by the youth whom she had before considered incapable of a base action, she, to avoid the shame and disgrace which she was likely to incur, as well as the just resentment of her injured parents, formed the desperate resolution of quitting their hospitable mansion, in the dead of night, and seeking among strangers an asylum, where she might be permitted to remain until she could return to her friends, without exciting their suspicion.—She said that she had been two days in town, and had not been enabled to find any one willing to employ her—that she had not an acquaintance in the place, was destitute of money, and of almost every article of necessary cloathing!—here she burst into tears, and in broken accents, seemed to reproach herself for her folly in thus quitting a peaceful home, and kind and indulging parents.—She said that she was an only child of wealthy and respectable parents, who resided in or near the town of Marshfield, in Plymouth county—and that her real name was ELIZA BOWEN, but the better to evade the pursuit of her friends, she had assumed that of *Louisa Baker!*

From the artless manner, in which this then pitiful object rehearsed her tale of sorrow, I could not reasonably discredit the truth of what she had told me—nor could I myself refrain from shedding tears, when I saw her apparently ready to sink under the weight of her afflictions!—but this base girl, has now the ingratitude to term them "hypocritical tears!" Actuated by the pure principles of benevolence, I did indeed assure her, that she might now consider her troubles at an end, and that she should find me a *mother*, and my house an asylum, until such time as it would be prudent for her to return to her friends—but it is an absolute falsehood, that the "old fowl and her chickens" (as she has been pleased to term me, and my female boarders) had any inclination whatever to conceal from her, any thing that could excite her suspicion, that we were not of respectable standing—my girls had their company as usual, and the young huzzy was perfectly at liberty to make what observations she pleased.

After being with me a few months, she was confined, which was attended with great expence and trouble to me, and which after her recovery, she would have artfully saddled me with, had I not been seasonably apprized of her design, and adopted measures to prevent it—no compulsatory means or threats were however made use of by me, to prevent her return to her parents, as she has falsely stated—I merely suggested to her, the unfairness of her thus quitting me, without indemnifying me for the expence and trouble which her sickness had subjected me to.[1]

"From this moment (says she) this antiquated hag, and her not less cunning pupils, began by degrees to unfold to me the important secret, which they never had before thought proper to disclose—no pains were spared to decoy me from the paths of virtue and innocence, and fit me for their market! and O! must I add, to my everlasting shame, that they at length fully succeeded in their nefarious schemes, and rendered me the object they so much desired—I was soon pronounced a forward scholar by my arch preceptress," &c.—Such was she indeed—never had I [a] boarder that made such rapid progress in all the deceptive arts of harlotry, as ELIZA BOWEN—that she knew "how to entrap the amorous youth, and to send him pennyless from her bed!" many an injured youth, of this town, can testify to—the public may rest assured that it did not require a great deal of pains "to decoy her from the paths of virtue and innocence!"—the sacrifice, however great it may be considered in the eyes of the world, was a voluntary one on the part of the relenting Penitent![2]

"For three years (adds she) I continued an associate of the detestable harlots who inhabit those vile brothel houses which the Hill contains—in which time no one could have had a better chance to become acquainted with their dispositions, their habits, and their wicked and deep concerted plans to decoy the unheeding youth, who too frequently resort there to witness the midnight revel—many of these scenes I shall in course record, and to YOUTH impart that advice which I hope may prove to their advantage," &c. What a pity it is that the repentance of ELIZA, did not come sooner—how many wretched Youths would have been thereby saved from a state of shame and infamy, into which they have plunged themselves, for the sake of this now relenting strum[pet]![3]—she advises them now to beware of those "deep concerted plans" by means of which she well knows that she has been enabled to beguile hundreds of them!—she advises them never to resort to the Hill, although she acknowledges that she has taken an active part to decoy them there!—that she was "an associate of the detestable harlots" yet now in the language of Shakespeare, threatens to—

——"Disclose *our* hidden vices,
"Acts of black night, abominable deeds,
"Complots of mischief and villanies
"Ruthful to hear."—

As to the true character of ELIZA BOWEN, and the probability of her becoming a *sincere* penitent, I appeal to those who were best acquainted with her while an inhabitant of the Hill—I am confident that they will agree with me in saying, that there could not be a more "detestable harlot" among those with whom she associated—she took as active a part at the "midnight revel" as any one, and was as forward to "complot mischief!"—not a night passed but she resorted to the dancing-halls, where she seldom failed to obtain a cully.[4] With her it was a common observation that "as she made a voluntary sacrifice of all that could render her respectable, it was in vain to think of ever again enjoying the good opinion of her friends!"—for more than two years she never expressed a wish to see her parents. In her book she mentions that her friends traced her to Boston, but could obtain no further information of her—this is false—for she was soon after discovered by an acquaintance in a dancing-hall, who giving information to her parents, a number of their neighbours were dispatched in quest of her, but she evaded them by secreting herself in a private room of my house.

"After a three years residence (says she) with these vile prostitutes, I became disgusted with their wretched habits, and was resolved to quit them at all hazards—accordingly, a short time after, a favourable opportunity offering, I, clad in a male suit, escaped from my "fair Shepherdess" unsuspected. I walked through many public streets in Boston, and finding that no one had the least suspicion of my sex, I resorted to a public rendezvous in Fish Street—here, agreeable to a former notion, I formed the desperate resolution of entering as a Marine on board the Frigate CONSTITUTION!" &c.

In these particulars, this modern Amazon, does not confine herself altogether to facts;—the plain truth is, she did not become so much disgusted with the "wretched habits" of her female associates, as she became enamoured with a young man, who had entered on board the Frigate *Constitution*—she did indeed resolve that she would "quit me at all hazards," as at all hazards, she was resolved to follow him—he was the principal instigator—he procured her a suit of cloathes, and introduced her to the recruiting officer as a cousin from New-York, who but the day previous had been discharged from public service, by which means she was enabled to evade the usual search—while on board he was of essential service to her, in enabling her to perform the duty of a marine, without exciting the suspicion of her shipmates; indeed he was the only person on board who had the least knowledge or suspicion of her being a female! To give her all the praise to which she is entitled, in justice to her, I must acknowledge that I have been credibly informed, that in time of action, she displayed much undaunted bravery, and became as expert in loading and discharging her musket, as any in her core!—the young man who accompanied her, and who has been since frequently at my house, gave me this information.

"Clad in a male suit (she observes) I escaped from my fair Shepherdess unsuspected!"—indeed after having manifested the greatest regard for me, I had very little suspicion that she would finally leave me in such a clandestine manner—surprized at her sudden disappearance, I made diligent search for her, concluding that she had been enticed to some of the bad houses on the Hill, but my search was fruitless, for I should as soon sought for her in the moon, as on board the *Constitution*. "Shepherdess" or not, had I found her, she certainly would have been detained by me, for she was honestly indebted to me to the amount of $90 dollars, being the amount of a year's board—her account I a few day's since took the liberty to forward to her husband in New-York! as (it being now improbable that I shall ever obtain a cent from Penitent Miss) I am determined to have the satisfaction of refreshing her mind with past scenes!

After the return of the *Constitution* from her last cruise, Miss B. observes that garbed in her military uniform, she frequently resorted to the Hill with her shipmates, where she recounted her sea adventures, and partook of the cheering glass, *unsuspected*—in this madam is mistaken; for although she indeed played the deceptive part extremely well, she was recognized in this dress by a miss COLLINS, one of her old associates, who the day following informed me that she had certainly seen ELIZA BOWEN, the evening previous, dressed in a marine's uniform, and in company with a number of the Constitution's men—but as I had at that time no suspicion of her having assumed that character, I thought miss C. mistaken.

The relenting girl relates (and apparently with a great deal of satisfaction) the manner in which she artfully succeeded in deceiving me, soon after her return from New York. If she is indeed the person who garbed like an officer spent an evening at my house the last summer, I must acknowledge that I was very much deceived in her person—but as she had been three years absent, and having been exposed to weather calculated to change the complexion, it is not so much to be wondered at that I did not recognize her at that time—had my boarders been present, she probably would not have succeeded so well.

The penitent Prodigal concludes the first and second volumns of her works, with an awful description of West-Boston Hill, and of the characters who inhabit it—subjoining a solemn warning to the Youth of the town, &c. I believe that I as much disapprove of many of the disgusting scenes of the Hill, as ELIZA BOWEN, and probably more so, for in them I have never acted so conspicuous a part as she has done—I wish not therefore to be considered as an advocate for the many foul transactions which characterize the place, but that the existence of such places are essential to the security of the innocent and defenceless, in large commercial towns and cities, I have no doubt. What would be the situation of Boston, and what the danger attending the evening excursions of its female inhabitants, were not a peculiar class of their fellow-creatures priviledged with a place of resort like the Hill?—should those of easy life, peculiar to sea ports, be denied a residence here, they would privately seek one in more respectable parts of the town—then would every female, however innocent and respectable, be liable to be insulted in their houses, and venture abroad in the evening at the risk of their lives—all whom necessity should call abroad at a late hour in the evening, unprotected, would be viewed as suspicious characters, and treated accordingly—sailors, soldiers, &c. who now uniformly resort to the hill, would then parole [*sic*] the public streets in search of company, and to whose insults and abuse every female, young and old, would be liable. Large towns and cities have found it always necessary to erect suitable places of deposit for all nuisances, filth, &c. whereby the health of its inhabitants are endangered—so for public good, in every large town and city, ought there to be a place allotted those who prefer a life of debauchery, and who are esteemed as a public nuisance—so far we consider the Hill, and its inhabitants (vile as they are represented by miss BOWEN) of public benefit to the town. Unquestionably it will be observed, that "for vice there is no apology,"—that such temptations to lewdness ought never to be encouraged, and that the proper way to remedy the evil, is to teach all mankind the propriety of departing from evil ways, and adhering to moral principles!—if such was human nature, it would indeed be a happy thing—but as to reform *all* mankind, would probably prove more than *one* day's work, I think I shall decline so arduous a task, and leave it for those to perform whom may suppose it practicable!

As to the "beguiling of innocent youth," there is no doubt frequent instances of it—but I have always strictly forbidden my boarders taking any advantage of strangers—I believe they have always dealt upon honourable terms, notwithstanding they have been charged with designingly upsetting decanters of wine, that their gentlemen might apply to me for more!—if there was ever an instance of this, it was without my approbation or knowledge. I do not consider myself accountable for the conduct of every inhabitant of the Hill, among whom there are no doubt many as wicked and abandoned as madam represents them to be—but these creatures are confined to their own habitations, and own circles of acquaintance, and are never permitted to enter my dwelling, or to associate with my boarders. If innocent and unsuspecting youth will suffer themselves to be beguiled by such disgusting objects, the fault must lie at their own doors.

Miss B. has said much about the "midnight revel," &c. but none was more fond of frequenting the dancing-halls, than she—it was there she spent a great proportion of her time, and strove as much (by a false decoration of her person) to beguile youth, as any one, and was not less forward to disburthen them of their loose change! Yet she has now become one of the greatest advocates of virtuous habits! This may pass well among those who are less acquainted with her than myself.

If miss B. became truly penitent, and sensible of the importance of leading a more virtuous life, why did she not immediately on leaving the Hill, return to her afflicted parents, who probably had not heard a syllable respecting her for more than two years?—why did she prefer garbing herself in man's apparel, and going on board a public ship, and there among four hundred men, and without another female on board, run the risk of exposing herself? Why did she not immediately after her discharge from the ship, return to her parents—why did she continue with her shipmates to lurk about the Hill, a place which she speaks of with so much abhorrence? Why (after her return to her parents, and from whom she met with such a cordial reception) did she express a wish so soon to leave them and again garbed in her uniform, make a tour to the southward? Why was she at the expence of procuring an officer's uniform, in New-York, and why did she there continue garbed in this suit, imposing upon a respectable family, calling herself Maj. B.? Why did she on her return again visit Boston, and once more exhibit an inclination to resort to the Hill, to try her skill at deception, and to witness scenes which she represents so disgusting? Why was she pleased in her new uniform to parade through the most public streets in Boston, and then resort to Fish-street, in search of some of her shipmates? Was all this to "try her skill at deception,"—or was it to discover if possible the young man who procured her a birth on board the Constitution? These I consider as strange proceedings indeed, for one who had been so "thoroughly awakened to a due sense of their shameful career!"

"I am aware (says miss B.) in attempting to warn youth of the fatal effects of an immoral life, I shall expose myself to the censor and ridicule of such as yet may have doubts of my *sincere repentance,* and question the propriety of my admonishing youth to beware of vices which I for three years industriously practised myself!—For the satisfaction of such, I now most solemnly declare, that I do feel that I have been thoroughly awakened to a due sense of my shameful career, while an inhabitant of the Hill—and if a prodigal could ever return penitent to her friends, I so returned to my afflicted parents, sincerely repenting of the evil of my ways;" &c.

I must (notwithstanding the solemn declaration of ELIZA) rank myself among the unbelievers of her "*sincere repentance,*" and do therefore "question the propriety of her admonishing youth!"—admonition would appear much better, and prove more effectual, did it proceed from some one whose life had been more exemplary—but in the present instance, those who had personal knowledge of LOUISA BAKER (so called) while an inhabitant of the Hill, are now unwilling to receive instruction from her.

She has furnished the public, in her second volumn, with a very affecting account of the seduction and untimely death of a youth, who had "unwisely yielded to the false allurements of the detestable harlots of the Hill!"—she has indeed wrought an affecting picture, which I hope may have its intended effect— but she might have subjoined a still more melancholly one, of an affair of a serious nature, and in which she took a very active part—as she has thought proper to disclose every secret of my family, which could tend to wound my feelings, or to injure the reputation of my house, while she has carefully avoided relating any thing of a criminal nature, which should implicate herself—I shall take the liberty so far to follow her example, as to furnish my readers with the particulars of an instance, which, in some measure, will serve to signalize her own depravity:—

Sometime in the fall of 1811, three or four girls that belonged to the Hill (among whom was miss ELIZA) proceeded to take an evening's walk in the Mall, where they fell in company with a young gentleman (who proved to be a Frenchman, and who had been but two days in the country) from whose genteel appearance, and the manner in which they were accosted by him, in broken English, they judged was a person of no mean extract, and consequently an object worthy their attention.—A plan was immediately devised by these arch girls to beguile the unsuspecting stranger—who, finding them very sociable, begged the liberty to attend them home, which the *ladies* (after some little hesitation) assented to. The young gentleman had been but a few moments in their company, when by his conversation, &c. it was evident that the bewitching charms of ELIZA had prevailed, as he was much more partial to her than to the others, consequently they were to perform their part, by doing all in their power to increase his esteem for this arch miss. They represented themselves as waiting maids to their young *mistress*, who were in the habit of attending her in her morning and evening excursions—the most elegant houses encircling the Common, and upon Beacon Street, it was represented to her young gallant, was the property of her father!—and even the State-House, it was hinted, was his, and built for a summer-residence!! The young Frenchman, who, although he understood the English language but imperfectly, understood enough to be led to conclude that the young lady must be a very great fortune [*sic*], as he had no suspicion of being deceived.

He was conducted by the girls to the best apartment of my house, where, the better to conceal the deception, and to make sure of their prize, they behaved indeed like waiting maids, or menial servants, to Eliza—while one was employed in combing and cirling [*sic*] her hair, another held for her a bason of water to wash her hands, and another in the mean time stood with a fan, to perform her office. The young stranger's attachment for the arch jade, was evidently increased, by a view of the great attention paid her—it led him to form a more exalted opinion of her worth!—wealthy and respectable as he was, he concluded himself by no means her equal, and with begging pardon for intrusion, would have withdrawn, had not Eliza, by her arch and insinuating behaviour toward him, given him to understand that his company was not disagreeable to her.

One of Eliza's "waiting maids" here took an opportunity (Eliza having withdrawn expressly for the purpose) to hint to the young gentleman the peculiar situation of her mistress, and why she was thus the inhabitant of so mean a dwelling, when she was an only child, and her father the possessor of so great a number of elegant houses!—Her story to the deluded and astonished Frenchman, was this:—that "the father of her young mistress was by far the richest man in the whole country, that in consequence of his great wealth, and the many accomplishments of his only child, Monsieur JEROME BONAPARTE (brother to the Emperor) when he visited this country a few years since, was induced to offer her his hand, but which offer she (contrary to the advice and consent of her parents) thought proper to decline!⁵ Her father (who was always very partial to the French) highly displeased with her folly and disobedience, immediately ordered her to retire to one of his meanest habitations, and there to remain, attended by only three domestics, until such time as she should find some *Frenchman* of distinction, whom she would consent to marry, and who would enjoy with her, after his decease, his vast estate! This, Monsieur (continues the artful jade) will account for the liberty which was this evening granted you to attend her home—she perceived that you was a Frenchman, and as it is the will of her father that she either marry one of your nation, or forfeit all claim to his immense property, she was not without her hopes that you might be the lucky person, whom providence had conducted thither, to bring about the much wished for conciliation, between her and her father—and if I am not much mistaken this will yet prove to be the case, for she has declared to me, that although she has declined the offer of hundreds of your countrymen, she does not know that she should have any objection to form an union with you, as there is something in your appearance that has secured her affections—it is therefore now in your power to make your fortune, if you wish it— and should it prove agreeable to you, and my young mistress consent to become yours, I should advise you not to delay the marriage a day, nor an hour, lest some unforeseen occurrence should deprive you, of not only the possession of an independent fortune, but of one of the most amiable girls on earth!"

The harmless Eliza now made her appearance, between whom and the gulled stranger, the business was soon settled to her mind—the nuptial ceremonies were that night to be performed—a priest was sent for, and who soon favouring them with his attendance, after swearing the bridegroom to be kind and obliging to his wife, and to indulge her in every reasonable request, pronounced them man and wife!—Here it may be well to mention, that the priest was no other than one of the girls, clad in man's apparel!

The artful Eliza having so far succeeded in her object, to her deluded cully, now suggested the propriety of his immediately removing his effects to her lodgings—a porter was accordingly that very night procured, by whom property of the silly dupe to a very considerable amount, was conveyed and deposited with his pretended wife. Unfortunately for the girls (who intended the next day to have obsconded with the property) the deception was discovered in season the next morning, by the friends of the Frenchman, to frustrate their plan—with the assistance of a constable most of the property was recovered!

Such my readers was ELIZA BOWEN, while an inhabitant of the Hill—the miss who now attempts to convince you of her "sincere repentance!" while she endeavours to stigmatize me, as one of the most abandoned of the human race! If she has indeed reformed, I rejoice for her parents sake—for there was never one, to my knowledge, whose "shameful career" bid more fair to bring them finally to an untimely end.

Whether a sincere penitent, or not, she has indeed effected one object by her publications—she has obtained a husband!—who I am informed is indeed a gentleman of respectability, of the city of New-York, but whose real name is WEBB, and not WEST, as represented by madam W.—Her object in assuming so many fictious [*sic*] names, is undoubtedly so to blind the public, that they may never be enabled to determine who she really is!—nor should I, for her friends sake, have taken so much pains to expose her, had she not so unjustly imputed her "shameful career" altogether to me![6]—I therefore now furnish the public with a true statement of the whole affair—let the candid examine and judge for themselves.

THE SURPRISING
ADVENTURES

of

Almira Paul

ALMIRA PAUL,

A YOUNG WOMAN, who, garbed as a Male, for
of the last preceding years, actually served as a comm
Sailor, on board of English and American armed vessel

THE

SURPRISING ADVENTURES

OF

ALMIRA PAUL,

A YOUNG WOMAN, who, garbed as a Male,
has for three of the last preceding years, actually
served as a common Sailor, on board of English and American armed vessels, without a
discovery of her sex being made.

In 1812 (at 22 years of age) she shipped at Halifax, by the name of JACK BROWN, as *Cook's
Mate*, on board the Revenue Cutter—since
which, she has been in active service on board
a number of English Privateers and Ships
of War &c.—once on board an Algerine
Corsair—and once on board the American Ship Macedonian.—Has been
in many engagements, and was once
severely wounded.

☞ *The said ALMIRA PAUL is now in* BOSTON
—*and in presenting the public with the particulars
of her curious Adventures, they may rest assured
that we present them with* FACTS, *confirmed by
a number of respectable gentlemen, now in this town.*

————— ✻◉✻◉✻◉✻ —————

BOSTON—Printed for N. COVERLY, jr.—1816.

Frontispiece (*opposite*) and title page of *The Surprising Adventures of Almira Paul* (1816),
probably another fiction concocted by Nathaniel Coverly Jr. or his hack. Courtesy, American Antiquarian Society.

THE
SURPRISING ADVENTURES
OF ALMIRA PAUL, &c.

I WAS born in Halifax (N.S.) in the year 1790, of reputable parents.—At the age of 15, I was married to a sea faring man, by the name of WILLIAM PAUL, by whom I had two children, and with whom I lived happily until the year 1811—when he having entered on board the British Privateer Swallow, was unfortunately killed in an engagement between the Swallow and an American Privateer, on the 20th February, 1812. I was now left in very indigent circumstances, with two children, yet too young to earn their bread, and without a friend whose situation would enable them to afford me assistance. I now very sensibly felt the irreparable loss of a kind and indulging husband, who had lost his life in his laudable endeavours to obtain a humble subsistance for his family, as well as in defence of the rights of his country. As he had fallen by the hands of the Americans, I conceived them alone the authors of my misery, and regretted that my sex prevented my placing myself in a situation, in which I might possibly be enabled to revenge his death.

It was not, however, until I found myself destitute of every means to support myself and family, that I formed the determination, of placing myself in a situation, which might not only enable me to gratify myself in this, but which most probably would be productive of something that might serve to alleviate my pressing wants. Having committed my children to the charge of my mother, for a few months, I, unknown to any of my friends, garbed myself in a suit of my late husband's cloathes, and thus disguised, shipped myself as Cook's Mate, on board his majesty's cutter Dolphin!—so well did I act the *man*, that I am confident no one on board had any suspicion of my being a *woman*—the only question asked me, was, whether I had ever been to sea—to which I answered in the negative;—to guard myself well against every risk of exposure, I procured a pair of sementers (a close garment) which I wore continually—I had too the precaution to keep constantly with me a suit of my own apparel, in case by accident a discovery should be made.

In June, 1812, the Dolphin put to sea, when I entered upon the duties of my birth, which my readers may suppose that I was not a stranger to, indeed I was very soon acknowledged to be an excellent cook—as I was not obliged to stand my watch at night, and in the day time was only at the command of the chief cook, I should have passed my time as merrily as any of my shipmates, had I not for the first two weeks suffered much from sea-sickness, so peculiar to persons unaccustomed to the water—but this at length subsiding, I soon found that I gained much more strength, and a better appetite, than what I before possessed—that I could eat and drink my allowance with as good stomach as any on board.

We had excellent officers, a good ship and pleasant weather—and not a complaint was uttered on any other account than our not being enabled to meet with the "*cowardly Yankees!*"—for such indeed were they termed by all on board. On the 19th August, being in lat. 41° 42, we for the first time had the satisfaction to descry a yankee frigate, with one of his majesty's frigates in chase—as we had been led to believe that the raw and unexperienced yankees, with a few rotten frigates, would never dare risk an engagement with any of our ships, of equal force, we considered the capture of the American frigate as certain—his majesty's ship (which proved to be the Gurrierre) passed within a short distance of us, and in signification of their intention to *treat* the yankees, as they passed us they hoisted a keg of molasses and water, which the yankees term switchel, and of which they appear extremely fond. We soon had the satisfaction to observe the Gurriere overhaul her antagonist (which proved to be the Constitution) almost within gun-shot—but what was our chagrin and disappointment in beholding at this moment his majesty's frigate tacking, and the Yankee in turn pursuing!—"There must be some mistake (exclaimed our captain, biting his lips) for surely a British frigate would never run from one of Jonathan's fir frigates, with strips of striped bunting at her masthead!" The Constitution bore down upon the Guerriere, as if with an intention to bring her immediately to action, as soon as she got within gunshot, she received the broadside of the Guerriere—at about 6 P. M. both ships being within half pistol-shot, a desperate engagement commenced on both sides—such a tremendous cannonade was kept up for the space of 10 or 15 minutes, as our oldest seamen observed that they had never before witnessed!—we were all eye witnesses of the engagement, our officers standing each with his spy-glass, in anxious expectation to see the yankee colours soon come down—but, in less than 15 minutes, they had the mortification to see the Guerrier's mizen-mast go by the board, and in 12 or 14 minutes after her mainmast and foremast, carrying with them every spar except the bowsprit!—the Constitution now ceased firing, and having succeeded in getting along side of the Guerriere, soon compelled her to surrender!—O, it was indeed a mortifying sight to all on board of us, to see the complete destruction of one of his majesty's best frigates, in half an hour—and that too by the Yankees, of whose naval abilities and courage, we had been led to form the most contemptible opinion!—As the Constitution appeared but little injured, and might soon be put in a sailing trim, we conceived it most prudent to sheer off, lest we should receive similar treatment from her—from this moment I began to harbour a more exalted opinion of the Yankees, and to despair of very soon meeting with an opportunity to revenge the death of my husband!

It was now nearly six weeks since I entered on board the cutter, when, being off Georgia Islands, we fell in with one of his majesty's ships of war, which having manned many prizes and being in want of men, myself and 12 others were put on board—a short time after we captured the American privateer Dart, and three days after fell in with and engaged for 15 minutes the French frigate Fair Play—the bullets whistled about my ears, but I think I was much less terrifyed than what many *women* would have been in my situation—we had 5 men killed in the engagement, among whom was our boatswain; when he fell, I was standing by his side, and perceiving that he was mortally wounded, I unperceived slipped my hand into his pocket and took his Call, which I deposited in my chest and have now in my possession—we captured the French frigate after a short but severe engagement, when I with a number more of our crew were put on board of her, with orders to conduct her to Barbadoes.[1]

At Barbadoes, we were ordered on board his majesty's sloop of war Sea Horse, which in 8 days proceeded on a cruize.—On board this vessel I served in my old capacity as cook's mate, but soon found that the chief cook (who had the principal controul of me) was of quite a different disposition from others whom I had served in that capacity—every thing that was vile, malicious and inhuman, appeared as if concentred in this man: whose greatest delight appeared to be in cuffing and unmercifully beating me for the slightest offence, and frequently for no offence at all!—my readers must naturally conclude that to be at the mercy of such a ruffian, a *woman* (and one who was a *mother* too) must be placed in a very unpleasant situation! As he continued to use me with great severity, I conceived him my greatest enemy, and no longer felt a disposition to retaliate upon the Americans, for the distress which they had caused me in depriving me of my husband—his fate was the fate of war, he voluntarily entered to contend and dispute rights with a foreign enemy, by whom, in fair and equal combat, he was slain—my case was materially different—patriotism had induced me (a female) to volunteer my services in the cause of my country; I entered as a youth unaccustomed to hardship, and a stranger to a sea faring life—and although they had no knowledge or suspicion of my being a female, yet, as I had behaved myself well, and they could not impeach me with cowardice in time of action, I conceived that

I had just claim to, and could not but reasonably expect good treatment from my own countrymen!—but such was not the case, the cook's unmanly behaviour toward me, formed an exception, and which at length drove me to the awful determination of seeking revenge, even at the expence of his life!—an opportunity soon offered—as I one evening saw him stooping over the ship's side, to wash a bucket, I could not let pass so good a chance to carry my long premeditated plan into effect—I gave him a gentle kick, and overboard sent master cook with his bucket—he bellowed like a boatswain—and contrary to my expectation, and almost my wish, with the assistance of some of my shipmates, he was resqued from his perilous situation, where he had been nearly 15 minutes exposed to the sharks! As soon as he reached the deck, he alledged that he was indebted to some damn'd scoundrel for his evening's bathe, who had taken the liberty to kick him overboard! I feigned as much surprize as any one, and probably should never have been suspected, had not the boatswain, unfortunately for me, witnessed the whole transaction—he charged me with the fact, which I was soon compelled to acknowledge—information was lodged with the officers, who sentenced me to be flogged at the gangway!—Never could a poor female feel worse than I did at this moment!—to be whipped and lashed like a fellon (although inconceivably shocking) was not the most I had to dread!—in striping [*sic*] my back naked, I certainly should be exposed, and thereby, should the whipping then be inflicted, I should receive double punishment!—but, providentially, things turned out much better than what I was at first apprehensive of—I was only stripped to my shirt, and wearing always a tight waistcoat around my body next to my skin, the lash made a much less impression than what it would have done had it been applied to my naked back—indeed, pleased to think that I was at this critical moment enabled to conceal my sex, I bore the punishment with all the fortitude of a heroine.

Although I at the time conceived this as an unhappy circumstance, yet I had escaped with no other injury than that caused by a few stripes—but, a far more serious accident attended me a few days after.—It was now almost six months since I first commenced my sea-faring life, during which time I had been but a few days on shore, having been almost constantly on ship-board, I became habituated to the sea—pleased to think to what length a female might carry her adventures, what hardships she could endure and what dangers brave, and all without betraying her sex! I frequently amused myself in my dexterous feats aloft, by walking upon the yards, and leaping from one piece of rigging to another!—it was in one of those presumptious performances that my feet slipped, and I was precipitated from the main yard to the deck!—by this dreadful fall, my skull was fractured, and my face mangled in a shocking manner—I was deprived of all sense, and unconsciously conveyed below—the surgeon, who at first pronounced my wounds mortal, afterward suggested that by trepaning, my life might possibly be saved—I accordingly underwent the painful operation!—for seven weeks I was confined to my birth, at times delirious!

As soon as I had so far recovered as to be able to walk the deck, I returned to my duty—but in consequence of the severe wound which I had received, my head remained for a long while so disordered, and my senses so effected, that from this period I was called "Ratling Jack" by all on board—having assumed the name of Jack Brown, which they supposed my real name. My readers will doubtless be anxious to learn, by what means I was enabled to conceal my sex from the surgeon, and others, during my extreme illness—I cannot impute it to any thing but the close garments which I constantly wore under my shirt, to prevent such a discovery, and the little trouble which they gave themselves to examine more critically, to see if I had not received wounds or bruizes upon other parts of my body—as soon as I recovered my senses, it was unnecessary, for being sensible of my situation, I assured the surgeon, &c. that my head alone was injured.

During our cruize we fell in with the American frigate President, Com. Rogers, which pouring a broadside into us, killed 2 of our crew and wounded 3, cut our sails and rigging, and otherwise crippled us very much; but by our superior sailing, we fortunately escaped.[2] Our commander now found it necessary to enter the port of St. John's to repair damages, as our ship was almost in a sinking condition.

At St. John's we found the English privateer schooner Flora, ready for sea, but was detained on account of the difficulty of procuring her compliment of men. Our captain proposed that 5 of us should enter on board—observing that if we went voluntarily, we would be entitled to a bounty and prize money, but compulsion would debar us from the recovery of either. As the reader may suppose, I did not fail to embrace this opportunity to free myself from the tyrannical cook—myself and four others stepped out, and signified our willingness to go on board the Privateer.

I entered as an ordinary seaman, and for the first time exchanged the dish-clout for the swab—no person perhaps in my situation could have made a greater proficiency in seamanship, than what I had done for so short a period—solicitous to obtain a complete knowledge of a seaman's duty, and to convince the world that the capacities of *women* were equal to that of the *men*, there was not a piece of rigging on board a ship, but what I could name, and no duty but what I could perform.[3]

The Flora proceeded on a cruize up the Mediterranean—on the 10th October, then in sight of Gibaraltar, we espyed a large sail bearing down upon us, which we supposed an American privateer of the first class—we hoisted American colours, but finding the enemy still bearing down upon us under a press of sail, to facilitate our escape, we threw overboard a part of our shot, all our spare spars, and cleared every thing off deck, as well as from below, to lighten as much as possible—the enemy notwithstanding still gained fast upon us, and at half past 3 P. M. being within pistol shot, commenced a brisk and well directed fire upon the schooner, which cut our sails and rigging very much—we were still under American colours, and as our antagonist had shown none, we yet mistook her for an American, who regarded our colours only as a stratagem made use of by us to escape from them;—At four P. M. the enemy's bowsprit ran athwart of us, which affording them an opportunity to board, although we had some moments previous hauled down our colours, as a token of submission—they boarded us with the fierceness of lions, and with their swords, pistols, dirks, boarding pikes, &c. attacked our whole crew with unprecedented outrage![4]—we now for the first time discovered that our antagonist was not an American, but an Algerine brig of 18 guns!—it was in vain however that we attempted to signify to them that we were English, with whom they were at peace; they, pointing to the American flag which lay on our deck, continued to maim and beat us—scarcely one of our crew escaped being wounded—I received a severe cut from a sabre across my left arm, which penetrated to the bone. The barbarians finding that we were no longer in a situation to resist, put us all in irons and confined us below, and with their prize proceeded for port. In five days we were off Algiers, where we were very fortunately visited by the English consul, who demanded and obtained our liberty, as his Britannic majesty's subjects.

I here obtained my discharge from the Privateer, in consequence of the severe wound which I had received, and having remained on shore until it became in some measure healed, I took passage for Cadiz, where I shipped on board an English merchantman, bound to Rottordam, where we arrived in safety after a long and tempestuous passage—from Rotterdam the ship a few weeks after proceeded for Bristol (Eng.) and from thence to Portsmouth, where all hands were discharged. As my wages amounted to considerable, like a real bred tar, I now felt a disposition to enjoy myself for a short time, at least, on shore. I took board with a number of my shipmates at a house of their acquaintance, a widow whose husband lost his life in the famous battle of Trafalgar—she was about 39 years of age, of a pleasing disposition, and well calculated to please and to obtain her share of boarders, who were principally sea faring people—to convince myself that this woman had no suspicion of my being one of her sex, I, after a short acquaintance, proposed marriage to her, which she conditionally acceded to, and after another cruize we were to be united as husband and wife! This was not the only instance which served to convince me, that the Portsmouth females were not suspicious of my sex—I did not fail to make my evening excursions with my shipmates, to see the pretty girls, with whom RATLING JACK was as great a favorite as any one.

After a six weeks recreation at Portsmouth, I obtained a birth on board the Ship Mary-Ann, bound to Jamaica, where not meeting with a market, we proceeded for Martinique, and from thence to Liverpool, where I received my discharge. As my wages again replenished my pockets, like every generous hearted tar, I was resolved now to remain in port while there was a shot in the locker. I found Liverpool a fine place for sport, abounding with Sailor's Landlords, Landladies and Sweethearts, who profess peculiar friendship for them while their money lasts, but there is neither love nor pity for poor JACK after that!—it does not become me however to censor the former, for their prodigality, for I had not been in port three days before I found myself more encumbered with sweethearts, than loose change!—by them I was frequently pronounced a *man* of uncommon generosity, because I would permit them to pick my pockets, without soliciting any favours within their power to bestow![5]

After I had spent nearly two months in Liverpool (in which time I had foolishly squandered away a great part of my wages) I began to harbour serious thoughts of returning home to my children and friends, from whom I had been more than 18 months absent. As there was no vessel in port bound directly for Halifax, I took passage on board one which was to touch at Demarara, and from thence proceed immediately for New-York, where (peace having been happily concluded between Great Britain and America) I thought it very probable that I might obtain an immediate passage for Halifax. We safely arrived at Demarara, but being there detained much longer than was expected, I was unfortunately taken ill with the fever peculiar to that unhealthy climate—I was conveyed to the hospital, and the vessel procceeded without me—as my illness increased, I was not without my apprehensions that I should now no longer be enabled to conceal my sex—but, fortunately for me, a woman of colour was my nurse, to whom I took an opportunity to suggest, that labouring under a natural infirmity, my situation required that I should constantly wear a close garment, which it would be improper for her or any other person to divest me of, and which it was my sincere wish might not be removed—this injunction was strictly adhered to by the nurse, whose business alone it was to change my linen, make my bed and to administer the medicine prescribed by the visiting physician. I was dangerously indisposed for several weeks, and in consequence of the weak and emaciated state to which the fever had reduced me, it was two months before I recovered strength to enable me to quit the unhealthy climate.

As my sickness had cost me nearly all that I possessed, and as I was determined not to return pennyless to my friends, I once more had recourse to the sea to replenish my pockets. I shipped on board an English brig, bound to the Havannah, and from thence returned to Liverpool, where I was happy to meet with many of my old female acquaintance, who welcomed "JACK's return" with cheerful hearts—but as I was determined that they should not filch JACK of his hard earnings as they had done, they probably did not think me half so much of a *man* as before!—in vain these arch girls strove, by their expressions of *love* and regard for me, to decoy me into their favorite ports; where they might be the better enabled to induce or *compel* me to part with a few guineas—No, rattle-headed as I was, I had seen too much of the world thus to be made a prize of in port.

I remained on shore but two weeks, when I entered on board an English brig bound to the Straits—in consequence of a very long passage, and the bad weather which we experienced, the brig had sustained so much injury when we arrived at Gibaraltar, that she was there condemned, and her crew paid off and discharged. There being no immediate opportunity to return to Europe, I was again compelled to remain a while on shore, although much against my inclination. With my shipmates I spent my time very agreeably, but always continued garbed in my pea-jacket and trousers, and used the utmost precaution that my sex should not be discovered. As we were one day taking a sail in a small pleasure boat, a few miles without the harbour, we saw what we supposed an English brig, under easy sail, about five miles to leeward—as we had all become heart-sick of Gibraltar, this we thought might present us with an opportunity to return home—we steered immediately for the brig, and when within hail, enquired where from, where bound, &c. and in plain English, was informed by those on board that they were bound on a cruize, and were in want of hands.—As we were all extremely anxious to quit Gibraltar, after a few moments consultation, we agreed to go on board and offer our services, without any further enquiry. As soon as I reached the deck, I recognized in the principal part of the crew, that savage appearance peculiar to the natives of the Barbary coast—they indeed proved to be Algerines, cruizing for Americans—those on board who could speak English, informed us that they were in want of hands, and strongly urged us to enter—as they were in want of a steward, I accepted of that birth, as did the remainder of my shipmates of births that were offered them.

Three days from that of our first entering on board, the brig chased an American privateer ashore near the Rock, where she was abandoned by her crew—the Algerines finding that she could not easily be got off, after stripping her of almost every article that was moveable, set fire to her. Five days after we were fallen in with by some ships of the American squadron, commanded by Com. Decatur, destined against Algiers.[6] As soon as the barbarians descryed the yankee stripes, they beat to quarters, and swore that they would defend the brig while a shot remained, although one of the enemy's ships was apparently of three times their size. The Macedonian bore down upon us, while the silly barbarians lay to, making preparations for their reception—a few shots were exchanged, when a broadside from the Macedonian compelled her antagonist to yield.

The Americans took possession of their prize and made prisoners of her crew, but fortunately for me (having represented my case fairly to the officers) I was set at liberty, and was permitted to enter on board the Macedonian. Of two evils, it may be truly said I was choosing the least—had I not declared myself by birth an Englishman, and voluntarily entered into the American service, I should have been retained as a prisoner of war, and as such, my sex might have been exposed. Yet, although I was now with a people who spoke the same language, and whose manners and customs were familiar to me, my new situation was not agreeable— although I had been greatly mistaken as to the courage, and naval skill and abilities of the yankees, yet I could not even regard them as friends in peace—the wound inflicted by the death of my husband, was not yet healed—beside this, it was certain that if I continued in their service, it would be attended with many inconveniences to myself, it would prevent my immediate return to my family and friends, which I had resolved to do the first opportunity that should present— hence I formed the determination to quit the yankee service, the first chance—an opportunity soon offered—being sent with several others of the ship's crew to water, I improved my liberty, and succeeded in getting on board an American Fishing Schooner, bound to Baltimore, to which place I agreed to work my passage, and where we safely arrived after a passage of 45 days.

I now for the first time, found myself safe on yankee ground, although as poor as a church-mouse—I was extremely anxious to see my children and friends, and could have obtained a passage to Halifax, but the thoughts of returning pennyless to a place, where from poverty and want, I had suffered so much, deterred me. The work which I was enabled to do on board vessels, the wharves, &c. procured me a sum sufficient to defray the expence of board—but, I had not been thus three weeks employed, when I was informed that the return of the American Squadron, from the Mediteranean, was daily expected. As it was uncertain what port they would enter, I was not now without my apprehensions that I should be discovered and recognized by some of the crew of the Macedonian, and apprehended as a deserter!—to avoid this, I was at length induced once more to reassume my female dress—thus, after having been three years garbed as a male, the greater part of which I had been at sea, performing the duty of a seaman, and having never once betrayed my sex, prudence now dictated that I should exchange the jacket and trousers, for the gown and petticoat, for a short time at least.[7]

But, in my true character, how was I now to procure a humble subsistance among strangers?—although perfectly acquainted with and accustomed to house work, yet the three years that I had been employed in quite a different capacity, had rendered me less able and less disposed to perform work better adapted to more delicate hands. As for the three years I had been almost wholly confined to the company of Sailors, both at sea and on shore (although I solemnly protest that not one of them had any knowledge of my being a female) I had become so habituated to their customs and manners, that I must indeed acknowledge, I even yet felt a disposition to associate with them. Thus disposed, and a willing inhabitant of a neighbourhood (Fells-Point) where prostitution bears unlimited sway, it would be absurd for me to impute the first cause of my immoral life, to fatal *seduction,* as many probably with less propriety have done—no! of virtue, RATLING JACK, made a voluntary sacrifice! I took board at a house of ill-fame on Fells-Point (Baltimore) where I rather invited than objected to the company of such as are in the habit of spending their cash, much easier than what they earn it.

I continued in Baltimore but six weeks—unaccustomed to continue long in one place, I took passage on board a small schooner for New-York—where I obtained board for a few weeks at a house situated at Powles Hook—it may perhaps be almost unnecessary to inform the reader, that I here too sought to obtain my bread, by other means than that of honest industry. Although I had thus prefered a life indeed the most wretched, and fondly sought the company of those as abandoned as myself—yet, permit me to say, I was not without my sober moments—shameful as was my career, I could not forget that I was the mother of two innocent children, and that as a parent, I ought rather by example to teach them the importance of cherishing virtue in their youthful days.

I continued in New-York nearly five weeks, when I formed the determination that I would (notwithstanding my impoverished situation) return to my friends, from whom I had now been more than three years absent—but finding that I could not obtain an immediate passage from New York to Halifax, I was advised to visit Boston, as a place from which a passage might most likely be obtained. I accordingly obtained a passage for Newport (R. I.) and from thence was conveyed to Boston in the mail stage.

But here I was not more fortunate to find a vessel bound directly to Halifax; I concluded however to remain in Boston, until an opportunity should present—I obtained a place to do housework for a few weeks, in Fish Street; where I soon attracted the notice of those who boast of a wife in every port—by them I was persuaded to become an inhabitant of West Boston Hill, where (as the reader will naturally conclude) no great persuasion was necessary to render me a distinguished character of the sisterhood—here, like almost every other female in a similar situation, I involved myself, in consequence of the extravagant price charged me by my landlord for board—I was unable to satisfy his demand against me, and he in consequence a few days since committed me to jail—where I at present remain.

BOSTON GOAL, July 16, 1816.[8]

A BRIEF ACCOUNT

of the

Origin and Progress
of
The Boston Female Society for
Missionary Purposes

A BRIEF ACCOUNT OF THE

ORIGIN AND PROGRESS

OF

The Boston Female Society for Missionary Purposes.

WITH

EXTRACTS FROM THE REPORTS OF THE SOCIETY,

IN MAY, 1817 AND 1818,

AND

EXTRACTS FROM THE REPORTS OF THEIR MISSIONARIES,

REV. JAMES DAVIS,

AND

REV. DUDLEY D. ROSSETER.

Go into all the world, and preach the gospel to every creature....*Jesus,.*

BOSTON :

PRINTED BY LINCOLN & EDMANDS,

No. 53 Cornhill.

[1818]

Title page of *A Brief Account of the Origin and Progress of the Boston Female Society for Missionary Purposes* (1818). Courtesy, American Antiquarian Society.

BRIEF ACCOUNT, &c.

"The Boston Female Society for Missionary Purposes," was constituted Oct. 9, 1800. Fourteen ladies, part of the Baptist and part of the Congregational denominations, composed the Society. The two first years after its commencement, its little funds were devoted to the aid of the "Massachusetts Congregational Missionary Society." After this, a Baptist Missionary Society being formed, it was agreed to appropriate the subscriptions of each member to her own denomination; and that both should meet together for prayer, and to conduct their usual business. The meetings to be holden the first Monday in every month.

Different sums have been collected from year to year, and applied to various missionary purposes as follows, viz.

The purchase of Bibles, Testaments, and other religious books, for distribution by missionaries in destitute places; to home and foreign missions of both denominations; to the translation of the scriptures into the oriental languages, and to the support of a mission in this town.

The Society by its constitution is at liberty to make such appropriations of its funds, as the openings of Providence suggest to be duty; whether in aid of foreign or domestic missions. It has increased to nearly 200 members.[1] Donations have been received from individuals and sister societies to the amount of $300, including which, $3825,39 have been raised by the Society since its formation, viz. 2219,69 by the Baptist, and 1505,70 by the Congregational branch, and $100 by voluntar [sic] contributions of both.

There are, it is presumed, many females in this place who would rejoice to contribute to the support of this Institution, if they knew such an one existed. As it will now be more generally known, it is hoped that persons of both denominations will come forward and aid the Society either by subscription or donations, which will be appropriated agreeably to the constitution. Though a large proportion of the present members, are "women professing godliness," others have united with them in promoting the best interests of their fellow beings; and some have received a blessing to their own souls while engaged for the good of others.

The following is extracted from the Report of the Secretary, in May, 1817.

"During the past season the attention of the Society has been particularly turned to the state of *our own town*. The multiplied exertions in favour of more distant objects have at length led us to look *at home,* (where charity is usually said to begin.) Viewing the destitute situation of a certain class of inhabitants, whose poverty forbids their appearing decent at public worship; and of others who have abandoned themselves to every species of vice, and are totally disinclined to go where the gospel is dispensed; and especially considering how few, comparatively, can be accommodated in our houses of worship, free of expense; we have thought it our duty to try the practicability of a new plan; and have accordingly appropriated the whole income of the year, which closes this day, to the support of two missionaries (for a few months, as an experiment) to visit and labour with the above description of people. May the Lord raise up and eminently qualify men for this important undertaking. . . . We therefore cherish the animating hope that some real good will result from this attempt, and that habitations which now echo with profanity and discord, will ere long resound with the mild accents of the gospel, and the voice of prayer and praise will be heard.

Should *only one immortal being* reap essential advantage from these labors, it will be an ample reward. But on the contrary, should they all, with one consent, put these things from them, and judge themselves unworthy of eternal life; we may conscientiously turn to some other object: and the ministers of Jesus may shake off the dust of their feet for a testimony against them.

It will be recollected by those who were present at our last meeting, that another important subject was brought forward. The question had been agitated—Should any of those poor unhappy females, who have wandered into the paths of vice and folly, and forfeited their good name and reputation, be disposed by means of missionary labors to reform and become correct in their lives,—*what is to become of them?* respectable persons would feel it unsafe to take them into their families; and their connections (if they have any) probably would have too little confidence in their reformation to receive them to their homes. To remain where they are, would expose them not only to sufferings, but to a liability of relapsing into sin. What then can be done? It was suggested, that if proper exertions should be made, an Asylum might be provided, to which those pitiable objects might resort, where they should be suitably employed, and the proceeds of their labour go to their support. Here they might be favoured with religious instruction and wholesome advice, until proof be given that their repentance is sincere. They might then be able to obtain an honest and reputable living for themselves. It was resolved that a close box, with an aperture in the lid, be kept in the Society for the purpose of receiving voluntary contributions for this object, should the attempt be made. This is indeed a small beginning, but the Lord is able to provide a sufficiency. The society by no means proposes to take a work of such magnitude into its own hands; but most sincerely and ardently recommends it to the consideration and patronage of the benevolent and virtuous; and would cheerfully help as far as consistent. Without boasting, it may be asserted, that many thousands of dollars have been raised in this town to spread the gospel in regions not favoured with its heavenly influence; we may therefore conclude that the friends of religion and virtue in other places would cheerfully contribute to an undertaking like this; particularly when it is considered, that but a small proportion of these unhappy creatures are natives of this place. They are collected from almost all parts of the country, and some even from foreign climes. The calamity is a *public* calamity; the cause of virtue is a *public cause,* and if good is done it will be felt by the community. There are several Institutions of this kind in Europe, which have proved a blessing to many. To check the torrent of vice, which is flowing with increasing impetuosity, and restore the wanderer to her father's house, must be truly gratifying to the benevolent mind. . . .

In answer to a Circular to similar societies, proposing a correspondence by letter and concert in prayer; communications have been received from 97 societies; and from information otherwise received, we find that many more have united in the prayer meeting. Thus, while the female of the metropolis rejoices to retire from her usual avocations, her sisters in the country also feel it their privilege on THE FIRST MONDAY IN THE MONTH, (a day favoured of the Lord;) to assemble with the thousands of Israel, and pour out their united supplications before the mercy seat."

Boston, May 5, 1817

Extracts from the Report, May, 1818.

"Through the good hand of our God upon us," we have been preserved another year.

When our Report was made the last May, we were in a state of suspense, waiting to hear from Missionaries, to whom application had been made to engage in the service of the Society. On the 16th of June Mr. Davis arrived in town, and commenced his labours the same week; and in October Mr. Rosseter also came. They both have laboured with little interruption to this time. . . .

Among the most promising projects of the mission is the establishment of religious meetings, and a school in a neighborhood of coloured people at the north part of the town. There ignorance and vice reigned, and their dread retinue of evils has closely followed them. Since these exertions, there has been a manifest alteration for the better, and one woman has been hopefully converted. It should be remembered that this unfortunate people were introduced into our country by the cruel hand of avarice and barbarity; and if there be a race of human beings, which have a right to *demand* our charity, next to the descendants of Abraham, these must have a claim. . . .[2]

Boston, May 4, 1818.

The following is extracted from reports of Mr. Davis, made to the Society at different times.

Whosoever shall convert a sinner from the error of his ways shall save a soul from death, and hide a multitude of sins.—James v. 20.

He that winneth souls is wise.—Prov. xi. 30.

And they that be wise shall shine as the brightness of the firmament, and they that turn many to righteousness, as the stars forever and ever.—Daniel xii. 3.

"Commenced my labours in the service of the Society, June 19, 1817. I have now been 3 months engaged in the work, and have preached in six different sections of the town, (a considerable part of the period, eight and nine times a week.) Have attended a number of prayer-meetings; visited between three and four hundred families; distributed several hundred religious tracts, and several dozens of Bibles. Numbers have with tears in their eyes, expressed a great sense of gratitude, in view of the attention paid to them, and *some,* apparently from the fulness of their hearts, after conversation and prayer, have said, "God bless you," &c.—In South-ark street, West Boston, the people are astonishingly destitute of the means of religious instruction, and appear not to have the fear of God before their eyes. Just in that vicinity, there are more than a thousand people who do not attend public worship, who are evidently hastening on with amazing rapidity the broad road to ruin. With propriety it may be said, *there* is the place where *Satan's seat is. There* awful impieties prevail; and all conceivable abominations are practised; *there* the depravity of the human heart is acted out; and from this sink of sin, the seeds of corruption are conveyed into every part of the town. Five and twenty or thirty shops are opened on Lord's days from morning to evening, and ardent spirits are retailed without restraint, while hundreds are intoxicated, and spend the holy sabbath in frolicking and gambling, in fighting and blaspheming; and many in scenes of iniquity and debauchery too dreadful to be named. The street is filled during the day with old and young of all complexions, numbers drunken and sleeping by its sides and corners; and awful noises and confusions are witnessed. Lord's-day evening is the period when greater numbers collect than at any other season of the week; *hundreds* of *boys* from all parts of the town, on this evening repair thither, where their ears are assailed with the dialect of the dark world; while all the oaths are uttered, which the powers of the mind, long exercised in the service of the adversary, and excited to action by a totally depraved heart, could possibly invent. Here these lads enter a school, calculated to give them an entire disrelish for all moral and religious restraint; and to cause them wholly to dis-regard parental authority and instruction:—A school pre-eminently calculated to erase from their minds all thoughts of God, and their accountability—a school, entirely suited to train them for the commission of all conceivable crimes, to be a disgrace to their family connections, to be pests in society, and subjects for a *world of despair.* Here, week after week, whole nights are spent in drinking and carous-ing; and as the morning light begins to appear, when others arise from their beds, these close their doors. Multitudes, evidently in different professions and employ-ments, clad in a manner indicative of affluence and high life, as soon as the sable curtains of the evening are drawn around them, pass and repass from one end of the street to the other; and beyond all doubt contribute much in different ways to the support and encouragement of the abandoned and the prostitute. Here in one compact section of the town, it is confidently affirmed and fully believed, there are *three hundred* females wholly devoid of shame and modesty. Their manner of life leads to the destruction of constitution and health. Wretchedness and misery ensue; disease and sickness bring great numbers to the alms-house. Multitudes of coloured people, by these examples, are influenced to habits of indolence. Hun-dreds are dispersed into different parts of the town, and are watching every opportunity to steal. Various articles of provisions are brought and sold here for a trifle. These depraved creatures, as soon as the darkness of the evening screens them from view, are thrusting themselves into entries and other places, and pilfering clothes of different kinds, which they pawn or sell. Children are continually begging from house to house, and are in this way trained up in habits of idleness: and while they collect provisions to support their parents and others, the examples they witness are calculated to confirm them in iniquity, and effect their everlasting ruin. Great numbers of coloured people, when the inclement season of the year comes on, are brought to circumstances of extreme suffering, being wholly destitute of food and clothes. Wretchedness, in all its forms, is experienced. Four or five of them have been seen lying on one floor without any bed, or articles of bed clothes: sick, and incapable of helping themselves; affecting spectacles of human woe!—they must be carried to the alms house, or die. It has been ascertained that such characters are to be found in many other streets. It is probable there are at least two thousand of them scattered over the town.

Being urged to attempt instrumentally to effect a reformation, or to remedy the evil, I appointed a religious meeting a little to the eastward of this street. Individuals were prevailed on to attend: the week after, I appointed to attend religious exercises a little to the south-west of this street; the number present was considerably increased, some were affected. These meetings have been continued, and evidently blest to the benefit of some precious and immortal souls.— In consequence of a death which took place in a house of ill fame, I was requested to call and attend prayer. The house was occupied by the worst of characters. The meeting was considerably numerous and very solemn. A woman, past the meridian of life, residing under the same roof, used profane language and uttered blasphemies in a distant part of the house during the season of worship; and a number of times afterwards disturbed the meetings by similar enormities; but was eventually constrained to request a meeting in her own room. A decent family, though in low circumstances, moved into this house, being ignorant of the character of its occupants. The eldest daughter, a girl about fourteen or fifteen years of age, who appeared discreet, was in a few days enticed and drawn away by the vilest of the vile; she soon became awfully profane in her language, and immodest in her conduct; she left the family of which she was a member, cast off all restraint, refused submission to her parents, and appeared to be on the brink of ruin. Being present in the time of solemn religious worship, she was seen to manifest a great degree of depravity, and a determination to rise above all fear of God, and the consequences of her daring impiety. She was excessive in her laughter and trifling; she was repeatedly conversed with and reproved. Her situation was represented to her mother, who was constrained to weep over her. Expostulations were reiterated, and means used abundantly to reclaim her. It appears the snare is broken, and the young immortal is escaped. Think, O think, ye affectionate mothers, how would your hearts be wrung with anguish, and your eyes run down with tears, in view of your amiable daughters, the objects of your tenderest solicitude, ensnared by the wiles of the ungodly, and falling victims to the vile lusts of brutes in human form. I have visited from house to house; in a variety of instances have been requested to pray with and for them; numbers, with tears, have related the manner in which they have lived, and expressed their determination to reform, and a strong desire to get away from that place. Some of those persons were brought there by fraud and intrigue, contrary to their inclinations, and wholly ignorant of the wiles which prevailed; concerning whom I had reason to believe they would leave the Hill, and reform, if any place could be provided for their accommodation, and means for their assistance."

From the encouragement that has been given by a number of respectable persons, that such a place would be provided, if sufficient evidence of their sincerity should be obtained; they have been informed of the benevolent design, and appear anxious for its accomplishment.

At another time Mr. Davis states:—

"A desire was expressed that religious meetings should be attended on Lord's-days. A large hall was therefore opened for this purpose; between two and three hundred crowded in, many were standing round the doors, all were attentive, some were affected: wildness, wonder, and surprise, were depicted in the countenances of many, and but very few appeared to have any idea of being seated. In the evening, religious exercises were attended in a chamber on account of a woman who was sick. She appeared to be much impressed through the week in view of her guilt and danger, and to have alarming apprehensions of future wrath; she frequently called upon me to pray with her, and inquired what she should do to be saved. Next Lord's day, religious exercises were attended again in the hall, and at evening, in the chamber just referred to. The house was occupied by a Mr. ——. A number of females came in, and some coloured men; but there was none on whom I could greatly depend for assistance or protection, in case of difficulty. Mr. —— and his wife came in and took their seats. About the middle of the exercises, Mr.—— left the room; his wife began in strains of awful profanity; and, uttering dreadful blasphemies and imprecations, went out and declared with an oath, if I came up the stairs again, she would break my neckt [*sic*]. At the close of the meeting she came to the woman confined to her bed, called her hard names, addressing her in language expressive of the greatest cruelty, and with threats and oaths, ordered her to leave the house and be gone. Next Lord's day morning, one week from this time, she was taken suddenly in the most distressing manner, and on Tuesday she died. God declares that he is angry with the wicked every day; that they shall not live out half their days. Truly it is a fearful thing for a sinner to fall into the hands of the living God.

After meetings had been attended a number of Sabbaths in the hall, religious exercises were appointed on the *evening* of the Lord's day: an unusual number collected. One evening a young man (it was said from the navy-yard in Charlestown) entered the hall with his hat on, spoke audibly, and manifested a determination to disturb the meeting. He was particularly addressed and cautioned. Before the week terminated, he was dead. Next Lord's day evening, in the same place, a sailor came among the assembly and made disturbance; within four or five days, he was called into the eternal world. Well may we consider the power of the Lord; his daring, implacable foes, should tremble. He says, a fire is kindled in mine anger, which shall burn to the lowest hell. . . .

It has been intimated to those unfortunate and abandoned females, that some place would be provided for them. Some of them are frequently inquiring *when* they shall have assistance to get away from the Hill? They express a great desire to leave the place. One woman remarks, that at the death of her husband, she was left in destitute circumstances, with a number of helpless children. She says she has conducted in such a manner, that the idea of seeing her family connections would be intolerable. Expresses much regret that she cannot get away. She says she has been all over town to try to get a place, but no one will take her in. Observed, she could not bear the thoughts of her children being reproached in view of their mother's continuing to be a prostitute. She manifested great earnestness to obtain a Bible. After saying every thing to her I could, for her present and eternal good, and obtaining promises relative to the manner in which she would improve this Holy Book; I put the sacred Volume into her hands.

As I was walking one day, I met a coloured man with his violin. I asked him, if he had not better lay aside that, and attend to the concerns of his soul? He replied, 'this is the way I have to get my living.' I urged the importance of an interest in Christ, of being prepared to die: said he, 'I have been encouraged for many years in my employ, as much by ministers as any class of people. They have sent their children to dancing schools and balls, and have themselves attended.' He appeared shielded against conviction, and disposed to justify himself on the ground of the countenance he had received from those who are reputed wise and good, as spiritual guides.

The sailors are a numerous, and in some sense an important class of people. I have attended a number of meetings, particularly with them; some of them appeared to listen with seriousness to the instructions of God's word. To a number of them I have given the Holy Bible, which has been received with expressions of gratitude. Appropriate tracts, also, have been put into the hands of many of them, which have interested their feelings. We have requests for meetings in almost every part of the town; those who have not been in the habit of attending meetings any where, manifest great satisfaction in view of the means used to promote their spiritual good."

Sept. 7, 1818, Mr. Davis closes by the following statement.

I have been fourteen months in the employ of the Society, have attended four hundred seventy four religious meetings, including morning prayer-meetings, seasons of fasting and prayer, religious worship on the sabbath, and lectures. I have distributed one thousand four hundred religious tracts, and three hundred Bibles and Testaments. I have received in payment for a number of Testaments, to the amount of seven dollars, which I have paid to the treasurer of the Massachusetts Bible Society. I have attended to the instruction of ninety persons, adults and children, in Sunday schools. Have sent away* eight unfortunate females, to their respective homes, or to places of service. I have visited families, and conversed with individuals as much as health and strength would admit, and have frequently been called to pray with the sick and dying. These services have been performed in twenty-six streets, of which I have the names; and in many alleys and courts, the names of which I cannot ascertain.

Of those who have frequented these meetings: there have been seventeen* hopefully turned from darkness to light, with these I have particularly and fre-quently conversed when in their distress, and constrained to inquire what they should do to be saved? These, in the judgment of Christian charity, have experi-enced a change of heart, have been made to embrace and love the truth, and have been brought into the liberty of the glorious gospel. We are assured that all who are born of the Spirit and from above, will be kept by the power of God through faith unto salvation.

----

*The persons here alluded to, as having been sent away, and those hopefully converted, are not the same persons hereafter mentioned in Mr. Rosseter's report. It should likewise be remarked that of those persons who have given evidence of a change, the principal part are from the more reputable (though poor) class of people.

Extracts from Mr. Rosseter's Reports.

". . . During a residence of 12 months in this town, in the performance of my missionary duties, I have not unfrequently been compelled to witness such a sad variety of human misery as could not fail to impress my heart with the most painful sensations. Alas! that rational and immortal beings, endued with capacities for the purest and noblest enjoyments, should sink even beneath the brute creation.

Since I commenced my labours in this place, I have visited 1896 families, distributed 54 Bibles, 68 Testaments, 45 Primers, and 1389 *Tracts;* have been called to visit 67 sick persons, and 19 in the agonies of death,—have attended 32 funerals, observed 3 seasons of fasting and prayer. Have attended meetings on Lord's-day in *Southark-Street,* and 10 other streets. Have held lectures in 36 different streets, and attended prayer meetings in 11, and visited 8 schools. I have also attended sabbath-schools in West-Boston and in the north part of the town.

In my daily visits I have generally met with the kindest reception; in some cases, however, have been received with coldness; but am happy to say, that in such instances they have almost invariably manifested a different disposition on my leaving them, and have often, with tears, solicited me to call again. In conversing with them I have endeavoured to bring into view the divine character, as excellent and terrible, and as angry with the wicked every day; have also sought to impress their minds with the exceeding sinfulness of sin, and the importance and absolute necessity of repentance and faith in the Lord Jesus Christ, in order to be accepted of him.

An astonishing degree of stupidity and ignorance pervades the minds of many. They scarcely know that they have a soul, and are wholly insensible that they are destined to the retributions of eternity. Some of them cannot read a word, and they often plead that, as an excuse for their total neglect of religion. Others have very incorrect views of the glorious plan of salvation, fondly imagining that a few prayers and alms-deeds will save them.

In visiting the sick and dying I have witnessed a variety of scenes, both pleasant and painful; have beheld some who were just launching into eternity, in the sweet hope of a glorious immortality; but, alas! the scene has been too often reversed. I have beheld many, who have lived without God, and without hope in the world, who have died either stupid or despairing. In one of my visits found a young female, who in a state of intoxication scalt [*sic*] herself in such a shocking manner, that there was no hope of her recovery. She had her senses, but appeared perfectly stupid as it respects the concerns of her soul, then just ready to sink into the fathomless abyss. Oh how distressing, to behold a being destined to an eternal existence, thus perfectly indifferent whether that existence be happy or miserable!

Called with a friend at a house in Southark-street. In the corner of a dirty room on a bed of shavings, lay a horrid object—the sad victim of iniquity and disease. So emaciated was her form, that there was scarcely a vestige of her former self remaining. So dreadful her appearance, that all who beheld her felt an involuntary emotion of terror. She attempted to rise, but her strength failed. She sunk back and exclaimed, Oh, Lord! have mercy upon me; my God, what shall I do? The scene was too affecting for language to describe. We endeavoured to converse with her, and to direct her to the cross of Christ. As she was destitute of every necessary [*sic*], we thought it expedient to remove her to the alms-house as soon as possible. This we effected; and here we must close her mournful story. She expired in one hour after her removal, without manifesting any hope; a dreadful warning to her surviving associates to shun her example. But alas! such scenes are too often witnessed by those miserable creatures to have the desired effect. As we left this abode of sin and sorrow, which was directly opposite one of the halls, we beheld at the door several of those deluded women; my friend endeavoured to converse with them, and pointing to the room we just left, entreated them to look there and be reminded of the dreadful end which awaited them, if they persisted in their vicious practices; but they scoffed and mocked, and replied in very indecent language.

As I was one day passing with a friend through Southark street, we met a number of these abandoned females. Said one—'there is a minister;' another said in a low tone of voice, not expecting me to hear—'will you preach me a sermon?' I asked her what she said; she replied, 'will you preach us a sermon?' I told her I would tell them a solemn truth in a few words, and that out of love to their souls. I then observed, that the course they were pursuing would lead them directly down to hell. I thought it not best to multiply words on this occasion, and left them, sincerely wishing that this solemn sentence might deeply impress their hearts; they stood amazed and made no reply. . . .

In visiting families in another part of the town, met with an unfortunate female whose history interested me much. She was a native of England, her father had been a military officer of some distinction, but unhappily for her he became dissipated, left her mother, took another wife, tore her from the arms of her fond maternal friend, and brought her to America; where she was educated for the theatre, and became a celebrated actress on the stage. Thus was she led on to ruin, by one, whom the laws of God and man required, should have guided her youthful steps, and imprinted on her heart the pure principles of religion and virtue. What a dreadful account must he have to give, when arraigned before the bar of Jehovah, who has thus been the very pander of his own offspring. She is now a miserable, abandoned, and wretched woman; but of late I have frequently seen her at meetings; she appears solemn, and often weeps: expresses a great desire to leave her vicious courses, and return to the paths of virtue. She is very desirous to get a situation in some family, where she may obtain an honest livelihood—says she has not a friend to assist her.

As it respects a part of the Hill at West-Boston, I think it of momentous importance, that something should be done. It is impossible for any one, not acquainted with circumstances, to imagine, or for me to describe, the awful deeds of darkness which are committed with impunity in that most horrid sink of pollution. What scenes of agonizing misery, and hopeless death, are there to be met with! There no soft sympathizing tones meliorate the agonies of despair, no hand of affection wipes from the pallid face the cold sweat of death. There all the feelings of humanity are obliterated. 'Like brutes they live, like brutes they die.' Perhaps many, who are now a disgrace to human nature, were once the idols of their fond parents, who cherished them with the tenderest affection; and while lovely in innocence and purity, they reclined on their parental bosoms, have looked forward with delightful anticipations to the period, when their beloved daughters, happily established in the world, would be the support and solace of their declining years.

I have, with a friend, improved Saturday afternoons, for a number of weeks, in visiting on the Hill, from house to house, and from hall to hall. Sometimes we have witnessed scenes which were solemn and affecting; at others, our hearts have been pained to behold the extreme sufferings and distress of our fellow creatures. Not unfrequently have a number of them gathered around us, and listened with seriousness and attention to what was communicated,—have appeared deeply to regret that such has been their manner of life, and promised that they would in future pursue a different course.

We called one day at one of the halls; eight or ten of those abandoned females came around us with countenances expressive of the deepest solicitude to hear, and most of them were in tears. One of them said, that she had written to her parents, entreating them to receive her home; humbly imploring their forgiveness, and promising repentance and reformation."

At another time Mr. Rosseter states:—

"I have for a fortnight past made every exertion to obtain all possible information respecting the situation of West-Boston, and am now prepared to say, that many appear truly desirous to leave, have expressed the strongest anxiety, and have followed me from house to house, weeping and entreating me to assist them in

getting away from the Hill. I am aware that it will be objected, that little dependence can be placed on their mere assertion; but from what I have daily
witnessed, I will venture confidently to affirm, that should an opportunity offer,
many would immediately and joyfully embrace it. In confirmation of this assertion, it is necessary to mention, that all, with but one exception, for whom means
have been provided, have immediately left; *and that one* died in a most shocking
manner, entreating her companions to take warning from her dreadful fate.

Have sent nine from the Hill, one a young girl who had been sometime resident
there, and had sadly departed from every thing amiable and lovely in the female
character—who had even threatened to destroy the life of her only parent, a fond
mother. Distressed and wearied with her infamous mode of living, she at length
formed the resolution to abandon forever a place where there were so many
records of her shame and folly; and if possible to be reconciled to her parent. She
went to a lady requesting her assistance, which she readily granted; and went in
pursuit of her mother, and at her house they met; an affecting scene ensued. The
injured parent was willing to forgive her unhappy daughter, in case of a reformation. It was thought best for them to go immediately to —— where they have
friends. Some necessary articles of clothing were obtained for the girl; my friend
paid the expenses of their passage; and I saw them on board a vessel, which sailed
in the evening.

Another, who for a long time has expressed a most fervent wish to get away, and
leave those dominions of sin, has, whenever she has seen me, in an affecting tone
of entreaty, inquired of me, Have you, sir, got a place for me yet? It has pained my
heart that I have so often been compelled to answer in the negative. I trust that a
reformation in her conduct took place last winter, from which I have reason to
believe she has never swerved, though assailed with repeated and inveterate
enemies.

A pious and respectable man lately informed me, that there was one of those
unhappy females who wished to leave the Hill. She had written to him repeatedly,
requesting him to get her away, and said that she not long since called at his house,
entreating him to use his influence with a friend of hers, that she might be
admitted into her family, until she could obtain a place. He accompanied me to
where we saw and conversed with her. She appears truly penitent for her past
errors, and heartily wearied with the detestable vices she had for years past pursued. She expressed a willingness to go any where, and do any kind of work. The
gentleman who was my companion, obtained consent of her friend to receive her
to her house. She was supplied with some necessary articles of clothing by a lady;
and she that evening we hope bade a lasting adieu to those shameless haunts of
infamy and prostitution. She has since, as far as I can learn, conducted [herself]

with strict propriety.[3] I have often seen her at meeting, where she always appears solemn and affected. A sister of hers, who had once been a companion with her in this broad road to destruction, had some time previous to this been rescued in nearly the same manner by the same gentleman. She by an undeviating course of good conduct has obtained a place in a very reputable family.

With respect to my meetings, I am happy to state, that they have generally been well attended; and a very flattering degree of solemnity and attention have been conspicuous in my little auditories. In some instances the house has been so crowded that many have been compelled to retire. . . .

In March I established an inquiring meeting at my house—the first evening there were 25 present, the next 27, and sometimes the house has been crowded so that some were unable to be seated. . . .

Prayer meetings have been peculiarly solemn and interesting; and we humbly trust that the Lord, by the influences of his Holy Spirit, has condescended to be one in the midst of us, and bless us. As far as we can ascertain, there are in the judgment of charity 20 hopeful converts, some of whom have connected themselves with different churches; and thirty or forty, who are, we trust, now anxiously inquiring what they shall do to be saved. . . ."

REMARKS.

. . . It is contended by those who are not friendly to this mission, that it is unnecessary; that there are houses of worship in the town; and if those people were disposed, they might have opportunity to hear the gospel occasionally. This is true in a certain sense. But are not the free seats in all our houses of worship, where the unadulterated truths of the gospel are maintained, fully occupied on Lord's-days? And would the generality of those persons meet a welcome reception into pews, that are owned or hired, even when they are not filled? There are, it is true, occasional lectures, on which some might be permitted to attend (should they take a distant seat) if they were *disposed*. But the grand difficulty with most of them is, they are NOT disposed. The duty then devolves on christians to visit, or employ others to visit them in their own abodes, and endeavour by every possible method to awaken them to a sense of their lost and wretched condition, and the immense value of their immortal souls. Should we see our neighbour's house at midnight enveloped in flames, could we content ourselves with the idea that he was asleep, half suffocated, and thereby *indisposed* to arise and flee from the impending ruin? Would it not be our duty to alarm him, and convince him that his situation was dangerous?

The pastors of our churches have a great variety of cares, and their time must be occupied in attending to their own immediate charge. And it is a well known fact, that there are thousands of our inhabitants that are not attached to any congregation, and have no minister on whom they can call as their pastor. There is also demonstrative evidence that numbers will attend on the preaching of the word, if they can have the opportunity free of expense, in their own neighborhoods, among their own associates, and in their usual attire.

After weighing those considerations, what reasonable objection can be made to this undertaking? Besides all the arguments which may be brought to prove that it is the duty of christians to seek the good of their neighbour, there is much reason to believe that the Lord has condescended to own the labours of his servants by making them instrumental of the salvation of some precious souls. In this, as in all similar cases, we must calculate on disappointments. We cannot expect that *all* those persons who have entertained hopes of mercy, will prove the genuine disciples of Christ. There always have been "tares among the wheat." Impositions were practised upon the apostles themselves; and human depravity is the same in the present as in past ages. If only half the number of supposed converts have in reality "passed from death unto life," heaven has been filled with the acclamations of angels; and the hearts of believers should swell with emotions of adoration and joy.

It is duty to acknowledge the kindness and liberality of a number of respectable brethren who have frequently accompanied the missionaries and otherwise contributed to the support of the mission. Also a vote of the selectmen, granting $30 from the legacy of the late Mr. Abiel Smith, "for the benefit of Africans," to aid in supporting the African school at the north part of the town.[4] Individuals have likewise contributed to this object, so as to enable the Society to continue the school till the commencement of winter, with the hope of opening it again in the spring.* The adults in this school have lived in a state of degradation and wretchedness, and the children have been exposed to the worst examples.[5] It must therefore require the continued exercise of patient, persevering efforts, to effect important and lasting advantages. Sufficient improvement, however, has been made to induce a belief, that with the same facilities for instruction, their progress would be equal to that of the whites. But a considerable lapse of time, with proper information and encouragement, are requisite to wear away that dullness and depression, incident to their humiliating condition. A number of the children can now read with a degree of accuracy; and have committed portions of scripture, hymns and catechisms; and have made as much proficiency in writing and sewing as could be expected. The rent of the school room has been principally paid by the scholars.

It would be a very important acquisition to the mission, if small buildings could be erected or hired, as places of worship, where the poor might assemble without embarrassment. When the blessed Saviour commissioned his disciples to go forth and publish the gospel, he prefaced the mandate by this powerful argument, "FREELY YE HAVE RECEIVED, freely give." Christians may shortly feel it their duty and privilege to devise a plan for the accomplishment of this object. A number of halls at the west part of the town have been opened for religious exercises: but a place appropriated for the purpose, would be less exposed to interruptions, and be far more convenient for preaching.

Another subject of vast importance presents itself while perusing the foregoing Reports, viz. The necessity of an institution for the reception of those unhappy

---

*A Sabbath school will be kept up during the winter.

females who are weary of a life of infamy, and are willing to labour for their support, if employment could be provided for them. And likewise for the children, who are strolling our streets, begging from house to house; and frequently stealing in the most artful manner, as though deeply skilled in the practice. Truly it may be said, the sins of this people have reached up to heaven. And we may justly expect the judgments of a sin-avenging God will fall upon us, unless measures are taken to put away these abominations from the land.

The following observations, by a friend, are deserving the consideration of the public.

"Should the town see fit, (as it is hoped it will) to institute a work-house, or house of industry, where disorderly persons belonging to the town should be confined and employed, while others are sent to the towns to which they respectively belong, the benevolence of individuals might be exerted in behalf of those who conduct with the most propriety, by providing an Asylum, upon the same plan with those in London, and other parts of Europe.

"Vagrant children might be taken up in a similar manner, and placed under the care of masters and governesses, who should possess the requisite qualifications, where they should be taught to do all kinds of work suited to their age, and calculated to prepare them for future usefulness.

"By these means united, the growing evils under consideration would be in a very great degree counteracted; the property of our citizens would be more secure; and a new tone would be given to the morals of the lower classes of society."

We conclude our remarks by observing,

. . . Those who engage in benevolent operations must expect to meet discouragements and opposition in all their forms; but while imploring the influences of the Spirit, and relying on all-sufficient aid, let this animating portion of holy writ be kept in perpetual remembrance. *Be not weary in well doing, for in due season ye shall reap, if ye faint not.*

The following piece (copied from the Boston Gazette of Oct. 1, 1818,) is subjoined as a testimony that there are pious heads of families in this place, who feel anxiously solicitous that proper measures should be put into operation by the guardians of the town, for the prevention of those evils heretofore brought into view.

"*Messrs. Printers,*

"I was highly gratified on perceiving in your paper of the 17th of Sept. an address, (the publication of which entitles you to public esteem) by 'Phylanthropos' to his fellow citizens, on the importance of some measures being adopted to renovate the morals of a certain class of our population, and thereby prevent the destruction of thousands, as yet untainted with the dreadful poison. I have been expecting, with solicitude, that some ingenuous mind would imbibe the spirit of that friend to mankind, and zealously contribute its influence in support of an object so vastly interesting to the community. But disappointed in this, and being the father of a rising family, whose present comfort, and future happiness are tender as the strings which twine about my heart, I feel compelled (though far less qualified than many others) to call on all virtuous heads of families to afford their individual aid to this momentous concern. Never was there a subject presented to the consideration of the public, more deeply fraught with consequences, important to society, than the one now suggested. What will all the improvements in education, in arts and elegance avail, if the morals of our children become vitiated? What will it avail for us to accumulate a property sufficient to establish them in business, or to settle them in life, if, during the period of minority, they are exposed to the artful machinations of the profligate, and the cunning of that detestable character, described by Solomon, Prov. 2nd, 5th, and 7th chapters? The almost certain consequences of such an exposure, is, the destruction of health, character, property, and life itself: and with those, the happiness of themselves and friends.

"It is a well known fact, that houses of ill-fame have multiplied exceedingly within a few years; and are scattered through every part of the town. Our children, therefore, are necessarily liable to temptation; and however secure parents may feel, as respects the safety and virtue of their children, many of them can form but a faint idea, what company their sons are in, when out of their sight. There are few young minds (unless fortified by real religion, and a sense of the heinousness of sin in the sight of God) that are capable of resisting the fascinating allurements of an artful female, combined with the sneers of older and more depraved associates. Those enticing creatures have been seen, not only in parts of West Boston, but elsewhere, beckoning to young persons as they passed the street. Curiosity at first may induce a compliance, the intoxicating draught inflames the passions and overpowers the judgment, till the *inclination* is won; a repetition of the scene indurates the mind; the habit is formed, and the 'good name' is lost. Unlawful means must be resorted to, in order to meet expenses; thus every species of iniquity are linked together, and the wretch becomes a willing captive. What must follow? The susceptibility of a parent shrinks from the heart-rending recital.

"The question now forcibly presents itself; *what can be done?* Let parents be fully aware of the exposure of their beloved offspring, and they cannot long remain inactive, they will intercede with the fathers of the town, to adopt, and perseveringly execute, some suitable measures to correct, and prevent those enormities, (which, ere long, must draw down the righteous indignation of Heaven,) and thereby give an evidence to the world, that such disgraceful conduct shall not be suffered with impunity, in the metropolis of Massachusetts."

A FATHER.

TEXT NOTES

THE FEMALE MARINE
FIRST PART: NARRATIVE OF LUCY BREWER

1. Interpolated text from *The Adventures of Louisa Baker* (New York: Luther Wales, [1815]), 9.

2. Compare that passage to the nearly identical passage in Susanna Rowson, *Charlotte Temple: A Tale of Truth*, ed. Cathy N. Davidson (New York: Oxford Univ. Press, 1986), 32.

3. Bracketed words in this paragraph have been interpolated by the modern editor for clarity. The bracketed "I" also appears in *Adventures of Louisa Baker*, 12; its omission in the "Tenth Edition" is probably a printer's error.

4. Interpolated text from *The Adventures of Louisa Baker* (New York: Luther Wales, [1815]), 13.

5. Interpolated word from *Adventures of Louisa Baker*, 14.

6. Interpolated text from *Adventures of Louisa Baker*, 14. In *Adventures of Louisa Baker*, the word "vulgar" appears as "vulgal."

7. In *Adventures of Louisa Baker*, 14, the phrase "worst of creation" appears as "filth of creation."

8. In *Adventures of Louisa Baker*, 15ff., the appellation "ma'am" consistently appears as "marm."

9. In the "Tenth Edition," the word "opprobrious" appears as "opprobious."

10. Interpolated text from *Adventures of Louisa Baker*, 15.

11. In the "Tenth Edition," the word "associates" appears as "asosciates"—an apparent printer's error.

12. Bracketed word interpolated by modern editor for clarity.

13. In *Adventures of Louisa Baker*, 16, the word "girls" appears as "bawds."

14. Interpolated word from *Adventures of Louisa Baker*, 16. In *Adventures of Louisa Baker*, 16, the phrase "misshapen person" appears as "misshaped stinkard."

15. This is an allusion to the work of Laurence Sterne (1713–1768), English novelist,

humorist, and clergyman. Sterne was an early literary exponent and practitioner of "sentiment" and "sensibility."

16. Interpolated text from *Adventures of Louisa Baker*, 18.

17. Interpolated word from *Adventures of Louisa Baker*, 19.

18. Interpolated text from *Adventures of Louisa Baker*, 20.

19. Interpolated text from *Adventures of Louisa Baker*, 20.

20. For contemporary newspaper accounts of the *Constitution*'s defeat of the *Guerriere* on August 20, 1812, see *Independent Chronicle* (Boston), Aug. 31, 1812, [2]; *Columbian Centinel* (Boston), Sept. 2, 1812, [2].

21. Interpolated word from *Adventures of Louisa Baker*, 21. In the "Tenth Edition," the phrase "resorted for" appears as "resort fed or"—an apparent printer's error.

22. Interpolated text from *Adventures of Louisa Baker*, 21; this sentence was probably omitted from the "Tenth Edition" because the timing of the actions it describes seems to contradict the sequence of events as described in the next sentence.

23. For contemporary newspaper accounts of the *Constitution*'s defeat of the *Java* on December 29, 1812, see *Columbian Centinel*, Feb. 17, 1813, [2]; Feb. 24, 1813, [2]; *Independent Chronicle*, Feb. 18, 1813, [2].

24. In *Adventures of Louisa Baker*, 23, the word "calibreous" appears as "selibrious."

25. The period that ends this sentence appears as a comma in the "Tenth Edition"—an apparent printer's error.

26. Interpolated word from *Adventures of Louisa Baker*, 24.

27. Compare to passage in *Charlotte Temple*, 29.

THE FEMALE MARINE
SECOND PART: CONTINUATION OF
THE NARRATIVE OF LUCY BREWER

1. Interpolated text from *Adventures of Lucy Brewer* (Boston: N. Coverly Jr., 1815), 4, which contains other slight variations in phrasing.

2. In *Adventures of Lucy Brewer*, 7, the word "quitting" is spelled "quiting."

3. Interpolated text from *Adventures of Lucy Brewer*, 5–10.

4. In *Adventures of Lucy Brewer*, 11, the phrase "domestic scenes" appears as "more romantic scenes"; this paragraph in *Adventures of Lucy Brewer* contains other slight variations in phrasing. In the "Tenth Edition" the word "home" appears as "ohme"—an apparent printer's error.

5. In *Adventures of Lucy Brewer*, 12, the word "unmannerly" appears as "unmanly."

6. Bracketed word interpolated by modern editor for clarity.

7. In the "Tenth Edition" the word "acknowledgment" appears as "ackuowledgment"—an apparent printer's error.

8. Interpolated text from *Adventures of Lucy Brewer*, 15.

9. William Hogarth (1697–1764) was an English painter and engraver of the eigh-

teenth century, famous as a pictorial social satirist; see Sidney Lee, ed., *The Concise Dictionary of National Biography* (1903; rpt. London: Oxford Univ. Press, 1925), 628.

10. Interpolated word from *Adventures of Lucy Brewer*, 16.

11. In the "Tenth Edition," the word "yield" is followed by a period rather than a semicolon (despite the fact that the "b" in "but" is lower-cased).

12. Interpolated text from *Adventures of Lucy Brewer*, 17.

13. Interpolated text from *Adventures of Lucy Brewer*, 18.

14. Interpolated text from *Adventures of Lucy Brewer*, 19, which contains other variations in phrasing.

15. Interpolated text from *Adventures of Lucy Brewer*, 19.

16. Interpolated text from *Adventures of Lucy Brewer*, 20, which contains other variations in phrasing.

17. Interpolated text from *Adventures of Lucy Brewer*, 21.

18. In *Adventures of Lucy Brewer*, 22, the departure from New York is placed on August 29. Interpolated word from *Adventures of Lucy Brewer*, 22. The abbreviated "incog" may have been used here playfully to avoid applying the gender-specific alternatives, "incognito" or "incognita," to the gender-flexible heroine.

19. Interpolated text from *Adventures of Lucy Brewer*, 22, where the phrase "small military hat" appears in place of "chapeau."

20. Interpolated word from *Adventures of Lucy Brewer*, 23. In the "Tenth Edition" the word "curtsey" appears as "curtesy."

21. Interpolated text from *Adventures of Lucy Brewer*, 24, which contains other slight variations in phrasing.

22. In *Adventures of Lucy Brewer*, 27, the phrases "man of colour" and "young gentlemen" are both italicized.

23. Interpolated text from *Adventures of Lucy Brewer*, 27, which contains other slight variations in phrasing.

24. Interpolated text from *Adventures of Lucy Brewer*, 30, which contains other variations in phrasing.

25. Interpolated word from *Adventures of Lucy Brewer*, 30.

26. Interpolated text from *The Adventures of Lucy Brewer* (Boston: H. Trumbull, 1815), 31. The copy of Coverly's edition of this title at the American Antiquarian Society lacks all pages after 30; consequently, all subsequent interpolations will be taken from Trumbull's edition, published at about the same time. In *Adventures of Lucy Brewer* (Trumbull), the phrase "young lady" appears in quotation marks.

27. George Barnwell was the main character in George Lillo's *The London Merchant, or the History of George Barnwell*, a prose tragedy produced in 1731. As the story went, Barnwell was seduced by a prostitute and murdered his uncle at her instigation; they were both hanged. See William Rose Benét, ed., *The Reader's Encyclopedia* (New York: Crowell, 1948), 77.

28. Interpolated word from *Adventures of Lucy Brewer* (Trumbull), 32. In the "Tenth Edition," the second set of parentheses is not closed—presumably a printer's error.

29. *Adventures of Lucy Brewer* (Trumbull), 33, contains slight variations in phrasing.

30. Interpolated text in this paragraph from *Adventures of Lucy Brewer* (Trumbull), 33–35, which contains other slight variations in phrasing.

31. Interpolated text from *Adventures of Lucy Brewer* (Trumbull), 36.

32. Interpolated text from *Adventures of Lucy Brewer* (Trumbull), 36.

THE FEMALE MARINE
THIRD PART: AN AWFUL BEACON

1. Interpolated text from *The Awful Beacon, to the Rising Generation of Both Sexes* (Boston: N. Coverly Jr., 1816), [3], which contains other variations in phrasing.

2. Interpolated text from *Awful Beacon*, 4, which contains other variations in phrasing. There is no space between the words "to" and "relate" in at least one surviving copy of the "Tenth Edition" (but not in another).

3. Interpolated text from *Awful Beacon*, 5.

4. Interpolated word from *Awful Beacon*, 6.

5. Interpolated text in this paragraph from *Awful Beacon*, 8–9, which contains other variations in phrasing.

6. Interpolated text from *Awful Beacon*, 12–13, which contains other variations in phrasing.

7. Interpolated text from *Awful Beacon*, 13.

8. Interpolated text from *Awful Beacon*, 14, which contains other variations in phrasing.

9. Interpolated text from *Awful Beacon*, 14–15, which contains other slight variations in phrasing. In the "Tenth Edition," the interpolated word "time" appears as "return."

10. Interpolated word from *Awful Beacon*, 16; in the "Tenth Edition," the interpolated word "or" appears as "of"—a probable printer's error.

11. In *Awful Beacon* 20, the phrase "great importance" appears as "the greatest importance." For more on the gale discussed in this paragraph, see the contemporary newspaper reports cited in the notes to the modern editor's introduction.

12. Interpolated word from *Awful Beacon*, 21.

13. Interpolated text in this and the previous paragraph from *Awful Beacon*, 22–23. Compare some of the passages in those paragraphs to the following passages from [Henry Trumbull], *History of the Discovery of America, of the Landing of Our Forefathers, at Plymouth, and of Their Most Remarkable Engagements with the Indians* (Norwich, CT: Published for the Author, 1810), 14–15, 22: "as soon as on shore they fell upon their knees and returned thanks to the Almighty for enableing them to reach in safety their place of destination.—But, although they had thus far succeeded in their views, although they had been enabled to flee from persecution, to cross a wide and boisterous ocean, what was their situation now!—sojourners in a foreign land!—

traversing the broken and unwrought shores of a wild and unexplored country!—they found here no friends to welcome them, or house to shelter them from the inclemency of an approaching winter!—on one side they beheld nought but a hideous and desolate wilderness, the habitation of wild and verocious [*sic*] animals, and probably the abode of a race of beings not less wild and unmerciful!—on the other, the briny ocean foaming and with tremendous roar dashing against the huge and projecting rock, which as far as the eye could perceive, marked the sea-beaten shores! . . . they had not penetrated the woods above three miles when they discovered five of the natives (which were the first seen by them since their arrival) they were cloathed with the skins of animals, and armed with bows and arrows. . . . thus it was, that in the course of a very few years, a great part of *New England,* which so late was an uncultivated forest, resounding with the yells of savages, and beasts of prey, became the place of abode of our persecuted forefathers." For the possible significance of the similarity of the passages, see the modern editor's introduction, notes 18 and 63.

14. Interpolated text from *Awful Warning,* 24–25.

15. Interpolated text in this paragraph from *Awful Warning,* 26, which contains other slight variations in phrasing, as does the following paragraph.

16. Interpolated text in this paragraph from *Awful Beacon,* 26–27, which contains other slight variations in phrasing.

17. Interpolated text in this paragraph from *Awful Beacon,* 28, which contains other variations in phrasing.

18. Interpolated text in this paragraph from *Awful Beacon,* 29–30, which contains other slight variations in phrasing.

19. Interpolated word in this paragraph from *Awful Beacon,* 30, which contains other slight variations in phrasing.

20. Interpolated text in the last two paragraphs from *Awful Beacon,* 31–32, which contains other slight variations in phrasing.

21. Interpolated text in this paragraph from *Awful Beacon,* 33, which contains other slight variations in phrasing.

22. Interpolated text in this paragraph from *Awful Beacon,* 34, which contains other slight variations in phrasing. In *Awful Beacon,* the narrator describes her stay among prostitutes as lasting "six years" rather than "three years."

23. In the "Tenth Edition," the word "by" in the first sentence of this paragraph appears as "hy"—an apparent printer's error. The narrator's characterization of brothelkeepers as women is consistent with Marilynn Wood Hill's claim (with reference to New York City) that "in contrast to later periods, management of the prostitution business in the early and mid-nineteenth century was very much dominated by women. Women owned or managed the businesses as madams or prostitution boardinghouse keepers." M. W. Hill, *Their Sisters' Keepers: Prostitution in New York City, 1830–1870* (Berkeley: Univ. of California Press, 1993), 94.

24. In the "Tenth Edition," the word "us" appears as "as"—an apparent printer's error.

25. Interpolated text in this paragraph from *Awful Beacon*, 37–38.

26. Interpolated text from *Awful Beacon*, 39–40, which contains other slight variations in phrasing. The bracketed letters have been interpolated by the modern editor for clarity.

27. Interpolated text in this long paragraph from *Awful Beacon*, 40–44. A couple of apparent printer's errors in the last rambling sentence of the paragraph have been silently corrected by the modern editor.

28. In *Awful Beacon*, 44, the word "unconsciously" appears as "unconsciouly"—an apparent printer's error.

29. In *Awful Beacon*, 46, the word "contempt" appears as "can tempt."

30. Compare the rhetoric in this paragraph to that in *Charlotte Temple*, 28–29.

31. In *Awful Beacon*, 49, the word "shunned" appears as "shuned."

32. Last twenty paragraphs of interpolated text from *Awful Warning*, 44–59.

33. Interpolated text in this paragraph from *Awful Beacon*, 59.

34. Interpolated word in this sentence from *Awful Beacon*, 59.

35. Interpolated advertisement from *Awful Beacon*, 60.

A BRIEF REPLY TO THE
LATE WRITINGS OF LOUISA BAKER

1. In the original edition, 8, the word "falsely" appears as "fasely"—an apparent printer's error.

2. The bracketed word has been interpolated by the modern editor for clarity.

3. The bracketed letters have been interpolated by the modern editor for clarity.

4. In the original edition, 10, the words "took as active a part" appear as "took as an active part."

5. For the true story of Jerome Bonaparte's abortive marriage to a young American woman, presumably the inspiration for this fanciful tale, see entry for Elizabeth Patterson Bonaparte in *Dictionary of American Biography*, 11 vols. (New York: Charles Scribner's Sons, 1964), vol. 1, part 2, 428–29.

6. In the original edition, 24, the word "determine" appears as "determined."

THE SURPRISING ADVENTURES
OF ALMIRA PAUL

1. In the original edition, 7, the word "Islands" near the beginning of this paragraph appears as "Isands" and the word "ships" is mistakenly given an apostrophe: "ship's."

2. Commodore John Rogers (1773–1838), sometimes spelled Rodgers, was the U.S. Navy's "ranking officer in active service" during the War of 1812. See *Dictionary of*

American Biography, 11 vols. (New York: Charles Scribner's Sons, 1964), vol. 8, part 2, 75–77, quoted at 76.

3. In the original edition, 13, "seaman" is spelled "seamen" and "seamanship" is spelled "seamenship."

4. In the original edition, 13, this rambling passage includes a number of printer's errors or irregularities in spelling that have been corrected here: "colours" appears as "colous"; "antagonist" appears as "antogonist"; and "athwart" appears as "atharwt."

5. In the original edition, 16, the word "soliciting" appears as "solicting."

6. Commodore Stephen Decatur (1779–1820), U.S. naval officer, was a hero of the Tripolitan War (1801–5), commanded with mixed success during the War of 1812, and led a successful campaign against Algiers, Tunis, and Tripoli in 1815. See *Dictionary of American Biography,* vol. 3, part 1, 187–90.

7. In the original edition, 21, the word "seaman" is spelled "seamen."

8. The original edition ends here, 24, with a comma rather than a period, suitably punctuating the end of a careless printing job.

A BRIEF ACCOUNT OF . . .
THE BOSTON FEMALE SOCIETY FOR MISSIONARY PURPOSES

1. In all three surviving copies of the original edition of *Brief Account* examined by or four the modern editor, the number "200" in this sentence has been altered by an early hand to read "260."

2. On African Americans in the North End of Boston during the early national period, see George A. Levesque, *Black Boston: African American Life and Culture in Urban America, 1750–1860* (New York, Garland, 1994), 32–34 and passim; also see James Oliver Horton and Lois E. Horton, *Black Bostonians: Family Life and Community Struggle in the Antebellum North* (New York: Holmes & Meier, 1979). Until the black "migration" to the West End that began during the late eighteenth century, most black Bostonians had lived in the North End; however, some African Americans continued to live there during the first half of the nineteenth century.

3. Bracketed word inserted by modern editor for clarity.

4. On Abiel Smith and his charitable support for the education of African Americans in Boston, see Levesque, *Black Boston,* 167–72; Horton and Horton, *Black Bostonians,* 71.

5. In the original edition, 20, the word "wretchedness" appears as "wrethedness"— an apparent printer's error.

INDEX

vice districts (*cont.*)
  child prostitutes; procurers; prostitutes; West Boston Hill, as vice district
virtue, 8, 37 n. 39; destabilizing or subverting conventional conceptions of, 14; nature and value of, 131–32

Wales, Luther (pseud.?), 3, *27*, 32 n. 9
warnings, 6, 63–65, 82–83, 93–97, 118–31
War of 1812, ix, 1–2, 24
Warrior Women and Popular Balladry (Dianne Dugaw), 8
Watts, Steven, 24, 42 n. 64
Webb, Eliza (née Bowen), as true name of Lucy Brewer, 139, 147. *See also* Brewer, Lucy
West, Charles, 6, 19, 23–24, 89–90; courtship of Lucy Brewer by, 105–17; letter of, 105–6; portrait of, with his wife, *98*
West, Lucy (née Brewer). *See* Brewer, Lucy
West, Miss, 85–89, 105–6, 108
West Boston. *See* West Boston Hill
West Boston Hill (Boston, Mass.): as African American neighborhood, x, 15, *16*, 29, 44 n. 73, 68, 69, 91, 171–72; Almira Paul works as prostitute on, 163; as home of Rachel Sperry, 137–47;

Lucy Brewer works as prostitute on, 15, 68–70, 83–84, 139–47; map of, *16*; music on, 91, 174; as vice district, x, 15–18, 28–29, 66–71, 83–84, 90, 91–93, 94–97, 118–27, 137–47, 163, 170–80, 185. *See also under specific streets*
West End (Boston, Mass.). *See* West Boston Hill
work-house. *See* House of Industry
World War I, 20
Wright, Amos, as father of Nathaniel Hill Wright, 3
Wright, Lyle, 15
Wright, Nathaniel Hill, 3, 5, 19; author of *Boston: A Touch at the Times* (1819), 5; biographical information on, 3, 5, 32 n. 11, 33 nn. 12, 14, 15, 17; marriage of, 5, 33 n. 14; as probable author of *The Female Marine* (and related pamphlets), 3, 5; as probable "hack" for Nathaniel Coverly Jr., 3, 5; in Vermont, 5, 33 n. 15

young people, as customers of Nathaniel Coverly Jr., 5. *See also* child prostitutes; children; youths
youths: corruption of, in vice districts, 68, 94–97, 119, 124–27, 171–72, 184–85; farewell address of Lucy Brewer to, 118–31. *See also* child prostitutes; children; young people